The Lives in Objects

The Lives in Objects

Native Americans, British Colonists, and Cultures of Labor and Exchange in the Southeast

Jessica Yirush Stern

The University of North Carolina Press CHAPEL HILL

This book was published with the assistance of the Anniversary Fund of the University of North Carolina Press.

Library of Congress Cataloging-in-Publication Data
Names: Stern, Jessica Yirush, author.
Title: The lives in objects : Native Americans, British colonists, and cultures of labor
    and exchange in the Southeast / Jessica Yirush Stern.
Description: Chapel Hill : University of North Carolina Press, [2017] |
    Includes bibliographical references and index.
Identifiers: LCCN 2016019957 | ISBN 9781469631479 (cloth : alk. paper) |
    ISBN 9781469631486 (pbk : alk. paper) | ISBN 9781469631493 (ebook)
Subjects: LCSH: Indians of North America—Southern States—History—Colonial
    period, ca. 1600–1775. | Indians of North America—Southern States—Economic
    conditions. | Whites—Southern States—Relations with Indians—History. |
    Southern States—History—Colonial period, ca. 1600–1775. | Southern States—Ethnic
    relations—Economic aspects—History—17th century. | Southern States—Ethnic
    relations—Economic aspects—History—18th century. | Ceremonial exchange—
    Southern States—History—17th century. | Ceremonial exchange—Southern
    States—History—18th century. | Southern States—Economic conditions—17th century. |
    Southern States—Economic conditions—18th century.
Classification: LCC E78.S65 S73 2016 | DDC 975/.02—dc23
    LC record available at https://lccn.loc.gov/2016019957

Cover illustration: Philip Georg Friedrich Von Reck, Indians going a-hunting, detail, 1736.
Royal Library, Copenhagen, Denmark.

Portions of chapter 2 were previously published as "The Economic Philosophies of Indian Trade Regulation Policy in Early South Carolina," in *Creating and Contesting Carolina: Proprietary Era Histories,* ed. Bradford Wood and Michelle LeMaster (Columbia, S.C.: University of South Carolina Press, 2013). Portions of chapter 4 were originally published as "Native American Taste: Re-evaluating the Gift-Commodity Debate in British Colonial Southeast" in *Native South* 5 (2012). Both are reprinted here with permission.

For my aunt, Ruth Stern.

Contents

Illustrations

Acknowledgments

As a person seeped in the theories of gift exchange, I am particularly aware of the debts I have accrued while researching and writing this book. Some feelings of gratitude stretch back even further than the beginning of this project and will extend well past this book's appearance in print. I will forever be grateful for my undergraduate advisor at Reed College, David Harris Sacks, and my graduate adviser at Johns Hopkins University, Jack P. Greene. They both believed in me, nurtured my "historical creativity," and served as model professionals. There are a number of individuals whom I have come to consider unofficial advisors over the years: Philip Morgan, Michael Johnson, Toby Ditz, and John Marshall, from my formative graduate student days, all sit on my shoulder at various times when I am researching and writing. Amy Turner Bushnell has always gone out of her way to attend my presentations when she is anywhere nearby, has provided astute feedback, and has opened her and Jack's home to me when I am in Rhode Island. Jane Guyer introduced to me the exhilarating world of economic anthropology and inspired the topic of this book. Robbie Ethridge has guided me at crucial points in my career, from an early conference presentation when I was a graduate student, to publishing the last article I needed to get tenure while she was the editor of the journal *Native South* (which comprises part of chapter 4 in this book), to suggesting that I work with editor Mark Simpson-Vos at UNC Press, and all the way through to reading and critiquing this entire work.

During the research phase of this project I have been fortunate to receive financial support from the Johns Hopkins University; California State University, Fullerton; the Institute of Southern Studies, affiliated with the University of South Carolina; and the American Philosophical Society through the Phillips Fund Grant for Native American Research. The staff at the South Carolina Department of Archives and History (particularly Charles H. Lesser), the South Caroliniana Library, the South Carolina Historical Society, the Georgia State Archives, the Georgia Historical Society, and the Newberry Library guided me through their vast collections and helped me pinpoint key sources.

I was at the mercy of archaeologists and anthropologists to help me understand how to decipher archaeological reports and literature—and what a fine group to be at the mercy of! Keith Derting at the South Carolina Institute of Archaeology and Anthropology took me under his wing and helped me understand the state of archaeology in South Carolina and put me in contact with specialists in the field, namely, Charles DePratter, Eric Poplin, and Martha Zierden. Gregory Waselkov shared his and Ashley Dumas's groundbreaking and exhilarating manuscript, "Cultural Revitalization and Recasting Identities in the Post-Mississippian Southeast," before it was published, and also read my first chapter and offered valuable insight. In the middle of a dig he was conducting, Jon Marcoux took time to answer my questions about the beads found at Southeastern Indian sites.

I did not start asking for help from other historians as early as I should have, and found only at the end that my shyness was unmerited. Thank you to David Silverman, who answered my questions about the gun trade and shared an early draft of his manuscript about guns with me. Cole Jones read over a key account book I was using to help me determine whether the goods it listed may have been used by British soldiers. Max Edelson was always there for me when I queried him about colonial surveying methods and the economic and social mentality of South Carolina agriculturalists. Tyler Boulware, Noeleen Mcilvenna, and Rebecca Batement all shared unpublished or soon-to-be-published manuscripts with me. Brad Wood and Michelle LeMaster both read and critiqued an earlier version of chapter 2, part of which was included in their fine edited book, *Contesting Carolina*. And Josh Piker and Coll Thrush gave me suggestions about how to improve chapter 1.

The individuals at University of North Carolina Press have been a pleasure to work with. Mark Simpson-Vos has been clear, honest, and encouraging throughout this process, as has Lucas Church. I do not even have words for the appreciation that I feel for my external readers for the press, Robbie Ethridge and Timothy Shannon. They spent more time with the manuscript than I could have hoped for and provided the perfect mixture of encouragement and straight-to-the-core critiques. The book is infinitely better because of how seriously they took their charge.

I am also thankful for the feedback I received from participants at the conferences at which I presented portions of this work: the Harvard University Atlantic World Seminar, the McNeil Center for Early American Studies, the North American Fur Trade Conference, Haifa University,

Dalhousie University's Stokes Seminar, the Omohundro Institute of Early American Studies Annual Conference, the University of British Columbia Global Encounters Initiative Conference, the American Historical Association Annual Conference, the American Society for Ethnohistory Annual Conference, and the American Origins Seminar at the Huntington Library. Though the audience members at these venues are too large to recount, I would like to thank the few individuals whom I can remember (and, at this remove, I do not trust my memory to be exhaustive), for asking particularly probing questions, answering my follow-up questions, making astute suggestions, and sharing their own inspirational work: Sharon Block, Heidi Bohaker, Amy Turner Bushnell, William Carter, Laura Johnson, Susan Juster, Andrew Lipman, Ann Little, Peter Mancall, Paul Otto, Arthur Ray, Dan Richter, Laura Sandy, Carole Shammas, Timothy Shannon, Terri Snyder, Danny Vickers, and Bruce White.

At Johns Hopkins I was blessed to be surrounded by a group of incredible peers whose influence is unending: Joe Adelman, Rich Bond, Jeremy Caradonna, Katie Jorgensen Gray, Amanda Herbert, Carl Keyes, Gabe Klehr, John Matsui, Andrew Miller, Mary Ashburn Miller, Catherine Molineux, Kate Murphy, James Roberts, Justin Roberts, Jessica Choppin Roney, Leonard Sadosky, Dave Schley, Eran Shalev, and Molly Warsh. And at Cal State Fullerton I have joined a group of accomplished, dedicated, and supportive colleagues. Benjamin Cawthra marshaled those of us who live in LA and Long Beach into a writing group; this LA/LBC cohort, comprising Natalie Fousekis, Allison Varzalley, Margie Brown-Coronel, and Kate Burlingham, kept me on track to finish this book and provides me with constant motivation as I start my next project. Gayle Brunelle offered feedback on portions of the manuscript and serves as an inspiration in her ability to balance a robust research agenda with a four-four teaching load. I was lucky to have Nancy Fitch as my junior faculty mentor, and now as an incredibly supportive departmental chair. It saddens me greatly that Gordon Bakken did not live to see the release of this book. Perhaps if I had heeded his constant encouragement and finished the book more quickly, he would have gotten to hold it, and I would have gotten to see that full-of-pride smile of his.

Many of my colleagues listed above became my dear friends and, as we traveled the sometimes-perilous road of academia together, they were crucial in providing the support any author needs in researching and writing a book. I am also grateful to my friends who are not historians who gave me welcome relief by urging me out of doors, giving me a chance to talk about subjects other than Early America, and, when I could not help but talk about history, helped me refine my ideas as I struggled to present them in a more engaging manner. They are Hannah F. R. Caradonna, Nina Malakooty, Heather Mund, Bonnie Shaner, Rhea Patenaude, Jenny Suter, the Boozy Brunch Crew (Truc HaMai, Kimberly Marar, Julie Tarango, Jill Tarango, and Amanda Donohue), and, more recently, as I neared the finish line, the regulars at the Adjacent Playground (Marielli Cardona-Rivera, Lisa Eiler, Michelle Kelly, Amanda Lamont, Christine Ostander, Courtney Smith, and Aaron Smith).

My children, Eva and Jacob, were born when I was in the midst of finishing this book. One might think that would have interrupted the completion of this work, but in teaching me to be efficient with my time, and foisting routine breaks on me, they just may have given me the space I needed away from the work to be creative and clear when I returned to it. Jacob, my two-year-old, is a sweetheart who is always up for a stress-relieving hug. And although Eva, at four years, is too young to understand the argument in this book, I can tell, already, that she will be as intense and compassionate an observer of the past as she is of the world around her. God knows she will have much to say about the Southeastern Indian fashions in chapter 4. As much as I am enriched by my time with them, finishing this book would have been impossible if not for the staff at LePort Montessori in Huntington Harbor who provided a home away from home for Eva and Jacob during the weekdays. In particular, their teachers Emmy Zappa, Alejandra Tryon, Isabel Espinosa, Carelia Altamirano, Veronica Jaramillo, and Deysi Carrera made it clear that sending them off to LePort each day benefits their intellectual development as much as it benefits mine.

My family has been unfailing in their support of me and their infinite faith in my intellectual abilities. My mom, Beth Ladin, has modeled creative analytical thinking throughout my life. On a more mundane level, she came down to stay with us on multiple occasions to take over household responsibilities in order to give me more time to work. Beyond serving as a role model for me—he sits down every morning to write his pages—my father, Howard Stern, read the entire manuscript right before I sent it off for its final voyage, and did as any good father should: he told me it was perfect. Both he and my brother, Robert Stern, spent several days with me in the archives at various points in the research process, when the loneliness felt unbearable and the eighteenth-century handwriting felt too illegible to be deciphered by my eyes alone. Even as he has entered deeper and deeper into the medical profession, Robert continues to be one of the most interesting people I know with whom to talk to about history and cultural encounters. I credit his bright and worldly wife, Melanie Todman, for keeping him grounded and well read, and I cannot wait to meet their two daughters, Lilah and Madeleine, when they enter this world. My aunt, Ruth Stern, is one of the best writers I know. When Timothy Shannon rightly took me to task for being overly theoretical and prone to jargon in my writing, I turned to Ruth for help. She not only flagged unclear passages, but she added a sprinkling of flare and panache to the writing style.

It was my husband, Craig Yirush, who convinced me to pitch this project as a book instead of publishing it as a series of articles. Along the way, he has treated each success, no matter how minor, with gleeful celebration (and chocolate), and each setback, no matter how major, with motivating encouragement (and chocolate). His was the last pencil to mark up the pages of the manuscript which, as I write this, seems to me less important than all of the other shadow ways that he helped me complete this project—the love, the joy, and the love!

The Lives in Objects

Introduction

In the summer of 1716 a Cherokee man walked into a store in Charles Town, South Carolina, and offered the shopkeeper ten beaver skins for a gun.[1] The shopkeeper did not haggle for a higher price, suggest other items the man might afford, or extend a line of credit to make up for the difference in cost. Instead, he turned the Cherokee man away, dutifully abiding by the official oath he took two days earlier, in the wake of the Yamasee War, not to trade directly with Native Americans. Despite this restriction, the Cherokee man did leave Charles Town ten skins lighter and one gun heavier. The storekeeper had apprised the Commissioners of Indian Trade, the governmental body in charge of Indian affairs, of the failed sale. On the Commissioners' instructions, Governor Robert Daniel, instead of endorsing a commodity purchase, staged a gift-giving ceremony. Presenting a gun to the Cherokee man, the governor expressed his appreciation of the man's role in overseeing the Cherokees who carried skins from Cherokee country to Charles Town. In return, the governor accepted the Cherokee man's gift of ten beaver skins.[2]

This episode, which features a Native American who is comfortable with commodity exchange and a European community that is not, is at odds with the predominant historiography depicting Native Americans as gift givers and the Europeans as modern economic actors. As one book states, trading with Native Americans "was more akin to an exchange of gifts between allies." Historians who adopt the Native gift / British commodity duality have argued that, in colonial America, exchanges with Native Americans often had to bear close resemblance to gift giving. In their view, Native Americans were not fluent in the economic parlance of European market transactions.[3]

The above episode suggests a different, and unexplored, story, one in which the British, and not the Southeastern Indians, were uncomfortable with commodity exchange, and at times regulated trade so heavily that it became akin to gift exchange. In early modern European marketplaces that relied on the extension of credit to execute most transactions, and thereby forced many economic networks to follow the trail of familial and ethnic connections, it is not surprising that trade and gift exchange often resembled each other. Far from being impersonal, for the British commodity exchange was dependent on, and sustained by, healthy personal relationships, as were gifts.[4] Distinguishing between gift and commodity exchange in the early modern period thus requires a matrix that addresses more attributes than whether there was an existing relationship between the two parties bequeathing goods.

This book seeks to untangle the different forms of exchange operating in the colonial Southeast. In both Southeastern Indian and British cultures the similarities between gift and commodity exchange outnumbered their differences. Both were reciprocated. With the exception of the rare free gift, an offering had to be repaid with a counter-offering. Well-formulated (though at times contested) rules that established value equivalency and propriety governed both. And both had the ability to create and dissolve social relationships. By analyzing numerous exchanges between the British and the Southeastern Indians during the colonial period, this book demonstrates that all participants were acquainted with a wide array of exchange modes. Included in this examination are asocial forms in which parties had no preexisting or future relationship (such as individuals trading with strangers off the coast), transactions that required trust because reciprocity would be delayed (such as items traded on credit), and gifts and counter-gifts of sentimental or diplomatic value but little utilitarian use.[5] This book suggests why certain goods circulated as gifts and others were distributed as commodities, and how the form of exchange influenced cross-cultural social relationships and material cultures.

One cannot fully catalogue and understand the variety of exchanges that operated in early America by merely analyzing the moment when goods changed hands. Yes, gift exchanges looked different than commodity exchanges, as they were often encumbered with rituals that emphasized each party's relationship with the other and reinforced the ensuing obligations carried with these gifts. But if we freeze the frame on that single episode, we will miss the larger story. How an object was created and how it was consumed contributed significantly to its classification and social significance. Was the gun that Governor Daniel ceremoniously handed to the Cherokee man really a gift, despite the fact that it had been produced by indifferent hands alongside guns destined for the market and used by the Cherokee man in exactly the same way he would have used it if he had purchased it in the store, as he originally intended to do? I suggest not. To fully classify modes of exchange and understand their social and cultural dimensions, we need a more expansive scope than existing studies allow. We must examine production (chapter 1), exchange (chapters 2 and 3), and consumption (chapter 4).

This book suggests not only that we must trace the lives of objects, but also that we must examine the lives that made, exchanged, and consumed these objects. At the center of this book is the supposition that objects that wove their way through the continent and over the Atlantic were not inert material; they contained identities, and they provoked actions—there were lives in these objects.[6] These life-containing objects forced social and political reckonings. Southeastern Indian and British colonial societies were drawn to reflect on the value of labor invested in making these items, the status of the individuals who traded them, and, once in hand, the uses to which these foreign objects were put.

The book starts at the beginning of an object's life, with its production. Chapter 1 explores the different ideologies that British and Southeastern Indian individuals developed to explain the significance of the labor they invested in making the consumables and manufactures that were central to the cross-cultural trade. Many British and Southeastern Indian myths and ideologies about production were in conflict. Publicly, Southeastern Indians promoted an ethos of labor that harkened back to sacred law and community collaboration, even as they increasingly adopted individualistic labor practices. British colonists in the Southeast, on the other hand, fervently gave voice to the notion of individualism based in labor; yet they relied on slaves to do the work.[7]

These ideologies about production serve as the backbone of the entire book. We see debates about labor come to the foreground, and become reconfigured, when individuals exchange and consume items. The Cherokee man in the opening scene, for example, insisted that the labor he invested in procuring, preparing, and transporting the beaver skins was worth a gun; the Commissioners disagreed, perceiving that it was his service to the colony in overseeing the transportation of the skins that had value. The astute reader will note that in a reversal of the myths that dominated the Southeast, the Cherokee man was clearly presenting himself as an individual laborer, while the South Carolina officials were asking him to see himself as a manager for a corporation. This incident hints at a phenomenon fully discussed in chapter 1: neither Southeastern Indians nor British colonists were united in their beliefs about which type of labor was most valuable to society, who had the right to control that labor, and who should reap the rewards of that labor. Individuals in both societies were able to shape their cultures through their actions as traders and consumers.

How an item was produced and how it was exchanged had repercussions for consumption as well. As anthropologists have explained, gift givers often expect their presents to harbor their identities and be used in a particular way; commodities rarely carry similar obligations.[8] As shown in chapters 2, 3, and 4, actors in the colonial Southeast subscribed to this general rule. The governor and commissioners for the Indian trade expected the Cherokee man above to use the proffered gun to promote English colonial interests (in fighting wars against English enemies or protecting a trading party bound for the colonies, for example), a message that they conveyed repeatedly to other Southeastern Indians who received their gifts. Southeastern Indians encoded their own expectations into their gifts to the colonists as well, asking them to honor treaties, act as good neighbors, and acknowledge their right to land. Both parties had to decide whether or not to honor the intentions of the group who gave them an item by using it according to their wishes. Would gifts become a mechanism of collaboration across cultures, or would they reify cultural chasms?

Commodities held a different place in colonial history. These were goods that were created by anonymous hands, purchased by strangers, and worn on unknown bodies. The British, who saw Native American consumers as central to their mercantilist mission, were most intent on catering to the tastes of Southeastern Indian consumers. They demonstrated little interest in influencing those tastes. The Southeastern Indians believed likewise. As shown in chapter 4, Southeastern Indians, like other consumers in a market economy, were comfortable expressing their commodity preferences by both purchasing and refusing items without regard to their cultural origin. Southeastern Indian and British consumers further commodified items they purchased by refashioning them according to their own distinctive tastes, thereby removing all traces of their natal culture. If gifts are repositories of memories, it becomes clear, despite the claims of some scholars, that not all European items that flowed into Native American towns were gifts. It takes a careful examination of consumption habits to fully reveal this fact.

Some scholars have argued that European goods were ultimately harmful to Native American societies. They claim that Native American consumers became dependent on European objects and allowed their own skills to wither away. This view implies that Native Americans, once a self-sufficient people attuned to their environment, abandoned their heritage to the Europeans and their trade items. In the 1770s William Bartram wrote, "The Indians who have commerce with the whites make very little use colours or paints of the native production of their country, since they have neglected their own manufactures for those supplyd them cheap & in abundance from Europe—I believe they are in general ignorant themselves of the virtues of their own country productions." Bartram conceded that the "Poccoon or *Sanguinaria, Galium tinctorium,* bark of the *Acer Rubrum, Toxicodendron radicans, Rhus triphyllon* and some other vegetable pigments are yet in use, for the women yet amuse themselves in manufacturing some few things, as belts & coronets, for their husbands, feathered cloaks, macasens, & c." He concluded, however, that the Southeastern Indians had lost an important inventive capacity because of their reliance on European goods, and he trivialized their current creative expertise.[9] Some historians agree with Bartram's claim that the adoption of European goods promoted the atrophy of the skills needed to sustain a self-reliant society.[10] This book rejects that assumption and argues that, far from passively accepting European manufactured goods, Southeastern Indians rejected most of the textiles and clothes available to them. In fact, they refashioned even those items that they did embrace. If the adoption of certain European manufactures led to a loss of some traditional craft skills, it also led to an opening up of new avenues of creativity. Native American women diverted their energies from extracting natural dyes for painting deerskins to decorating fabrics with countless varieties of threads, ribbons, tapes, and beads. The consumer revolution in Indian country expanded, rather than constricted, Native American creative potential.

This book also examines how the realities in colonial America accorded with early modern British economic thought and policies.[11] South Carolina and Georgia were settled in the late seventeenth and early eighteenth centuries on the cusp of significant economic changes in England. Manufacturing output began to equal agricultural production, labor was increasingly divorced from capital, production occurred at sites more distant from consumption, professions became more specialized, trade regulations were reworked, and more people gained access to previously exotic goods. A Tory world order, which posited that all wealth and political power grew naturally out of land, was challenged by a Whig worldview, which held that other forms of labor, improvement, and trade added value to natural resources. Tories and Whigs were also at odds about trade regulation. Because they believed that wealth was rooted in the unchangeable land, and thus that resources were finite, Tories were mercantilists who argued that trade was a zero-sum game that was best orchestrated by a royal monopoly. Whigs, on the other hand, retorted that wealth was expansive, and thus economic models that promoted the involvement of more British citizens added to, rather than jeopardized, Britain's economic health.[12]

These neat categories broke down in South Carolina and Georgia.[13] Both colonies were aligned with certain Tory objectives: they would be devoted to agriculture, concentrate political power in the hands of the largest landowners, and, particularly in the case of South Carolina, participate in the mercantilist goal of helping Britain export more goods than it imported. But the overseers of both colonies embraced the Whig belief that labor, improvement, and trade could add to the natural value of land. However, the realities in the colonial Southeast pushed the founders to test how fully they believed in these tenets. For example, the Georgia trustees had faith in the sanctity of labor. Britain's poor, they argued, could turn barren land into bountiful land with the sweat of their brow. An interest in the value of labor reveals itself most fully in the debate that ensued almost immediately after Georgia was founded about whether to allow settlers to own African slaves, which the Georgia trustees originally forbade. Both opponents and proponents of slavery tallied the amount of produce a single man could yield with his labor alone, underlining their nearly universal Lockean belief that land did not just naturally produce wealth.[14] But despite acknowledging that laborers were economically valuable, the trustees doubted their social and political value and deprived them of self-government. The trustees also narrowly defined value-added labor to mean manual labor and were skeptical of the claim that scientific improvement, plantation management, and trade were useful activities.

While Georgia officials and colonists elucidated the turn-of-the-century debates about labor, South Carolina officials and colonists came head to head with debates about international trade policies. These thorny issues were foisted on them; because a useful agricultural commodity was not immediately discovered, early South Carolinian colonists were kept afloat by trading with neighboring Native American groups for deerskins and slaves, a pursuit that kept them solvent but that also forced them to rely on commerce instead of land. This mode of commerce placed unprecedented economic and diplomatic power in the hands of the lower-class peddlers who ventured back and forth between the colonies and Southeastern Indian territory, and begged a question similar to that which would be begged in Georgia: Should these individuals who added wealth to the colony in nontraditional ways be accorded social and political positions of power? Few South Carolinians were willing to answer in the affirmative. South Carolina officials also revealed that, when push came to shove, they looked more like Tories than like Whigs when crafting their trade regulation policies. Despite the fact that the proprietors and the South Carolina Commons House initially embraced the new antimonopolistic trade models advanced by the Whigs, their fear of an unregulated trade, and their belief that trade was a game of scarcity and volatile competition, always lurked in the background. Both the proprietors and the successive legislatures occasionally erected monopolies, and even when they dismantled these monopolies, they instituted a range of regulations. The Yamasee War (1715–16), which settlers blamed on the Indian trade, convinced the South Carolina Commons House of the need to heavily regulate the Indian trade, imposing the kind of constraints that forced the storekeeper in the opening vignette to turn away the Cherokee man with ten beaver skins. These regulations were largely replicated in Georgia, perpetuating the belief that the expansion of trade between poor whites and foreigners was a dangerous affair. Thus, rather than mounting a sustained challenge to Tory mercantilism, events in the Southeast reveal how traditional economic ideologies continued to influence government officials and merchants alike.

SOUTHEASTERN INDIAN SOCIETIES were also in a state of flux, a condition reaching as far back as the Mississippian era (ca. A.D. 1000–ca. 1600). A combination of environmental instabilities, resource depletions, and the very nature of the chiefdom structure itself caused communities to regularly relocate, or collapse and rebuild.[15] Subsequent to contact with Europeans, most of these chiefdoms broke apart and recombined, giving rise to the larger coalescent groups encountered by British colonists. In determining how to structure their society, these coalescing groups had a wide variety of models from which to choose.[16] Over the course of the Mississippian period, some chiefdoms built strict, hierarchically organized societies with multiple administrative layers. At the top sat an autocratic leader, called a *mico*, who could control surplus labor and goods and whose opulent lifestyle distinguished him from other members of society. At the other end of the spectrum were

Mississippian chiefdoms that were more corporate in nature. Despite their emphasis on elite lineages, they had diffuse political structures, shared decision-making responsibilities, and were composed of members who did not differentiate themselves by what they wore or ate or how they lived.[17]

Within the variously organized chiefdoms, there were multiple ways that chiefs and elites attained and legitimated their positions of power. Some leaders were able to rule by coercion. In other chiefdoms, unbridled factionalism among qualified elites necessitated that *micos* use persuasion to lure community members into the fold and keep them there. The extent to which a *mico* could take care of his town or region—be it by providing food during times of famine, defense during times of warfare, or mediation during times of internal strife—could bolster or diminish his standing. In some chiefdoms, a *mico* reigned supreme when able to prove himself adept at creating relationships with distant towns and using those networks to coordinate mutual defense and/or obtain prestige goods. In these prestige-good polities, foreign trade items became emblems of power which a *mico* could distribute to potential rivals in an attempt to keep them as allies. A leader's kinship connections and exalted relationship to the supernatural world were also a means of solidifying his or her place of honor. Ideology and religion, as well as economics and warfare, are essential to an understanding of the political and social systems in the Southeast.[18]

Mississippian chiefdoms were pushed to the limit during and after Hernando de Soto's mid-sixteenth-century rampage through the Southeast. De Soto's decimation of food reserves precipitated Southeastern Indian military losses. The Southeast, which was capable of absorbing the collapse of one or two chiefdoms, simply could not rebound from widespread regional devastation.[19] A century later the British brought diseases that the Southeastern Indians had previously escaped. The British also introduced an American Indian slave trade, burdening the recovering communities both directly and indirectly by supplying certain groups with guns and ammunition and inciting them to raid other territories in search of slaves. Chiefdoms, already structurally inclined toward political instability and still reverberating from de Soto's *entrada*, could not withstand these additional colonial onslaughts. By the early seventeenth century, chiefdoms had collapsed across the region. In the ensuing crisis, countless migrations of fleeing refugees created coalescent societies incorporating people from different chiefdoms.[20] The Creek

Indians, who had gradually achieved a loose political unification during the eighteenth century, were a fusion of groups that remained after the major chiefdoms in present-day central Alabama fell in the mid-sixteenth century. The Creek also merged with individuals from more distant chiefdoms, namely the Yuchis, Alibamos, Shawnees, Natchez, Koasati, and Alabama, some of whom may have been victims of Westo aggression.[21]

In order to develop their political and cultural institutions, these new communities had to be flexible, often deviating from the Mississippian traditions of any single group. Linguistic and cultural diversity abounded. Spoken within these groups were dialects derived from at least five language families (Iroquoian, Algonquian, Muskogean, Catawban, and Siouan). Despite the political disunity of the Mississippian world, the people shared many cultural elements, though these were oftentimes local variations of a theme. Cultural affinities gave rise to unified cultural practices, such as the annual corn harvest ritual called the Green Corn Ceremony, hunting rites, and their expectations of gift and commodity exchanges. Coalescent societies also shared in, and responded to, dilemmas and opportunities encountered with the Atlantic trade. Although each group acquired its own particular history, unifying patterns emerged across the region and within most of the Native South. While historians have done a masterful job of recapturing the local variations that distinguished Southeastern Indian cultural groups and towns from each other, this book places less emphasis on the cultural variations that differentiated specific towns and ethnicities from one another in an effort to elucidate the broader pattern of responses to expanding marketplaces.[22]

This methodology extends to this book's treatment of the colonists in South Carolina and Georgia as well. Historians have revealed the ethnic diversity of the colonists in South Carolina and Georgia. This book argues that despite differences around the fringes, settlers in South Carolina and Georgia shared and forged a cultural language about economic practices and policies. This shared language allows me to use deep analyses of episodes and debates that occurred in subsections of these colonies to elucidate the range of beliefs shared by the culture as a whole. For example, chapter 1, which untangles British debates about labor, makes heavy use of sources produced by settlers in Georgia and those outside of Georgia who expounded about the vision behind Georgia. In justifying the creation of a colony meant for individual laborers, and in defending that vision against proponents of slavery, Georgians were forced to

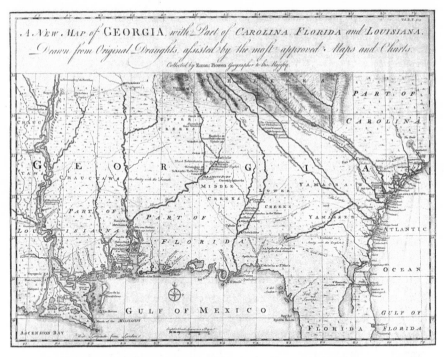

MAP 1. Eman Bowen. A New Map of Georgia, 1748. Courtesy of Hargrett Rare Book and Manuscript Library, University of Georgia Libraries, Athens, Georgia

articulate the range of debates that occurred in the South about labor. South Carolina writers, on the other hand, have center stage in chapter 2, on exchange, for they were the architects of the regulatory system that structured the deerskin trade in the Southeast in the colonial period. Through noting the different business strategies utilized by towns, ethnicities, and colonies within the regional marketplace, this book is more concerned with the spectrum of ways in which the Southeastern Indians and British colonists interpreted and reacted to colonization and the Atlantic trade.[23]

While not primarily interested in comparing and contrasting different towns or ethnicities, this book is interested in the different market responses that coexisted within the Southeast. In both English and Southeastern Indian ideologies of production, exchange, and consumption, there were gaps and ambiguities that allowed individuals to challenge the predominant beliefs, or to use those beliefs to gain social advantage within the existing system. Individuals in both British and

Southeastern Indian societies were familiar with power structures built on the ability to control access to wealth (in the form of objects or land), to amass wealth (and perhaps redistribute it), and to exert control over labor (either directly or through regulations). On the frontier of the globalizing marketplace, increased access to trading routes also offered pathways to power that were previously unavailable. Those leaders who staked their position on their command of networks to secure rare items became especially vulnerable. Porous trade lines, and the ease with which goods could be illicitly obtained, allowed individuals to accumulate the resources needed to compete for positions of authority, a process that had been in place long before contact. By disregarding the decrees of their leaders, these mercantile upstarts could stake a claim to a new position. It was not simply the fact of contact that introduced a new form of regional upheaval for the Southeastern Indians. The European manufactures furnished novel opportunities for individuals to compete for power within the existing system.[24] For Southeastern Indian leaders who hailed from a tradition in which authority was premised more on the ability to protect one's people than on one's control of resources, contact also provided new ways to prove one's worth.

It is important to underline this point. Whether intentionally or not, scholars sometimes give the impression that the Atlantic trade was responsible for toppling indigenous political structures (largely by bestowing gifts on individuals who had no hereditary stake to glory) and shifting the ethos of indigenous peoples from communal to individualistic. This book advances an alternative theory. Cultures are resilient. When individuals who had previously been deprived of goods are given unprecedented access to them, they often accept or reject those goods in accordance with cultural norms. If individuals act contrary to accepted traditions, communities devise regulations, such as sumptuary laws, or they engage in social shaming, to curb unauthorized behaviors and the use of forbidden goods. What looks like an irrational response to wealth, such as spending all of one's resources on ribbons and gold buttons instead of on garden hoes, is perfectly rational in that specific culture of consumption. And what appears to be perfectly rational behavior, such as buying locks to secure one's possessions, would seem peculiar to cultures lacking a long-standing sense of private property.[25] Cultural shifts, even significant ones, are possible, but in their wake they leave evidence of struggle. I did not, in my research, find the type of struggle one would find if the Southern Indian economic ideologies had, indeed, been wholly reconfigured by European contact.

While cultures are resilient, they are also more expansive than some historians have acknowledged; a single culture can hold a myriad of different variations on a single theme. Whereas I did not see evidence of a complete toppling of the Southeastern Indian culture, I did find examples of one belief gaining traction over another belief. Thus a more apt model for understanding the effect of commercial contact in the colonial Southeast is Karin Barber's generative model. She "envisages a productive field of potentialities, from which multiple performances emerge. At every point, creators . . . are expanding and concretizing one potentiality and in the process bypassing others." This bottom-up approach starts from production "and inquire[s] how what is produced *comes out of* existing repertoires, procedures, and habits."[26] As Ann Stahl suggests, such an examination "attends to moments when the habits of taste are diverted or interrupted," a procedure that pushes us to "resist the notion of fixity and gain an appreciation for the extent to which the habits of taste are not a 'finished set of rules' but rather a 'repertoire of possibilities.' "[27] The colonial Southeast, with its numerous combinations of cultures within each community, is perfectly suited to a model that shifts the focus from fixed institutions and objects of trade to the actions individuals and groups employed within and outside these frameworks.[28]

This theory illuminates British economic cultures as well. Like the Southeastern Indians, British settlers employed economic ideologies and conducted the Indian trade in a variety of ways. At the edges of the British Empire, settlers had the opportunity to establish economic networks with Southeastern Indians and thereby amass deerskins (the primary form of wealth in the early Southeast), creating significant diplomatic relationships with indigenous communities. How these white deerskin traders (called "Indian traders") interpreted these powers, and their place within the empire, varied. As this book shows, some individuals staked out a new path to independence, undermining their leaders' right to control their economic and social lives by disregarding colonial regulations. Others attempted to assume positions of political prominence by exploiting strands of Whig ideology. Despite the fact that they did not own land, they argued, their participation in the Indian trade was crucial for the colonies' economic success and security. And yet others saw the Indian trade as one step toward their ultimate goal of gaining power in the traditional way, by purchasing land. By and large, evidence suggests that the majority of nonelites in both societies staked new claims to authority using the available methods of their cultures. Far from being an area devoid of state power, the borderlands allowed traders not only to reinforce colonial notions of power but to assert their own relationship to the government.[29]

Because there were traders who used the cover of the borderlands to enact a free-trade model and assert political power, the southeastern region became rife with political debate throughout the colonial period. In South Carolina, Georgia, and Southeastern Indian country, those in power clung to a system of tightly regulated trade that barred upstarts from prestigious positions. Lesser elites and commoners, like the Cherokee man in the opening vignette, pushed the American economy toward deregulation and increasing individual freedom. Though wider access to trade goods did not inspire a steady march toward more individuals gaining the ability to participate equally in economic and political systems, there were revolutionary moments. Much of the Proprietary Era of South Carolina's history saw limited governmental involvement in the Indian trade. Even following the imposition of regulations after the Yamasee War, traders were able to successfully shape policies about debt and credit and gain the ear of colonial officials who saw relationships with Native Americans as crucial to their colony's health.

Evidence suggests that trade with Europeans contributed to the consensus-based form of government gaining precedence over the authoritarian form of government in Southeastern Indian society. Instead of clustering their polities in centralized power structures, as some chiefdoms did during the Mississippian period, southeastern groups emphasized the corporate decision-making strategy perfected by other Mississippian chiefdoms. This practice was better suited to uniting different ethnicities in confronting the challenges posed by European contact.[30] Instead of handing over control of their economy to headmen, more and more Native American households moved further from town centers and replaced community granaries with their own food storage structures.[31] Some southeastern elites opposed these changes and persisted in believing that they controlled the distribution of food and manufactured goods, and thus the social order. They retold fables like the Corn Mother myth and enacted annual rituals like the Green Corn Ceremony in part to bolster their control, but also in an effort to insulate Southeastern Indian culture from the potentially pernicious effects of the Atlantic trade. In these myths and rituals they reminded themselves of their long histories and their control over their economic lives. Ultimately, as this book maintains, headmen ceded some of their control over production and distribution to other individuals. In the course of doing so, they reenvisioned their role as advocates for their townsmen in their trade with Europeans. As many European visitors noted, this trend manifested itself on the bodies of indigenous leaders who used their dress to show solidarity with, instead of distance from, their peers.

In some regions, British-American colonists similarly found that colonial officials who put the corporate needs of the settlement before their own interests were better suited to the New World than those who used prestige goods to set themselves apart from the group.[32] In South Carolina and Georgia this was not always the case, begging the question why the material and economic realities of the American colonies led to the democratization of political systems in some places and not in others. As suggested earlier, this is partly due to the fact that, in the Southeast, non-elites perpetuated traditional notions of power. But it also highlights the fact that institutions matter, and that those who controlled these institutions, particularly during the first generation of colonization, were able to define the relationship between property and power. In the initial decades of colonization, South Carolina leaders had to loosen their grip on economic control and cede a lot of freedom and authority to lower-class deerskin traders who kept the economy afloat. Eventually, the interests of merchants (many of whom dealt in deerskins) and planters, though initially at odds, melded in support of a plantation economy.[33] And while South Carolina had an unusually powerful legislative branch, this was largely the result of the maneuverings of a faction (the Goose Creek Men) whose goal was to use the legislative process to perpetuate the Indian slave trade and regulate competitors out of existence.[34] In the eighteenth century, all of the members of the South Carolina legislature owned a substantial amount of land and numerous slaves. They were thus able to use their power to restrict the economic and political potential of future Indian traders.

Control over labor was central to these machinations, as individuals debated how goods destined for trade would be produced and for whose benefit. In early Georgia, where a Whig labor ideology drove the colonial mission, history charted a different course. As was mentioned earlier and will be discussed in chapter 1, though the Georgia trustees advanced the ideal that individuals should control their own labor and thereby construct autonomous lives, they created the only government within the colonies without a legislative branch.[35] Like the Goose Creek Men in South Carolina, those who agitated for more representative government in Georgia did so in order to have access to slave labor.[36] In the early years after South Carolina's and Georgia's founding, it seemed possible that the founders' belief in the right of individuals to control their own labor and economic relationships might steer the colonies toward democracy and the equality of white men. Instead, as this book argues, largely due to the significance of trade with Native Americans for deerskins and slaves, the South based its conceptions of freedom on the right to control and exploit the labor of others, whether directly through slavery or indirectly through gifts and regulations.[37]

THIS BOOK IS STRUCTURED according to the lives of objects, beginning with their production in the first chapter, following them in transit through their exchange as gifts and commodities in the middle two chapters, and ending with their consumption in the final chapter. Although the bulk of the analysis of each of these categories takes place in its designated chapter, the interconnectivity of some objects and exchange modes upsets this neat structure at moments. For example, as I argue in chapter 3, both the Southeastern Indians and the British colonists demanded that their gifts be used in specific ways. Therefore, I discuss both the exchange and consumption of gifts in chapter 3. Commodities, on the other hand, did not make demands on their consumers, allowing me to analyze commodity exchange in chapter 2 and commodity consumption separately in chapter 4.

I also found in my research that certain goods traveled more regularly as gifts, whereas others circulated as commodities. Guns, for instances, were mainstays at gift-exchange ceremonies, whereas textiles were most regularly traded as commodities. Therefore, one might note that guns are all but absent in chapter 4, on commodity consumption; fear not, as they are major actors in chapter 3, on gift exchange.

This book ends before the Imperial Crisis of the 1760s and 1770s. The French and Indian War, and in particular the Cherokee War (1759–61), greatly changed the dynamics in the Southeast. The Cherokee, in particular, were diminished numerically during the war, and the Creek Indians forfeited 2.3 million acres of their land when the Treaty of Augusta was signed in November 1763.[38] The colonial leaders in the Southeast, who once bent over backward to keep their Native American trading partners well supplied with European commodities, began discussing them as economically insignificant, and more deserving of gifts of charity. As suggested at the end of chapter 4, the Southeastern Indians doubled down on their commitment to remain serious members of the marketplace, but this required more struggle than before. Using the strategies they devised during the colonial period, the Southeastern Indians and Americans would reconfigure their economic relationships anew in the wake of war and revolution.

CHAPTER ONE

Production

In the summer of 1734 the Yamacraw Creek Indian leader Tomochichi, his family, and attachés visited England under the auspices of James Oglethorpe, leader of the new colony of Georgia. Georgia was founded in 1733 in part to buffer South Carolina from the frontier. One of Oglethorpe's first missions as a Georgia Trustee was to secure the friendship of Georgia's closest neighbors, the Yamacraw, a group of approximately 200 individuals who had separated from the Creek Confederacy. Oglethorpe hoped that this trip to England would cement a budding alliance. Before regaling his guests with theater performances, architectural tours, and meetings with royalty in London, Oglethorpe insisted they stop at a kersey wool production site in Godalming, Surrey, near his hometown.[1] The Southeastern Indians were passionate about British textiles, expending more of their yearly deerskins (close to 400,000 skins annually at the pinnacle of the trade) on cloth goods produced in Britain than on any other item.[2] Oglethorpe reasoned that the Yamacraw would relish a chance to see the creation and manufacture of the garments they regularly wore. The tour would also unveil a new production technique, one that the English usually attempted to keep secret.[3] As Tomochichi gazed out at the plant, he saw, for the first time, how the treasured fabrics came to life at the hands of British workers. Oglethorpe must have hoped that this sight would impress upon Tomochichi how the English government could command the labor of its citizens, particularly those who had previously been idle vagrants.[4]

On the Yamacraws' return home, the Georgia Trustees commemorated the voyage by sending Tomochichi two pieces of kersey, assuring him that it was "the same cloth he saw making at Godalming when he was at Mr. Oglethorpe's Country Seat."[5] Two years later, the trustees again sent a gift of red kersey to Tomochichi, insisting that the Georgia officials presenting it "must acquaint him it was made at Mr. Oglethorpe's order for him at Godalming in Surrey."[6] The trustees' pride in their manufactures, and their belief that their ability to provide such goods would secure Tomochichi's fidelity, were part of a long narrative that placed industry and technology at the heart of ideas about English colonization. From the earliest days of exploration, the English depicted Native Americans as bewitched by European technologies, affording the English both political and spiritual sway over the Indians and their environment. The "white man's power in native America," the historian James Axtell explains, "was his technological superiority."[7]

More than any other manufacture, wool textiles defined English nationhood and fueled the Atlantic enterprise. Colonial officials and British journalists alike lauded previously naked Indian consumers who enriched Britain's economy by purchasing its textiles and apparel.[8] Before the white man came, said Georgia officials, the "Red People being unacquainted with and unskilled in Arts and Sciences were under great Difficulties in clothing themselves, and had no ornaments for their women or themselves . . . but since the white people came among them they have been well clothed and gratified with a number of ornaments for their bodies."[9] The message was clear: the British made superior use of their labor.

The Southeastern Indians were unimpressed. Although they eagerly adopted European goods, they rarely glorified the labor that the British invested in these products.[10] Instead of celebrating the Godalming tour, as they did other segments of the trip, Tomochichi and the Yamacraw were silent about the textile production site. Tomochichi, who maintained relationships with officials he met in London and remarked upon other aspects of the trip in future meetings with Georgia administrators, made no mention of Godalming or Godalming kersey.[11] Despite the fact that he had gone to England to discuss the availability of trade goods, he did not ask colonial officials for looms, wheels, or balls of wool or flax. Nor did he add Godalming kersey to his litany of requests.[12]

Tomochichi's disinterest in Godalming kersey for mass import was due, in part, to the fact that most Southeastern Indians found the cloth's coarse quality unappealing.[13] More importantly, contrary to British expectations, Southeastern Indians were simply not dazzled by England's manufacturing prowess. Nor did the Southeastern Indians develop a competing rhetoric about the mystique of their own manufacturing skills. They did not attempt to hide production details from European colonists to foster curiosity about their productive capacities, nor did they argue that their rights to land and sovereignty over that land originated from the particular labor they invested in it.[14] White traders and travelers could easily examine deerskin and river cane production techniques, not because they were ceremoniously displayed, as in the Godalming tour, but because

they were performed in the open. The German traveler Philip Georg
Friedrich von Reck capitalized on this ease of observation in his careful
drawing of both a Yuchi woman weaving a cane basket and a Yuchi hunting camp (figures 1 and 2). Von Reck was too new to the area to have become a confidant, but his drawings show how even a casual visitor was
privy to indigenous production techniques. He sat so close to the weaver
and gazed at her with such concentration that he was able to accurately
capture her tattoos, despite the fact that their symbolism was undoubtedly a mystery to him.[15]

A handful of historians have studied the mechanics of Native American production techniques, but none have compared the meaning of
labor in Southeastern Indian and British colonial societies.[16] By analyzing
eighteenth-century myths and ceremonies of production, this chapter
seeks to compare ideologies of manufacturing between trading partners. British myths reveal how closely southeastern colonists connected individuals' standing in society to how effectively they and the
dependents they commanded could produce goods, either directly or
through managing plantations and slaves. This emphasis stood in marked
contrast to the Southeastern Indians, who, in their myths and rituals,
went to great lengths to disassociate an object from the individual who
created it. Southeastern Indians, therefore, were neither awed nor dis-
comfited by the way in which the Atlantic economy rendered producers

A Indien Camp.

FIGURE 2 Von Reck, An Indian hunting camp, 1736. Royal Library, Copenhagen, Denmark

and production instruments invisible to them. They did, however, find the new labor realities of the deerskin trade, which encouraged individual and nuclear family labor over communal labor, unsettling. Through their myths and rituals they regularly exalted the value of community, their sacred tradition, and their own political structures, thereby expressing a desire to maintain control over how their society was structured within an Atlantic market system.

CLEARLY, EUROPEAN COLONIZATION shaped the ways in which Southeastern Indians worked. As historians have amply demonstrated, Native Americans participating in the Atlantic trade invested their labor in the items that Europeans would purchase so that they, in return, could secure specific European goods (particularly textiles, guns, rum, and metal tools). In the Southeast, this desire for European goods increasingly limited the type of work that Native Americans performed. The first generation of settlers purchased foodstuffs and slaves in the greatest quantities, as well as a variety of skins and furs. The next generation was more discerning: though the Yamasee War, fought between South Carolina settlers and an alliance of Southeastern Indian groups between

1715 and 1716, did not eradicate human trafficking, it did reduce it. Although their seventeenth-century predecessors had purchased victuals from their Indian neighbors, southeastern colonists were, by the early eighteenth century, largely self-sufficient agriculturalists who grew most of their own food. Furthermore, the British market began rejecting all animal products except for deerskins.[17] Many Southeastern Indians responded by investing unprecedented amounts of their labor in hunting, harvesting, and transporting deerskins. While some Native Americans were paid directly by colonists to transport and prepare skins, most Southeastern Indians were self-employed and sold finished products to white traders. The archaeologist Cameron Wesson writes that the "average Tallapoosa phase [1715–1830] structure has six smudge pits within a five-meter radius, indicating [that] a tremendous amount of household effort was invested in the production of finished hides."[18] And the Chickasaws were probably not alone in developing advanced tools to process deerskins.[19] Most of the changes in labor practices, it appears, took place in Native American territory.[20]

Southeastern Indian communities retained substantial control over how they adjusted to altered labor demands. But their choices, never limitless, sometimes had unintended consequences. As they invested more of their time hunting deer and manufacturing deerskins over the course of the eighteenth century, their winter and summer hunts lengthened to the point at which hunting became a yearlong activity, consuming much of the town's labor. This trend affected social relationships. Ceremonies and other town activities were either postponed or had to proceed with reduced community involvement. Towns would all but empty for months at a time, the remaining inhabitants primarily women and elderly men.[21] Winter houses, once a staple in Southeastern Indian towns, disappeared because no one was there to occupy them.[22]

Changes in hunting techniques also created smaller social units. An earlier practice of using fire to herd deer required large groups to surround and slay the fleeing animals. Gathering with kinsmen and clansmen in large hunting parties provided opportunities for collaboration and interaction on the hunting field. But as the deer population dwindled over the eighteenth century, stalking individual and small groups of deer was more effective, a practice that was best carried out in smaller numbers. The residents of towns continued to leave for hunts together, but quickly broke off into groups of fifteen or fewer individuals, usually composed of nuclear families. These small groups hunted and dressed skins together and coordinated the sale and delivery of their product. The town's hunting parties usually tried to stay close enough to each other to provide mutual defense, but sometimes this proved impossible.[23] The shift to smaller, nuclear units on the hunting ground eventually transformed town dynamics. Southeastern Indian families became more self-sufficient and established residences further and further apart from each other.[24] A headman's authority was now based largely in his success at securing hunting grounds and acquiring guns for his townsmen.[25]

The Atlantic trade also influenced the gendered division of labor.[26] Though men and women continued to operate in their traditional spheres—"men apply themselves to the war and hunting, supply their Houses plentifully with meat, the women plant and howe the Corn," Thomas Nairne recorded[27]—the time they spent performing certain tasks, and the skills that they honed, reflected the new demands. In their contribution to the deerskin trade, Creek women and men were equal partners. On hunting trips, women tended the camp, gathered wood and food, cooked, and dressed the skins. For much of the eighteenth century a raw deerskin, unprocessed by female labor, either fetched less merchandise in trade or was rejected outright. Dressing a skin was a skilled activity that took about a week to complete. First, a woman scraped the tissue and fat from the skins. She let the skins dry, attached to frames, in the sun. After soaking the skins she was able to scrape the hair from the hides. A final soak in a solution of water and deer brains, a source of tannic acid, readied the skins to be pounded until softened. The woman then stretched and dried the skins and then smoked them over a fire pit (see figure 2).[28]

Yet despite a woman's contribution to deerskin preparation, her labor went unacknowledged as the skins wended their way to the colonies and across the Atlantic. A colonial law enacted in 1764 that stipulated that skins must be traded in towns instead of at hunting camps (where it would have been clear that women were processing the skins) hid women's contribution in the hunting camps from the view of colonial traders.[29] Women, no doubt, demanded that their partners purchase certain items with the skins they both produced, as evidenced by the variety of farming tools and haberdashery on trading lists most likely intended for women. But more often it was the male hunter who determined which European items to buy with the skins.[30] The fact that Native American women played a central role in the deerskin trade by forming romantic relationships with white traders, thereby ensuring reliable access to European goods, was also overlooked by white and Southeastern Indian traders alike when assessing their value to the trade.[31]

In conversations between male Native Americans and colonists it became clear that the male act of hunting, and not the female act of dressing the skins, conferred value on the skins. South Carolina governor James Glen said to a group of Cherokee men in 1753, "If you make good Hunts, that is the way always to have plenty of Goods."[32] Thus they should think of their "Women, and Children, and hunt briskley to cloathe them."[33] Southeastern Indian men, who already had a sense of obligation to their families, seized on this rhetoric of the male provider and deployed it in diplomatic settings.[34] Mingo Bemingo, who was part of a Chickasaw delegation to Georgia, invoked the similar gender norms held by the English and Chickasaw when explaining that he could not stay in Savannah very long because he had to return to his wife. "I believe every man would take care of his wife & therefore I would go as soon as possible," he explained.[35] Decrying the devastation of increased warfare on their communities, the Chickasaws complained that it was "impossible for us to kill Dear to buy Cloathing for ourselves, our Wives, and Children."[36] That the women were the ones who turned deer carcasses into usable leather went unmentioned.

Yet women were able to maintain control, both practically and ideologically, over their farms. As men invested more and more of their time in hunting and defending hunting grounds, the women who were left behind completed the agricultural tasks of the town in the common fields as well as the private gardens attached to each home. While men participated in some farming activities, such as planting, women were the primary agriculturalists. Many communities followed the example of one Cherokee headman: when the men were needed to wage war, "they would all go in a body and leave their women to hoe their corn."[37] It was not uncommon for travelers to find "Nobody at Home but a few old Women,"[38] and most of the reported murders of women occurred in the fields.[39] Left solely in charge, the few women who were not accompanying hunting parties were responsible for arranging crops, deciding which new seeds to import, and determining how to create stable microclimates to stave off pests and fertilize soil.[40] And unlike the deerskin trade, which obscured female labor, Southeastern Indian men and European visitors alike acknowledged women as the primary laborers in the field. Though Southeastern Indians rarely sold corn to the colonists, such business, when conducted, was transacted by women, a stark contrast to the trade in skins.[41] The same colonists who viewed male hunters as responsible for the deerskin trade determined that women were the owners of their fields. Indian trader John Buckles, for instance, reported, "Two Choctaws killed a Woman in her Plantation."[42] One could argue, then, that agricultural production was largely insulated from the Atlantic trade. The investment in deerskin and increased warfare undoubtedly made it more difficult for Southeastern Indians to grow the food vital to subsistence, but agriculture operated according to indigenous gender norms, and agricultural produce was not a primary export commodity.

It is no coincidence, then, that Southeastern Indians chose the agricultural realm, existing at arm's length from the Atlantic trade, to reinforce the very values that were threatened by colonial commerce: community cohesion and collaborative labor. In the period after contact, food production, particularly of corn, was dense with symbolism throughout the Native South. Corncob stamping of pottery replaced other patterns, and the Green Corn Ceremony (also referred to as the Busk) surpassed other rituals in importance. Though traditionally one of the Southeastern Indian leaders' primary roles was to oversee the production, collection, storage, and distribution of food for the public granary, the image of agricultural abundance did not dominate Native American art until the post-Mississippian period. This development suggests, I argue, that food production acted as the means by which revitalizing communities could negotiate social and political structures in the post-contact era.[43]

After the advent of the Atlantic trade, eighteenth- and nineteenth-century Creek and Cherokee myths about the origin of corn began to illuminate Southeastern Indian conceptions of the production of food and social relationships.[44] In both the Creek and Cherokee myths, young boys learning adult methods of subsistence became curious about the secretive production of food. Sick A Towah, who first heard the myth in the mid-eighteenth century, explained that, as the boys got older, it occurred to them that their mother "always disappeared when their provisions was exhausted, and always returned with a new stock. They were determined to find out how she came by the supplies with which she fed them."[45] But the woman refused to divulge how she procured the corn and beans.[46] In both the Creek and Cherokee myths, the curious boys secretly followed her to "a mysterious and secluded raised structure of logs, into which she shut herself."[47] Peeking between the wooden slats, the boys watched as she placed a riddle on the floor, stood "with one foot on each side of it and scratch[ed] from one of her thighs, whereupon corn poured down into the riddle. When she scratch[ed] her other thigh beans poured into the riddle."[48]

In both the Creek and the Cherokee myths the children reacted with absolute horror at the sight of their mothers' physical generativity. Sick A Towah identified the nature of their revulsion: "They could not comprehend the power by which their mother enabled them to be supplied from her own person.... Their minds were bewildered by their incapacity to understand her power."[49] In the Cherokee myth the sons "determined to slay her as an enchantress," and in the Creek myth the Corn Mother simply resigned herself to that fate.[50] "Before you leave," the Creek Corn mother instructed her son, "lock me up in this log cabin and set it on fire."[51]

The death of the Corn Mother provided both the Creek and the Cherokee with everlasting corn at the site of her murder. The Creek Corn Mother simply promised her sons that, when they returned, there would be corn and beans where they had set her on fire. The Cherokee Corn Mother, however, was more demanding and declared that her sons would have corn only if they dragged her body across the land and uttered "thanks and prayers in a series of devotional chants" while they plowed the land, and held an annual ceremony (probably the Green Corn Ceremony) to commemorate her.[52] She warned that she would always be watching over them from the sky to see if "they complied with her further instructions to tend the field through which they drew her at the various stages of her uprising in the shape of her corn,—by rooting out the weeds and lopping away the superfluous husks."[53] They were never to forget, as the Creek myth concludes, that "the corn was a person, that old woman."[54]

The Corn Mother myths reveal cultures that were deeply ambivalent about production as the fruit of humans. Instead of celebrating the human feat of reproduction, for example, the Creek myth divorces the process of creation from the body. The story, which begins with a birth, is careful to point out that the boy did not spring from the female body but rather from a mixture of dirt and blood in a jar. The Creek Indians built the fear of human reproductive capabilities into menstrual seclusion laws. Based on the belief that contact with menstruating women could bring disease and destruction, these laws ordered such women to live apart from men, use separate dishes, and not partake in communal meals.[55] As eighteenth-century European travelers and settlers noted, Creeks also downplayed the importance of birth, separating new mothers and children from the rest of the community and refusing to mark the event with public rituals.[56] Menstrual and childbirth seclusion laws were not indicative of, or based upon, a devaluation of women. In fact, many argue that, through the colonial period, women held a considerable amount of power in these matrilineal, matrilocal societies.[57] It was particularly the overwhelming power of female fertility that triggered fear, as witnessed by the sons in the Corn Mother myths who were terrified by the capacity of women to create living things from their own bodies.

While it is tempting to interpret the Corn Mother myth as targeting women, the treatment of hunters reveals that male productive capacity was also significantly tempered. Men, the myths emphasize, learned how to become successful hunters from women. In the Creek Corn Mother myth, when the son grew into a boy, the Corn Mother made him a bow and arrow and taught him which animals are suitable for eating. "What was the thing I saw flying from tree to tree?" he would ask. And she answered, "It is a bird. Go and kill it and bring it to me to eat."[58] Likewise, his social status was dependent on items produced by a woman. When the boy ventured out into the world, the Corn Mother made him a flute and a headdress from blue jays. These items endowed him with social prestige as he traveled past the mountains.[59]

While the Creek son willingly relied and thrived on the Corn Mother's guidance, the Cherokee myth offers a cautionary tale about the dangers of disregarding the wisdom and assistance of one's elders. The Cherokee sons tried to mimic their father's hunting technique before their lessons had concluded, and, in the process, released animals that were secluded in a cave, wreaking havoc. "Sons, you have said in your hearts, we can do even without our father;—and beware!—your father may leave you to yourselves," the father said in the myth.[60] As with growing corn, the father insisted that successful hunting must always depend on invoking the traditional instructions he imparts and on abiding by ritual purification.

The Southeastern Indians adopted the First Father's lesson in their daily life. Warriors relied on ritual and supernatural assistance for their success. On their hunts in the eighteenth century, Southeastern Indian men carried a buckskin pouch containing an array of magical objects that had the power to induce an animal to participate in his own slaughter. During his travels through the southern Indian country in the 1770s, William Bartram described one of these charms, the physic-nut, noting how the Creek, "when they go in pursuit of deer, carry this fruit with them, supposing that it has the power of charming or drawing that creature to them."[61] The Creek hunters also included fragments believed to be part of the mythical Horned Serpent's horns in their hunting pouches. The anthropologist John R. Swanton, writing in the early twentieth century, explained how the Creek believed that the power of the Horned Serpent was similar to that of the physic nut: "If any game animal, such as a deer, comes near the place where this snake is lying it is drawn irresistibly into the water and destroyed."[62] Hunters also carried the foot of a small deer, dressed as the animal they hoped to kill, and imitated "the voice of such an animal so well that the wild ones come near them, and their shot seldom misses."[63] These hunting tactics share one common trait: they all displace the skill and work of the hunter and, instead, emphasize the power of traditional, supernatural techniques. The animals were bewitched into succumbing to their own deaths.

Warfare was also punctuated by sacramental rites that linked a warrior to his ancestors, community members, and deities. In preparation for entering battle men completed communal purification rituals, such as abstaining from sexual contact with women, drinking "holy consecrated herbs and roots" for several nights, and fasting for the duration of the mission. They followed the lessons of their ancestors by abandoning their mission if the fire that they ceremoniously carried with them went out, if they encountered a wren, or if a warrior's dream predicted danger.[64] Like the disobedient sons in the Cherokee Corn Mother myth, the rare warrior who ignored these rituals was maligned as "irreligious" for "depending on the power of his own arms, instead of the powerful arm of the supreme fatherly chieftain, *Yo He Wah*, who always bestows victory on the more virtuous party."[65]

On their return, during an elaborate ceremony, headmen commended valiant warriors for their "strict observance of the law of purity, while they accompanied the beloved ark of war, which induced the supreme chieftain to give them the victory."[66] In conjunction with the emphasis on sacred tradition and purity, these warriors were individually celebrated. "I present you with a token of my valor at war," the warrior would declare while displaying the scalps that he seized in battle to the headmen and the town's esteemed beloved men. They would exclaim, "We thanks you." A beloved man would fetch some beads and deerskins from the public store and hand them to the headman, who would, in turn, bestow on each victorious warrior "a war name and a present." Since a warrior was eligible to receive a new name for each success in battle, it was not uncommon for a man to acquire twenty unique names.[67] These names ensured that successful men were marked in perpetuity. Their communities celebrated them as distinctive individuals in a way that female farmers, deerskin dressers, and male hunters were not marked. Accumulating these honors furthermore served as the basis for attaining political power.[68]

What was the specific type of labor that the Southeastern Indians were valuing so highly when they singled out warriors? In addition to celebrating these warriors for abiding by sacred law, the community believed that successful warriors were honorable, deliberate, and in control of themselves, as opposed to the "blind white man who rushed on with his eyes shut, improvident of danger." The Native American, because he "wisely considered that his bare breast was not bullet proof, . . . cunningly covered himself from tree to tree, and by his skillful conduct vanquished the hateful enemy, without exposing his own valuable life to danger."[69] While not producers per se, these warriors were charged with keeping people and property intact.

The Creek origin myth further reveals their mid-eighteenth century ideologies about production and warfare. Chigelly and Antiche, of the Lower Creek town of Coweta, reiterated these principles when performing the myth before a large audience of colonists in Savannah in 1735.[70] The myth, which underlines the Creeks' long history of commanding American territory and their ability to defeat all antagonizing forces, served as a warning to the colonial neighbors in the audience.[71] When they first emerged from the ground, Chigelly and Antiche related, the Creek were tormented by their environment: "a thundering hill forced them to live in fear, a noisy stick smashed their children to death, and a large bird came, killed, and ate their people every day."[72] Eschewing brute force, the Creek were able to gain strategic advantage over their enemies by harnessing the powers of the environment and manipulating the appetites of their aggressors. To combat the large bird (an eagle), for instance, the clever Creek created an object that resembled a woman. The eagle fell in love with the womanlike object, carried it away for a while, and returned it, heavy with child. After the woman gave birth to the child, a red rat, the Creek "consulted with the rat as to how they might kill his father," and devised a plan in which the rat ate the eagle's "bow strings so that the bird could not defend himself."[73] One would expect that in the next scene the Creek warriors would slay the defenseless eagle, but, alas, the myth omits this event. One is left with the distinct impression that the eagle killed himself out of misplaced lust for a man-made object, just as hunters' prey killed themselves by being lured by the hunters' sacred objects, and just, perhaps, as Chigelly and Antiche may have been warning their audience, the Europeans might lose the battle for America because of their greed, should they break their alliance.[74]

In addition to crediting their survival to clever strategies, in the origin myth the Creek attribute their success to their judicious use of nature. They fashioned the stick that once killed their children into a wooden tomahawk. The thunderous hill that left them cowering in fear gave them the holy fire and herbs which they used to honor each harvest during the Green Corn Ceremony.[75] And they "always carry the feathers of [the eagle's] tail when they go to war or peace."[76] If the English suggested that they were superior to the Native Americans because they were able to organize their labor to create cloth and guns, the Southeastern Indians retorted that their knowledge of the land and their ability to work as a group to harness the power of the environment made them formidable opponents.

The values presented in the origin myth—community labor, sacred tradition, and the prudent use of nature—were annually reinforced throughout the Southeast during the Green Corn Ceremony. The Green Corn Ceremony was *the* community event of the year. While increased hunting and military responsibilities routinely scattered a town, headmen could guarantee that "our People will be all in at the Busk."[77] As a communal gathering, the Green Corn Ceremony also became a time when headmen could discuss weighty matters with each other, tribes could consecrate alliances, and people who had attended meetings with the colonists could convey their agreements to the group as a whole.[78]

The Green Corn Ceremony was not only an opportunity for a town, or several allied towns, to reestablish their relationships; it was also a ritual that anchored the present to the past through sacred practice and ideology, and linked a people to their headmen and religious leaders. The relationship between the present and the past was undoubtedly open to interpretation. During the eighteenth century, therefore, the Green Corn Ceremony became a site of "elaborations and reorientations of earlier rituals" and was subject to constant reinterpretation.[79] Yet there were some central features that prevailed across eighteenth-century accounts, such as the main events and the order of those events. The Creek, Yuchi, and Cherokee Indians performed the Green Corn Ceremony every year in late July or early August, marking the ripening of the new harvest and the beginning of the New Year.[80] Spanning an average of four days, the Green Corn Ceremony involved cleaning, fasting, and purging in the beginning; a restatement of laws and obligations in the middle; and dancing and feasting at the end.[81] Town members extinguished all fires and finished last year's harvest so that they could produce a new fire and consume the new harvest from public lands. People purged, relearned their ancient rules, and were reborn in the river.

For Southeastern Indians in the eighteenth century, the Green Corn Ceremony symbolically recreated the Middle World (which, in their tripartite cosmology, was the realm inhabited by mortals).[82] During this recreation, it is not surprising that the Southeastern Indians harkened back to their founding myth of the Corn Mother. After they purged by imbibing the black drink at the beginning of the Green Corn Ceremony, the men metamorphosed into the sons at the start of the Corn Mother myth.[83] Central to this process (and to the myth), the men were kept willfully ignorant of the productive capacities of the women of the town, who were responsible for cooking all of the food during the ceremony. Men were sequestered in the town square, and all women, except for the Beloved Women whose obligations did not include cooking, were barred from entering the square until the last day.[84] Furthermore, women had to leave the food they prepared in their houses at the perimeter of the square to be collected and distributed to the men by religious attendants, a practice that set the Green Corn Ceremony apart from other ceremonies performed throughout the year.[85] The fact that Beloved Women were allowed to enter the square when other women were prohibited from doing so suggests that this ceremony was more concerned with isolating producers from consumers than with distinguishing men from women. By severing all interactions between consumers and producers, the Green Corn Ceremony recreated the original world in which the sons did not witness their female caretaker producing corn and beans.

By symbolically eradicating individual human producers, the Southeastern Indians were able to remind themselves that individual labor did not create and recreate their societies. Rather, it was their devotion to ritual and community that perpetuated their way of life. When the religious leader made a single offering to the fire at the end of the ceremony, he deliberately chose animal, herb, and vegetable, encompassing the labor of all sectors of society.[86] Similarly, multiple actors produced the food for the final feast. It contained the vegetables that were a product of community labor, taken from the communal, and not the household, garden. The women cooked the final feast on the New Fire, the product of the labor of the religious leader.[87] These choices masked individual labor and celebrated communal labor.

Headmen, Beloved Men and Women, and religious leaders stood at the center of the Green Corn Ceremony, thereby sanctifying their positions of authority and respect. The headmen were responsible for providing the "necessary Orders to be given for the Bus[k]."[88] During the ritual, the religious leaders acted as proxies for the sacred traditions that the Green Corn Ceremony renewed. At the climax of the Green Corn Ceremony, for instance, the town's religious leaders lectured the people about their ancient laws and obligations.[89] A nineteenth-century observer noted that these speeches were delivered "in a language that is partly lost—at least there is very little of it known now," suggesting that the Green Corn Ceremony was a call to honor the past and a reminder that the towns' leaders were the vessels of sacred and historical knowledge.[90] In this ceremony representing the restarting of the human world, these revered individuals were also charged with ordering society. They first leveled the society, erasing all rankings and inequalities, by doling out the black drink and small tobacco in personalized quantities.[91] Then, on the last day of the Green Corn Ceremony, they reestablished community rank through food distribution. While previously the religious waiters, charged with distributing food during the feast, had indiscriminately served meals to "the famished multitude" in the square, this time they allocated the food in order of social rank, from Headmen, Beloved Men, Head Warrior, warriors, and so on down.[92] During the remainder of the year individuals in the square were seated according to these social divisions and hierarchies.[93]

The religious leader's lofty position in society was also attested to by the fact that, during the Green Corn Ceremony, his labor was neither hidden nor diluted. This transparency of labor was first indicated in his new dress, which he had created, down to the sinew, from a single animal, instead of from multiple sources, as was the case with the other objects in the ceremonies.[94] Dressed in this garb, the religious leader created the New Fire, which, similarly, did not obscure or eclipse his labor. As he withdrew to the temple building in the square to make the fire, everyone was expected to stand at attention—the men in the square and the women in their homes—until he emerged with the fire. Multiple observers attested to the arduous task of making the New Fire from scratch.[95] After this feat the religious leader recreated his people as law-abiding members of the community, instructing them with sermons and reminding them of their obligations to their community and ancestors. As the most esteemed member of Southeastern Indian society, the religious leader was allowed to display the generative capacity that the Corn Mother and all other individuals in Southeastern Indian society had to conceal and obscure by mixing it with the labor of others.

The role of the religious leader during the Green Corn Ceremony suggests that Southeastern Indians fully understood that individuals could create objects themselves and, in fact, allowed the most powerful individuals to do just that. John Locke wrote in *The Second Treatise* that "reason makes the deer that *Indian's* who hath killed it," and, in practice, the Southeastern Indians would not disagree.[96] For Southeastern Indians, the idea that an individual's status in society was related to the labor he or she performed was not inimical. Property was individually owned, even though portions of that property were funneled to a central reserve for the community to use for gifts to other nations, to reward warriors for their valor, and to support individuals and the town when disaster struck.[97] Families consumed the produce they grew in the gardens attached to their homes and had a right to produce from the communal garden only if they labored in it; hunters got to take home most of the meat they shot themselves, and if they chose to trade the skins, they kept the trade goods; a woman's family wore the clothing that she manufactured.[98]

The inextricable connection between individuals and their property is most clearly seen in Southeastern Indian mortuary practices. Alexander Longe, who resided among the Cherokee from 1710 to 1725, reported that they believed that a person's soul could not leave his or her personal belongings, which prompted them to free the deceased from Earth by burning everything the person owned at the time of death.[99] Other observers claimed that the Southeastern Indians buried, rather than burned, their movable goods. A Georgia settler recorded that upon the death of a Native American man (probably a Creek or Yuchi Indian) who had settled among colonists at Purysburg, "some Indians assembled for his burial and interred him, according to their custom, in a sitting position, together with his hunting weapons[,] household tools, and clothes."[100] And James Adair, who called Southeastern Indian territory (particularly Chickasaw country) his home from 1735 to 1768, insisted that "modern

Indians bury all their moveable riches." The exception, he noted, was the Creek headman Malatchi, "who bequeathed all he possessed to his real and adopted relations," as well as the "Cheerake of late years" who had been persuaded by white traders to will their goods to their nearest living relative.[101] Whether the deceased's possessions were burned, buried, or bestowed, the Southeastern Indian mortuary practices reveal a clear sense of the individual's ownership of his tools and the items he created and purchased using those tools.

These customs raise the question of whether the Southeastern Indian myths and rituals accurately reflected the belief system of the majority. Perhaps these rites were rote practices carried out in honor of tradition, or perpetuated by an elite subsection of society who had a vested interest in their messages. Gregory Waselkov and Ashley Dumas have suggested that the Green Corn Ceremony was central to a revitalization movement during the post-Mississippian period. As the Southeastern Indians reeled from the disease and devastation of the Spanish expeditions, the collapse of the Mississippian chiefdoms, and the creation of new coalescent communities, a movement spread throughout the territory to revive old cosmographies such as the representation of the three-tiered universe. The Southeastern Indians then applied these models to new realities such as the collapse of hierarchal chiefdoms and the emergence of a more egalitarian, consensus-based social structure. Waselkov and Dumas surmise that the Green Corn Ceremony became the principal mechanism for enacting this revival—a means of reinvigorating traditional cosmologies in a nonhierarchical, community-wide setting.[102]

It is possible that Waselkov and Dumas overstate the Green Corn Ceremony's alignment with emerging social realities. Other evidence suggests that, rather than adapting to changing events, the myths and the Green Corn Ceremony attempted to buttress an image of Southeastern Indian society that was in jeopardy of eroding. The most striking example of this phenomenon appears in Alexander Longe's description of the final feast in the Green Corn Ceremonies he witnessed when living with the Cherokee. The headman was treated with the pomp and circumstance of a Mississippian-era chief. Longe recounts how, sporting the sacred crown, "the king is lifted up on four generals shoulders and carried round a great and spacious square," at regular intervals being cooled with fans. For the duration of the feast "they never let the soles of the king touch the ground."[103] This treatment was at great odds with the daily lives of headmen, who dressed, lived, and traveled like everyone else in the town.

The Green Corn Ceremony also glorified specific individuals in Southeastern Indian society, particularly religious leaders, as the purveyors of corn. In fact, Southeastern Indian families were increasingly controlling their own food production and diversifying their crops. Archaeologists have found that during the eighteenth century most nuclear family Creek Indian dwellings had their own storage pit for food, whereas in earlier phases it was more common for families to rely on public granaries controlled by the headman.[104] And, as they celebrated the yearly Green Corn Ceremony, the Cherokee were actually turning away from corn and toward other native crops and fruits that required less labor and insulated them against the risks of warfare, disease, and loss of labor to the deerskin trade.[105]

But did these changes alter the Southeastern Indians' evaluation of productive relationships? If so, were these changes beneficial or harmful to their societies? It can be argued that Southeastern Indian cultures and practices of production shielded them from some of the more potentially damaging outcomes of the Atlantic market system. Thus, old rituals were revived in order to preserve the bond between a new reality and a pre-contact system of ethics. It is telling that Southeastern Indians chose to situate their origin stories in cornfields. Europeans may have produced the Indians' guns and textiles, but Southeastern Indians continued to produce their own corn, to gift plants of corn to new settlers, and to sustain British soldiers who manned the forts in their territories by either giving or selling them corn.[106] Though diplomatic relationships with the Europeans and the deerskin trade pressured Southeastern Indians to conform to European norms, the realm of agriculture remained largely untouched.[107]

There is also an aspect of the Southeastern Indian ideology that can be read as protest literature if the cultural custodians were consciously revising the ceremonies and myths, or as a protective mechanism if they were not. Raised in a culture that was comfortable with items that obscured their individual sources of labor, the Southeastern Native Americans did not have to psychologically adjust to a commercial system that created a new distance between producers and consumers. This cultural system insulated them from the disruptions other peoples have faced when adjusting to an expanding market, which, according to Marx, can lead to fetishizing the commodities that distort traditional productive relationships.[108] Southeastern Indians were able to accept European products without overvaluing the productive capacities of Europeans and adopting the colonial rhetoric of Native American creative deficiencies. Accustomed to incorporating foreign goods into their communities, the Southeastern Indians could do so without lionizing the item's producer. The Green Corn Ceremony and their myths helped Native Americans to keep these relationships in proper perspective.

THE COLONISTS WHOM the Southeastern Indians encountered would have been familiar with, if not wholly sympathetic to, their labor ideologies. During the first few decades of the seventeenth century, Joyce Appleby explains, "the social purpose of labor predominated" in English thought.[109] In this period of food scarcity, grain producers were required to put the subsistence needs of the community above their own desire for profit, an expectation that was reinforced by biblical decrees. According to Appleby, an increase in agricultural productivity in the seventeenth century and abundant harvests after 1662 relaxed the pressure placed on farmers to invest all of their land and energy in supporting the community. Grain was then categorized in the same way as any other commodity. The land enclosure movement, which began in the mid-seventeenth century, signaled that society was embracing the value of individual labor and profit over community labor and welfare.[110]

But some historians question whether, as Appleby and others assert, there was a steady march toward liberal thought. Instead, they argue that this ideological shift happened slowly, unevenly, and, in some places, not at all.[111] Well into the eighteenth century, only about 30 percent of individuals sold their labor in a market; most people worked for family members, which enforced the connection between individual labor and corporate well-being.[112] In addition, religious and social mores limited the embrace of individualism in Britain. Despite the seventeenth-century movement to cede common land to individuals, for instance, English intellectuals and religious leaders regularly expressed their support of a common right to land. They argued that humans were simply stewards of God's land, and must honor God's wishes that the fruits of his land be shared with the poor.[113]

At least some southeastern colonists endorsed this social view of labor. One readily available pamphlet in South Carolina, Joseph Morgan's *The Nature of Riches*, published in Philadelphia in 1732, asserted that man's individual ownership of the products of his labor did not benefit society, but was a necessary evil that grew out of man's sinful nature. Ideally, said Morgan, "there would be no occasion for any man to have his riches or estate to himself."[114] Instead, man would "labour sincerely, in his calling, for the good of the whole. . . . And all that is produced, would be for every one as he needs."[115] But man's sinful nature prohibited the realization of this ideal society and determined "that each man be the proper owner of what his Industry raises."[116]

The southeastern colonists determined that laboring individually, and individual ownership of the proceeds of that labor, was more efficient and just than communal labor and the equal distribution of goods. Additionally, instead of believing that individual production and ownership were in tension with community welfare, proponents of southeastern colonization recognized that the success of the enterprise depended on individuals investing in their own prosperity.[117] The widespread adoption of this ideology, even by inhabitants who did not hail from Britain, can best be seen in the writings of the Salzburger settlers. The Salzburgers, who were Protestant German peasants, first settled in Georgia in 1734. They deliberately employed a corporatist labor philosophy to create a community reliant on communal labor and mutual ownership. They initially ordered their agricultural labor in a manner similar to that of the Southeastern Indians; men worked in a common field, and women tended gardens. All of the bounty was split evenly among the townsmen, a commitment to corporate living that not even the Southeastern Indians attained. But the Salzburgers were dissatisfied with relying on communal property alone and, as pastors Johann Martin Boltzius and Israel Christian Gronau explained, "also want to work for themselves." Because the cooler morning and evening hours were devoted to communal labor, they performed their individual work "during the time of the most intense heat," making themselves sick.[118] The following year the pastors concluded, "Communal work, in the way we have practiced it so far, is no good and brings little profit. If the people were given their own land and were allowed some freedom in their work and their arrangements, one would soon detect excellent gains."[119] By June 1736 all of the communal land was divided into private lots, and productivity increased greatly.[120] The Salzburgers thereby affirmed the Georgia Trustees' contention that those who worked "for their own Benefit, they are indefatigable, and outdone by none."[121]

The Salzburgers extolled individual labor, much like the most celebrated architect of South Carolina, John Locke. Locke was the coauthor (if not the sole author) of the first draft of the Fundamental Constitutions of Carolina. He oversaw its subsequent revisions, and received much of the credit for the political philosophy underlying its principles.[122] In part because of Locke's influence on South Carolina, Barbara Arneil argues, "'Industrious'... became the key word to the Lord Proprietors, for it was the labour of those who would work that brought value to the plantation."[123] The environmental conditions of the Southeast reinforced this high regard for human labor. In order to make the land profitable, the colonists had to transform the swampy wasteland into well-ordered plantations. In the process, South Carolinians embraced an "ethic of industriousness," and the Georgians rolled up their sleeves to conquer the American wilderness that the trustees had "opened for industry."[124]

This "ethic of industriousness" was premised on a theory of labor that differed from that of the Southeastern Indians. Unlike the depiction in the Corn Mother myth, where produce grew directly from the body or nature before the sons faltered, Locke argued that human labor was necessary to production, and that this was a good thing. With his labor, man removed natural products from their common state and "fixed" his property in them.[125] As Robert Markley concludes, "Locke emphasizes labor itself as the be-all and end-all of value, glossing over the dialectical transformations of humankind and landscape" to the extent that the "land itself becomes largely a function of labor."[126] For the Southeastern Indians, products were removed from their individual makers at moments in which they were reinvigorating their communities; for Locke, writes E. J. Hundert, humans continually "inject the very essence of their personalities into the object worked upon."[127]

By injecting his personality into an object he manufactured, a man created a perpetual bond with that object, a theme that Anglican ministers in London reinforced annually when they delivered their anniversary sermon extolling Georgia's future and past successes.[128] The preachers argued that because God manufactured man, God would always control him. Thus man was best seen as an extension of God, his maker.[129] Locke similarly argued that God, as the producer of man, would always be man's rightful owner, preventing him from destroying his body or selling it into slavery.[130]

This philosophy of production filtered into the missionary literature, where it was presented to Native Americans. Thomas Wilson, who wrote a conversion manual inspired by Tomochichi's 1734 visit to England, taught missionaries to reinforce man's obligation to God, his maker, when instructing the Native Americans in Christianity. First, tell the Indians that the Great God "made the World and all things in it, and in [his] Hands our Breath and Life is," Wilson instructed the missionaries. Next, remind the Indians "what Duties you owe to your Maker," underlining the endless debt one owed to God for the gift of life.[131] Unfortunately for missionaries and colonial officials, this argument did not resonate with the Southeastern Indians. Enmeshed in a culture that ritually divided manufactures and producers, the Southeastern Indians did not contemplate an obligation to their maker per se, but rather an obligation to their communities and their ancestors. They did not envision themselves as extensions of a deity or their manufactures as extensions of themselves.

Even southeastern colonists, who were primed by their European culture to see the connections between producers and products, could not always make these connections easily. Only the most simple of tasks allowed a clear line to be traced from a single laborer and his product. When multiple individuals invested their labor in the creation of a product, colonists had to determine who deserved the largest portion of the proceeds and what type of labor was the most valuable.[132] On this point, southeastern colonists were divided. Some argued that the manual laborers who directly created the food they needed to survive were the most virtuous members of society. Others asserted that the nonphysical labor of managing a plantation and instituting innovative agricultural techniques brought the most profit to the colony and thus should be the most revered. And still others believed that those who were able to wash their hands of the mundane tasks of production and concentrate on politics and intellectual pursuits sat at the pinnacle of society.

In Georgia, where, Jack Greene reminds us, settlers "had an unusually clear sense of what they hoped to do," the trustees asserted that the colony should be devoted to the men who directly harvested the land.[133] By providing Britain's disenfranchised with a place to flourish, Georgia did not stand apart from other British colonies.[134] But by restricting the amount of land that an individual could hold to 500 acres, preventing the private sale of that land, and outlawing the use of slaves, the Georgia Trustees signaled their determination to create a colony built on the "Labour of the industrious white People, for whom the Colony was principally intended," and not on the wealth of gentlemen.[135] Samuel Smith echoed these sentiments in his inaugural lecture before the Georgia Trustees. He envisioned that Georgia would provide a corrective to other settlements, in which "large tracts of land lie waste and uncultivated, that would otherwise furnish an ample provision for numbers of distress'd families, and open new fields of industry to the laborious planter."[136] Whereas others in the colonies devoted themselves to "Traffick" and "arts and sciences," and other colonies' governors were consumed with "Self Interested Views of raising private Fortunes, and by that means prostituting Justice, and oppressing the People to Accomplish Their Case, and Unworthy Ends," Georgia mimicked early Rome, where individuals of all stations "Laboured in Common with the meanest, for Their daily Subsistance Which Glorious example could not faile to inspire the breast of every Roman to labour and that with the utmost Chearfulness."[137]

In the Southeast, South Carolina promoters promised, men would not only transform the land, but the land would transform them.[138] Manual labor, geared only toward supporting one's family, Georgia's founders echoed, inculcated the values of diligence, duty, and honesty necessary to produce good citizens. The Scottish nobleman Sir Robert Montgomery, who created the first blueprint for Georgia, imagined a place where "poor labouring men, so secured of a fixed future settlement," would go "and act, when there, with double diligence and duty." These newly virtuous men would in turn "bring their children up honestly."[139] By securing a piece of land, people who were once "useless members" of society would learn to lead a "useful and significant" life, minister Samuel Smith proposed. For Georgia would provide "plenty of Materials for their Employment, and the Produce of the Labor will subsist them and their families."[140] Minister George Watts esteemed subsistence labor, pointing out that while God replenished the earth for the poor, people should not suppose "he would make every convenience rife up for their use, and remove every obstacle without any labour of their own." On the contrary, Watts maintained, "ye text expressly directs the hungry to prepare *themselves* a city to dwell in, *to sow their lands, and plant vineyards, to yield them fruits of increase*."[141] Chaplain Edmund Bateman, too, emphasized the necessity of "labours which were to be undergone on their part, before their happiness was to be complete."[142] While some of the ministers relied on the language of stewardship and the obligation of man to use God's land to distribute the profits fairly, most of the Georgia preachers directed men to use the products of their labor to better themselves— materially, spiritually, and civically.

The Georgia Trustees were optimistic that all men, if given the right opportunities and tools, could be productive. The charter posited that the multitudes of impoverished British subjects and foreigners seeking refuge in Britain, who "through misfortunes and want of employment [were] reduced to great necessity, insomuch as by their labor they [were] not able to provide a maintenance for themselves and their families," would, after settling in America and "cultivating the lands, at present waste and desolate," certainly "gain a comfortable subsistence for themselves and families."[143] But as in Britain, Georgia had to grapple with the birth of "the laboring poor," a new category of people who were destitute but not idle.[144] Facing sparse agricultural returns in the first decade of their experiment, some of the Georgia settlers were struggling to survive, and the trustees were unsure how to interpret this failure. Were the colonists simply unlucky, or was the trustees' premise that man would naturally work hard if given the opportunity to do so misguided? Speaking for the trustees, Benjamin Martyn lamented that among "the Necessitous, who first applied to be sent over, there were some, who had been reduced merely by Misfortunes, but still unused to Labour; and many by Idleness, who were as little accustomed to it. It was almost impossible to distinguish between them."[145] Instead of positing that Georgia could transform anyone into a virtuous laborer, in the 1740s the trustees began distinguishing between honest and dishonest individuals. Many of the poor who arrived in Georgia "shewed [that] they were brought into those Misfortunes by their own Faults; and when those who quitted their own Country to avoid Labour, saw Labour stand before their Eyes in *Georgia*, they were easily persuaded to live in *Carolina* by Cunning, rather than work."[146]

The trustees' ambivalence about the character of their laboring inhabitants is reflected in the governmental structure they created. At a time when every British North American colony had a legislative branch, the trustees chose not to offer the Georgia colonists a chance to participate in government. As other commentators have noted, the Georgia Trustees were not proponents of democracy; they were philanthropists who supported traditional hierarchies.[147] Until the inhabitants could prove that they could use their labor to improve their land, the trustees viewed them as dependent settlers, not independent citizens. Some servants thumbed their nose at the social hierarchies of their natal country, but such transgressions, instead of causing the gentlemen of Georgia to embrace a utopian vision of equality, drove them to rage.[148] The trustees walked a middle road. While they hoped that the settlers would "consider to whom they are indebted for their preservation, and from whom they must expect a blessing on their labours," they hoped that once the settlers were financially independent they could expect a degree of political independence as well.[149] Although some Georgia colonists countered that it was impossible for even an industrious man to sustain his family through his labor on the land alone, the trustees remained committed to the belief that as long as he had a strong work ethic he could convert his labor into independence and, eventually, citizenship.[150]

The alternative to the vision of the Georgia Trustees was not, in the minds of their opponents, the cultivation of different forms of cooperative, free labor. The solution was enforced servitude. By 1751, the trustees' dream of free labor and communal harmony had been supplanted by the economics of slavery when they finally succumbed to the aggressive campaign of a group of colonists, referred to as the Malcontents, and their sympathizers.[151] Unlike the trustees, proponents of slavery could not rejoice in the virtue of manual labor, for that would make slaves the most virtuous individuals in the South. They could not argue that the man who mixed his labor most directly with the land was the owner of the products of that land, for that would make black men and women wealthy beyond belief. Colonists in the Southeast were aware of these pitfalls and realized that, to some, their adoption of slavery marked them as unenlightened.[152] As the eighteenth century wore on, travelers from Britain and the North, who embraced the same labor ideology that graced the writings of early southeastern colonists, disparaged slaveholding southern elites as lazy and degenerate while praising the hard-working slaves.[153]

In response, southeastern colonists maintained that they were not lazy, but rather that there were other forms of labor that were more virtuous and made man more entitled to property. John Stewart, who had previously worked as a trader to Native Americans, mocked individuals who overvalued the "toil of the body" and the "labor and toil which every slave is capable of." He subscribed to the classical Republican view that the highest form of labor was intellectual and political, a calling that could be answered only when a man no longer needed to get his hands dirty. Stewart declared that "a more than ordinary desire to do somewhat greater tasks than that of negroes did excite me to consider Government."[154] Others, seizing on the concept of "improvement," averred that the overseeing of crops and labor was a far more estimable activity than working the land oneself. Slave labor alone could not create valuable commodities, Peter Gordon, the first bailiff of Georgia, argued when encouraging Georgians to permit slavery. It was rather "their Labour Joyned to the industry and good management, of Those who have hade the direction of Them," that led to commercial success elsewhere in the Atlantic world.[155] When determining the skills most valuable in running a plantation, colonists in South Carolina pointed to their agricultural innovations and their "hard-won experience by which they had learned to convert wastelands into productive fields," the historian Max Edelson concludes.[156] Proud of their ability to transpose human designs over nature—by introducing new crops and horticultural innovations—southeastern colonists deviated from the British belief that man was simply a steward of God's creation, as well as the Southeastern Indians' reverence for the rules of their ancestors when harnessing nature.

Regardless of what type of work the colonists most prized—be it physical, managerial, or intellectual—they were united in believing that a free white man had a right to the fruits of his labor as well as to those of the labor he commanded. Colonists viewed improvement in personal rather than corporate terms; a man's plantation was "a privately bounded domain for enterprise."[157] Even the argument posed by the Malcontents in defense of slavery marshaled the modern liberal economic claims for individual property rights that would later be used to bolster free labor ideologies.[158]

This relationship between an individual and the products of his labor was crucial to the eighteenth-century concept of liberty and a just society. As one colonist asserted, Georgia's promise of liberating the poor could become a reality only if "the Profits of his Labour be for his own Use."[159] The radical Whigs John Trenchard and Thomas Gordon observed that the essential component of liberty was "the power which every man has over his own actions, and his rights to enjoy the fruits of his labour, art, and industry."[160] The Southeastern Indians would not have disagreed with the proposition that man has a right to what he created. South Carolina governor James Glen acknowledged this when he said to the Creek headmen, "This you know is the Case among yourselves. You can oblige no Man to part with his Property unless he pleases."[161] What differentiated the southeastern colonists from the Southeastern Indians is that, rather than keeping this individualized vision of labor separate from their notion of community, the colonists believed that control over labor and property rightfully determined one's place in society. Trenchard and Gordon noted that "it is most certain, that the first principle of all power is property; and every man will have his share of it in proportion as he enjoys property, and makes use of that property." It was the law of natural power, they explained, that "men will ever govern or influence those whom they employ, feed, and clothe, and who cannot get the same necessary means of subsistence upon as advantageous terms elsewhere." On the opposite side of the coin, "men will contentedly submit to be governed by those who have large possessions, and from whom they receive protection and support, whilst they will yet always emulate their equals."[162] One's rank in society, in other words, naturally grew out of one's ability or inability to create and control property. One's position in Southeastern Indian society, by contrast, was determined by one's capacity to abide by sacred law and tradition. Year after year, at the Green Corn Ceremony, political and religious leaders reinforced this social structure built on ancient tenets.

AS TOMOCHICHI AND JAMES OGLETHORPE stood together, looking out at the textile manufacturers, they may have found common ground in recognizing the benefit of a group of laborers working side by side for a common goal. But both of them would have also known that this was not the primary way that labor was organized in the Southeast. Oglethorpe, as a Georgia Trustee, was invested in the ideal of the lone farmer. And while the members of Tomochichi's town pooled their labor at times, such as when the fields needed to be planted, nearly every other economic task— be it hunting, dressing skins, carrying skins to sale, harvesting crops, or fashioning clothing—was the work of small groups or individuals.

The textile tour displayed a form of labor organization that Tomochichi could not emulate. But there is a chance, given what we know, that this tour resonated with him. If Tomochichi was going to be impressed by any exhibition of English labor, this would be it. For even if the Southeastern Indians were spending little time laboring together, they were regularly reminded of the worth of communal labor. Far from the colonists' eyes they enacted rituals that turned what appeared to be individual activities into acts that emphasized collaboration and tradition— mixing food products created by multiple parties before consuming them; abiding by the hunting and warring rules of purification established by tradition; telling the cautionary tale of the sons who did not listen to their father. Even as the expanding Atlantic trade drove Southeastern Indian hunters to accumulate wealth in nuclear, instead of larger clan or town, units, the Southeastern Indian myths and rituals warned against adopting an individualist outlook. The textile factory, with its row upon row of laborers, seemed to exemplify that accepted mentality more cogently than the farmer with a hoe.

If Tomochichi deliberately ignored the Godalming tour, and the evidence suggests that he did, he most likely did so to protest the English claim that an object was an emblem of its producer. Oglethorpe wanted to impress upon Tomochichi that *the English* made these goods, and thus Tomochichi should respect these "makers." Pride in manufacturing is not necessarily nefarious, but in the colonial context it became a way that the English could claim superiority, and eventually sovereignty, over the Native Americans. Tomochichi may have suspected this. He did not want to walk around wearing the insignias of English textile manufacturers; he wanted to walk around wearing nice, soft woolens, refashioned by his wife. Tomochichi had come to England for one reason—to negotiate the best prices possible for the products he desired. He wanted, in other words, to procure and wear commodities.

CHAPTER TWO

Commodity Exchange

Determining how trade with Europeans affected Native American cultures, societies, and polities has been a central question for scholars who study early American history. When Tomochichi and other Native American leaders appeared before kings, governors, and colonial assemblies and advocated for better prices on a greater variety of goods, were they pioneering new roles or following in the footsteps of the *micos* who preceded them? Scholars who argue that there was continuity point to archaeological evidence that suggests that precontact Mississippian *micos* often served as portals through which foreign goods entered their territory.[1] Their role as gatekeepers was crucial to their ability to retain power. With foreign objects in hand, a *mico* could show that he was adept at creating and sustaining beneficial networks, confirm his supernatural power (if the goods were sacred), and gift these objects to potential competitors to keep them as allies.[2] Within the framework of continuity, the political significance of foreign objects explains why Native Americans eagerly acquired European goods. But these imports were double-edged swords, for while they could bolster the power of sitting leaders, they could also lead to their undoing. A clever upstart without a pedigree, skilled at acquiring these manufactures, could make a case that he was most deserving of a leadership position, thus upsetting traditional political structures. The flood of European manufactures into the colonies and the multitude of routes through which one could obtain those manufactures made it particularly difficult for Native American leaders to remain unchallenged.[3]

This perception of trade as a threat to established power structures is premised on a particular understanding of precontact society, one that is now being questioned. Some archaeologists have posited a more complex picture of Mississippian politics by demonstrating that there were multiple sources of authority in the Mississippian world, of which the control of prestige goods was only one. In upholding their right to lead, precontact *micos* and other elites relied upon their kinship connections and their relationship with the supernatural. They also proved that they were indispensable to their community's welfare by acting as judicial officers during periods of strife, coordinators of provisions in times of want, and orchestrators of defense in time of war.[4] Building on this modified view of Mississippian chiefdoms, this chapter proposes a revised understanding of the role played by Southeastern Indian leaders in the Atlantic trade. After contact, when the strict hierarchies known during the Mississippian period collapsed, headmen could no longer depend on their inherited place within a specific clan to stake their claim to power. Their monopoly over prestige goods was short-lived as well. To maintain their rank, this chapter argues, postcontact leaders emphasized their ability to protect their communities by enlarging their economic opportunities. Most individuals would become directly involved in foreign trade. Leaders thus envisioned themselves as overseers of commerce, seeking to ensure that their community members got the best prices for their goods, that the trade was carried out fairly, and that they had the hunting grounds and guns necessary to harvest deerskins. Instead of upsetting Southeastern Indian leadership patterns, the Atlantic trade pressed leaders to accentuate some skills over others.

In this context, it becomes clear why Tomochichi was not unduly impressed by the kersey that he "saw making" and was more intent on meeting the Georgia Trustees and King George, from whom he could request access to goods. Like other Native Americans who desired to cross the Atlantic, he was attempting to bridge the diplomatic chasm. Many wanted to meet "the Great King over the Great Water," for, as Creek leader Malatchi lamented in 1753, they had "never had the pleasure to see the great King George, nor to hear him talk."[5] The vastness separating England from America also troubled the Cherokee leader Connancaughte. He attempted to close the gap between himself and the Great King by giving South Carolina governor James Glen a "small leather bag in which was enclosed some Earth . . . desiring that it might be sent also to the Great King George."[6] Perhaps the most thoughtful gift that James Glen ever gave to Old Hop (or any leader, for that matter) was a box of maps and a magnifying glass. Because Old Hop was "not able to travel I am going to shew him other Countries in a Glass," Glen explained. Glen was shrewd enough to have figured out that Old Hop would want to "shew them to your People" as evidence that he was successfully linking his town to a vast commercial network.[7] For Southeastern Indians, the road to achieving leadership in the Atlantic economy was rough and uneven. With each step, they discovered that it was the distribution of goods, rather than the incorporation of technologies produced in remote locations, that spawned the greatest struggles within their communities.

For the English colonists, commodity exchange was equally fraught with dilemmas about political economy. They, too, debated whether distribution should be controlled by leaders, and if so, which leaders. In England, the decades surrounding the Glorious Revolution (the very era in which South Carolina and Georgia were created) brought the question of royal versus parliamentary control of the economy into sharp relief. But there were other controversies stirring as well. Markets were expanding over unprecedented distances, bursting out of traditional oversight networks. Could trade run smoothly by itself in borderlands, or must order be instituted? Those who claimed that oversight, particularly by governments, was unnecessary clashed with balance-of-trade theorists. Proponents of the mercantilist model of commerce were deeply suspicious of trade relationships, regarding them as inherently hostile. This balance-of-trade theory was premised on the belief that all global wealth—minerals and agriculture, for example—grew out of land. Because land was finite, an omniscient sovereign was needed to exert control over international trade and to ensure his or her country's accrual of the greatest amount of wealth. In addition to apportioning limited resources, regulation of trade was vital because individuals who dealt primarily in movable goods and owned minimal landed property were viewed as untrustworthy. They had no real stake in the community; unmanaged, they might harm a nation's security when dealing with foreign trading partners.

Some seventeenth- and eighteenth-century thinkers began to challenge the belief that land was the bedrock of wealth (and that landholders were the bedrock of society), arguing instead that the number of laborers and the efficiency of their work determined a nation's prosperity. Manufacturing output, after all, vied with agricultural production in the late seventeenth and early eighteenth centuries, forcing a reassessment of long-held assumptions.[8] English settlers in the Southeast, however, subscribed to the balance-of-trade framework because it dovetailed with their initial colonial mission.[9] Carolina's planners imagined Carolina as a plantation. True to the balance-of-trade goal of amassing global resources, Carolina promised to assist England in accumulating specie by supplying it, as well as its colonists in Barbados, with the agricultural goods they needed to become self-sufficient (so that they could minimize their imports) and luxuries England could sell to foreign countries (so that they could maximize their exports). There was, as well, a Whig strand of Carolinians' early writings that lauded the power of efficiently planned labor systems. Barbadian transplants sold themselves as "experienced planters" who would bring "there Negros and other servants fitt for such labor as wilbe there required," and be overseen by proprietors who were involved in other plantation colonies and various economic improvement programs. But despite this interest in optimizing labor potential, there was little question that the southeastern portion of North America would be divided among men who, through proper management, would create agricultural riches for England.[10] As in England, dominion over the land served as the basis for political power. Although during the last quarter of the seventeenth century a number of individuals in England were starting to consider manufactured, movable property to be as valuable to a nation as land, if not more so, South Carolina was founded just before this intellectual shift. Similar to Georgia, whose founding several decades after South Carolina was premised on the belief that England's poor needed a plot of earth to become virtuous, South Carolina's framers hewed to the belief that the only truly independent citizen was one who held land. The Fundamental Constitution concentrated political power in the hands of a small landed aristocracy in an attempt to stave off democracy.[11] Over the course of the colony's early history, South Carolinians remained steadfast in holding that mobile property created artificial men whose appetites for power had to be governed.[12]

A colony based in landed property served as the ideal model for Carolina. But it soon became clear that it was not the fruit of the soil that supplied the colony's riches. Slaves captured and deerskins harvested by Southeastern Indians were the only ready sources of revenue in the Southeast.[13] As the commerce in slaves and deerskins expanded, most of these transactions took place between Southeastern Indians and transient settlers. The economic realities of South Carolina forced settlers and officials alike to reassess the debate about balance-of-trade theory. They were actually witnessing how a society dedicated to landed property would react to an economy based in goods that moved across international boundaries.[14] In analyzing how the colonists engaged with mercantilist ideologies, I join those scholars who maintain that, rather than originating from the center, economic policies were the product of negotiations between the metropole and peripheries.[15] Moreover, this argument reaches even further into the frontier by showing the influence of the Native American trade on these debates. After an early period of very loose regulation, uncertainties in the Native American trade forced the South Carolina Proprietors and the legislative body, the Commons House, to move away from a freer-trade model. Instead, they instituted tight regulations on prices, trading locations, and trade partners, thereby reaffirming traditional economic mores. After its founding in 1732, Georgia adopted similar regulations, demanding that only individuals who took out a license yearly and posted a bond could participate in the Indian trade, assigning specific traders to specific towns and forbidding them to trade elsewhere, and charging a commissioner to listen seriously to accusations that Southeastern Indians made against white traders (called "Indian traders") and to execute a proper punishment (the officials did not trouble themselves to consider how to ensure that Indian traders' grievances were addressed).[16] Historians familiar with these guidelines argue that Native Americans were the main impetus for a highly regulated trade, for, they argue, Native Americans traditionally exchanged goods as gifts and were uncomfortable with market commodity exchanges. By situating the Native American trade in early modern English economic debates, this chapter demonstrates England's unease with expanding markets and cross-cultural traders, and further argues that colonial authorities insisted on the regulations that historians mistakenly attribute solely to Native American pressure. Southeastern Indian leaders promoted and embraced these regulations as tools to protect the economic health of their communities.

MANY HISTORIANS CONTEND that gifting was the first form of exchange to bridge cultures in North America.[17] But contrary to this supposition, in the history of economic contact in the Southeast, trade came first, and it came quite easily. After centuries of intertribal exchange and decades of trade with Spanish settlers, the Southeastern Indians approached British explorers with commodities to trade.[18] The first British voyagers noted the Southeastern Indians' eagerness to trade. As they made their way toward St. Ellens in 1663, Captain William Hilton wrote, there "came many Canoas about us with Corn, Pompions, and Venison, Deer-Skins, and a sort of sweet-wood," all eager to trade.[19] Seven years later, Captain Maurice Mathews recorded a similar willingness to exchange goods, noting that, as he was anchored in St. Katherina, "the Indians very freely came aboard . . . they traded with us for beads

& old Clothes, & gave our people bread of Indian Corne, Pease, Leakes, Onyons, dear skins, Hens, Earthen pots & c."[20]

Because this trade took place on the border regions of the North American ocean and shoreline, these early exchanges were markedly different from later interactions occurring on land.[21] Individuals, usually in boats, quickly negotiated trading terms, immediately gave and received goods, and then departed, usually forever. A deep understanding of each other's economic and material cultures was not a prerequisite for this type of exchange. The explorers did not record the names of their trading partners or the specific amount of items they traded. While reflecting on the image of first-encounter exchanges in general, the anthropologist Nicholas Thomas asserts that "what is most *telling* about the image of barter is that it does *not* speak: it is a spectacle of silent film in which we see things change hands."[22] The first economic contact between the Southeastern Indians and the British was, in many ways, asocial: it brought together participants who did not have an established relationship, and because of the transitory nature of the British seamen's venture, the relationship was unlikely to survive.[23] Additionally, these initial economic contacts were, essentially, commodity exchanges: the items traded were alienable, the exchange partners were independent parties, and the value of the goods was based on their suitability for exchange at the time of the transaction.[24]

If the story of colonial southeastern trade had continued to operate according to these early patterns, we could examine trade as a process independent of larger social dynamics.[25] But as the British built communities in the Southeast and established more permanent trading relationships with surrounding Native Americans, the process of commodity exchange demanded greater cross-cultural understanding. Carolina's planners did not foresee that trade with Native Americans would hold a central place within their economy. Yet, as the first settlers' provisions dwindled, they "were forced to live upon the Indians," creating a system in which trade with the Southeastern Indians for food and deerskin clothing touched the lives of almost everyone during and after South Carolina's founding.[26] Georgia, which was equally committed to an agricultural economy, followed suit. Initially, southeastern commerce consisted of the exchange of food and small amounts of manufactured goods. It quickly blossomed into a trade that funneled thousands of deerskins from Southeastern Indian country to Britain and manufactured European goods into Native American communities. In the initial decades of the

South Carolina colony, before the rice and naval store industries became established, deerskins and slaves supplied by the Southeastern Indians were the most profitable exports. Nearly all settlers earned at least part of their livelihood by trading with neighboring Southeastern Indians.[27] According to the most recent estimate, from 1698 to 1715 South Carolina colonists exported between 53,000 and 54,000 deerskins per year. The numbers climbed to nearly 400,000 skins in 1764 before declining after the American Revolution.[28]

For the settlers, commodity exchanges were inextricably linked to social and diplomatic relationships. Peaceful neighbors were defined as those who traded with them; menacing neighbors were those who refused to trade. The settlers, accustomed to England's use of trade to fill its own coffers, were surprised that these foreign Native American nations acted generously. In 1670 proprietor Lord Ashley's deputy Stephen Bull reported that they "sould vs Provisions att very reasonable rates & takeinge notice of our necessitys did almost daylie bringe one thing or another."[29] Similarly, settler William Owen relayed that their indigenous neighbors supplied their "want of provisions without inhanceing the price upon our necessity."[30] By disregarding profit, the Native Americans were behaving like *domestic* trade partners who were working alongside the English to bolster the Carolina economy. In this respect, the Southeastern Indians differed from foreign nationals who used trade to fill their own pockets at the expense of the settlers. Based on their cooperation, the proprietors speculated that Native Americans living within the patent boundaries would soon become members of the colony.[31]

Trade could undermine relationships as well as strengthen them. In the early years of colonization, officials either expelled or prosecuted Native Americans who surrounded the settlements but were not economically friendly.[32] The South Carolina Grand Council admonished Southeastern Indian individuals who threatened the settlers' subsistence by destroying their livestock. In all likelihood, Native Americans engaged in these acts to protect their land from destruction caused by pigs and cows. The council, however, interpreted this behavior as an act of aggression.[33] Economic assistance, on the other hand, was intertwined with friendship. Thus, the council presumed that the Kussoe Indians had become hostile and were conspiring with the Spanish because they had removed "a great quantity of Corne from time to time," thus choosing not to assist the Carolinians in subsisting, and had further withdrawn from "trading with our people." The council and the governor interpreted this refusal to trade as an indication that the Kussoe were "endeavoring and contriving the destruction of this settlement and his Majesties subjects therein."[34]

Early reports revealed that there was an even greater threat to South Carolina's existence than removed corn and slaughtered pigs. Stephen Bull juxtaposed his account of nearby peaceful neighbors with tales of the Westos, who would barrel down "in the tyme of their cropp & destroye all by killinge Caryinge awaye their Corne & Children & eate them & our neibouringe Indians."[35] As thieves and cannibals, the Westos represented a mercantilist's nightmare: a group that sought to arbitrarily destroy the colonists' livelihoods, with seemingly little gain for themselves.

In assuming that the international competition for finite resources was a volatile affair, the settlers adopted a mercantilist mentality. Since one party became enriched while the other party was impoverished, trading partners were yoked in a hostile relationship.[36] The establishment of a trade monopoly offered a solution to this problem. A monopoly not only appointed experts who ensured that England was seizing the biggest piece of the pie, but also created a central authority that could marshal a defensive army should the depleted party react violently.[37] Thus, to contend with the Westos, the proprietors (despite their standing as Whigs, the party that usually opposed monopolies) took control over inland trade beyond Port Royal. Trade relationships were unstable, and the proprietors reasoned that "if quarrels should arise [it] might extreamly prejudice [the Indians]."[38] In the frontier environment, the potential repercussions of these unstable trading relationships intensified. Weakening one's trading partner to the point of fury could pose an existential threat to the British colonies. Southeastern Indians' material dependence, though a boon for profits, could harm the colony by creating a population that would do *anything* for European goods. The proprietors noted this danger when explaining that the 1683 war with their neighbors was sparked by the Savannah Indians' "Covetuousness of your [Carolinians'] guns Powder & shott & other Europian Comodities," which induced them "to make war upon their neighbours" in order to seize slaves to sell to the Carolinians.[39] New World monopolies and participants in commerce walked a precarious line of attempting to exploit Native American trading partners while maintaining peace. As shown throughout this chapter, the assumption that trade created contentious relationships would underlie various officials' suspicion of colonists who traded goods with

Southeastern Indians, and would provide the rationale for regulating them throughout the colonial period.

Not only were profit and peace in tension, but the legality and popularity of trade monopolies were increasingly contested in the latter half of the seventeenth century. Settlers who opposed the proprietors' policies used this conflict to their advantage. Defenders of royally sanctioned monopolies (or, as they called them, exclusive privileges) argued that companies had the right and obligation to bar noncompany members from trading within a designated territory. The king, they reasoned, had a right to control trade with foreign non-Christians who could quickly become enemies and jeopardize the safety of the empire. Advocates of monopoly also maintained that only large companies had the economic power to orchestrate international trade for the benefit of England. The South Carolina Proprietors, who did not command a large company, rejected this assertion, although later Indian trading firms that were accused of holding a virtual monopoly endorsed it. Opponents of royal monopolies, on the other hand, doubted that company-run trade was safer than a freer-trade model. They argued that more individuals trading freely in movable property would enhance England's wealth, and that all British subjects should have the freedom to trade. Moreover, they claimed, only Parliament, as a representative body, had the right to regulate trade. The 1689 case *Nightingale v. Bridges* and the 1696 case *Dockwra v. Dickenson* dealt a blow to the African Company specifically and monopolies in general. Although it upheld the legality of the king giving specific companies exclusive rights to trade, it barred those companies from imprisoning noncompany individuals who traded within their bounds and from seizing their goods, and was thus interpreted as weakening the ability of monopolies to function.[40] New World monopolies faced uphill battles. In 1699 the Board of Trade, ruling in an East New Jersey dispute, refused the right of proprietary monopolies to restrict English colonists from trading. Knowledgeable colonists, repeatedly invoking English precedent, drew upon the anti–royal monopoly movement in England to defend their rights to trade freely with Native Americans.[41]

The Goose Creek Men, often at odds with the South Carolina proprietary monopoly, resisted control of the trade. Much to the proprietors' chagrin, the Goose Creek Men had established an extensive slave-trading corridor from South Carolina to Barbados and were becoming increasingly powerful in South Carolina politics.[42] In their 1690 address, the

Goose Creek Men rebuffed the proprietors' claim that a monopoly was necessary to "prevent quarrels and bludshed," and asserted that it was part of a larger "tirannicall" policy that violated the rights of the colonists. The proprietors, they declared, had jeopardized the public good in order to enrich themselves. The Goose Creek Men did not propose that the Indian trade should be unregulated. In fact, they conceded that laws were needed so that "the Colony should not be in any danger." Rather than making a free-trade argument, they were stating that a proprietary monopoly, and a corrupt one at that, was ineffective.[43]

Much to the delight of the Goose Creek Men (and largely due to their maneuvering), the South Carolina Proprietors' justification for maintaining a monopoly for the sake of the colony's safety was shattered in 1679. War with the Westo had broken out under their watch.[44] After much conflict with Governors James Moore and Nathaniel Johnson, the Commons House, as a representative body, was able to seize control of the trade. The proprietors and the consecutive governors were left with only their feeble powers of persuasion.[45] South Carolina became the only colony in the South in which the legislative body, and not the governor and council, controlled Indian affairs for most of the colonial period.[46]

Some scholars hold that 1707, the year the Commons House passed its full regulatory system, marks a watershed moment when trade went from being free to being regulated. These 1707 provisions, however, were minor compared to later policies.[47] In 1707 the Commons House demanded that traders take out licenses. It also appointed an Indian agent who spent ten months in Indian country resolving disputes, and it created the Commissioners of Indian Trade. This body, composed of nine members of the Upper and Lower Houses of Assembly, was authorized to try egregious crimes. But regulators did not, as they would after the Yamasee War (1715–16), set prices, assign traders to specific Indian towns, or limit the goods that could be traded beyond alcohol and certain weapons. Nor did they monopolize the trade.

The years from 1707 to 1715 are best understood as a time when fears about foreign trade relationships receded and officials trusted colonists and Southeastern Indian traders to devise their own trading culture. Instead of top-down regulation, the Commons House relied on the same outlet available to traders in England and the English colonies: a judicial body. In this case, it was the Commissioners of Indian Trade that worked to contain potentially hostile trading relationships by mediating disputes.[48] The proprietors had set the groundwork for this adjudication system to address disagreements between settlers and Native Americans outside of their monopoly boundaries. But the Commons House was unique in trusting the colony's safety (for they too, like the proprietors, believed that trade and peace were interconnected) to the efficacy of mediation to settle all trading disputes.[49] Realizing that "at this Distance" they would be unable to "restrane the Traders," the commissioners asked Southeastern Indian leaders and communities to take the lead in regulating the trade.[50] Southeastern Indians set the standard of conduct; the commissioners instructed the traders, simply, that "your Behaviour [should] be such towards the Indians that they may have no Reason or Grounds of Complaint."[51] They encouraged Native Americans to submit grievances to their local South Carolina agent, whom they commanded "to hear all their Complaints and to doe right and impartial Justice between them an[d] the Traders."[52] If the agent could not achieve a resolution, he would alert the Commissioners of Indian Trade, and they would summon the disputants for a hearing. The southeastern frontier was not a stateless area, but largely under the jurisdiction of Native American leaders who were attempting to shape economic life.[53]

The faith that the members of the Commons House had in peaceful negotiation and mediation suggests that they, like the Whigs in England, had abandoned the fears of international trade promoted by the Tories.[54] Instead of seeing economic culture as differing across societies and religions, they believed in the commensurability, if not universality, of trading norms. Significantly, neither the proprietors nor the Commons House officials distinguished between Native American and British property rights, and they stipulated that an exchange was legally binding only if both parties consciously and willingly agreed to its terms.[55] Accordingly, most of the cases the commissioners decided hinged on scrutinizing a transaction for evidence that both the Carolinian and Southeastern Indian traders consented to the exchange. Common disagreements involved questions about which items could be bought and sold (including slaves), at what price, and the time at which ownership would transfer hands. Instead of codifying rules of exchange, as they would later do, the commissioners simply voided disputed transactions. While not as critical of slavery as the proprietors, they regularly deferred to indigenous categorizations of slavery and spent much of their time freeing individuals whom Southeastern Indians claimed were falsely enslaved.[56] Oftentimes, instead of attempting to compel the disputing traders to understand each other's positions, they dipped into public funds and gave restitution to both parties, allowing everyone to walk away feeling that justice had been served.[57]

While the commissioners granted Carolinian traders a great deal of freedom, their choice of words reveals that they were quick to blame the malfeasance of white traders, not cultural differences, for conflicts with the Indians. The commissioners' use of the word "force" as a basis for invalidating commercial transactions underlines this predisposition. For instance, when Captain John Musgrove complained that the Creek Indians still owed him skins for powder and bullets, the commissioners released the Creek of their obligation to pay this debt, ruling that Musgrove "forced the said powder and bullets upon the Indians."[58] Unlike theft, in a forced trade the initiator foisted goods on the reluctant individual and seized other goods in compensation, usually at the standard rates of exchange. Indian Forster, a leader of the Tuscarora Indians, complained, "Daniel Callihaun had violently seized and taken a canoe from him, on pretence that he had sold it to him, the said Callihaun, for twenty shillings, current money, because Forster said he was willing to sell his canoe for money."[59] Although twenty shillings was on the low end of the scale for used canoes, it was not an unheard of price. This suggests that Callihaun, rather than being a cheat, held a different conception of the nature of a verbal contract or the time at which traded goods should change hands.[60] The case never reached a final verdict because Indian Forster chose not to reappear before the commissioners. Based on past decisions, however, it is likely that the commissioners would have determined that, because Forster and Callihaun did not agree about the specific terms of the exchange, the verbal contract was not legally binding. Further, instead of merely reading this case as a contract dispute or a cultural misunderstanding, the commissioners would have insisted that Callihaun had acted unethically by forcing the sale on Forster. By interpreting cases through a balance-of-trade lens, the commissioners were guided by the belief that it was likely that one party was walking away from the exchange with a less valuable object. As a result, they were prone to trust the account of the aggrieved Native American party.

Like Indian Forster, Carolinian and Southeastern Indian traders alike seldom called upon the commissioners to negotiate their disputes. Commissioners and colonial officials were thus relegated to the periphery of the emerging trading culture. In spaces far from colonial oversight, traders developed a commodity exchange system that, when viewed by colonial officials, smacked of anarchy. While colonial officials equated commerce with social and political relationships, there is ample evidence that Southeastern Indians (though perhaps not their leaders) and Carolina traders were more than comfortable with asocial exchange, a fact that frustrated and confused some officials. In his 1708 report, the first Indian agent, Thomas Nairne, complained that the Chickasaw Indians had "not a right notion of Allegiance" to those from whom they purchased commodities. "They're apt to believe themselves at Liberty, when they please to turn to those who sell them the best pennyworths," Nairne continued.[61] A South Carolina committee reported that the Southeastern Indians "indiscriminately visited and traded with the *French, Spaniards* and *English*, as they judged it most for their Advantage."[62] Though officials took "pains to instruct them" otherwise, the Native Americans held to the "erroneous doctrine" that one could trade with whomever one wanted.[63] Many Carolinian traders likewise believed that they were free to choose their trading partners.[64] They did not always share their government's political allegiances, and formed partnerships with individuals from rival European nations and sold goods to enemy Native American groups.[65] Their disrespect for the colonial officials and laws was palpable. The traders, Ludovick Grant reported, "do not observe the Law that was made and they heard read to them."[66] Agent James Wright reported that traders contemptuously tore up the commissioners' warrants right in front of him.[67] And a packhorse man who funneled goods to and from Southeastern Indian territory went so far as to assert that "he was not subject to any King and had Nothing to do with any King."[68]

Colonial officials put as many teeth in their orders as they could, but they recognized their limited ability to enforce some rules of trade, particularly their insistence that traders obtain licenses. The commissioners informed the agents: "You must be cautious how you deal with the Indian traders about paying their arrears of license money. You may threaten them with Warrants, and probably that way may persuade them into compliance, but upon considering the Act of Parliament we do not think we have sufficient power to prosecute the same."[69] The question of legality loomed throughout the colonial period; the argument that all "His Majesty's Subjects" had the right to "a free open and uninterrupted trade with the Creek Cherokee and other Nations of Indians in Amity & Friendship with his Majesty's Subjects" thwarted the attempts of specific colonies to restrict the trade to their licensed inhabitants.[70] In 1754 Virginia governor Robert Dinwiddie expressed doubt to Governor Glen that there were legal grounds for restraining colonists "from trading with any Nation of Indians in Amity with Great Britain."[71] The increasing openness of trade in Britain, brought on by the assault on royal monopolies, left colonial officials with few tools to restrain the traders, who were adopting a modern market exchange mentality faster than governmental officials.

The May 1714 case of the trader Alexander Longe finally convinced the commissioners as to the accuracy of the proprietors' belief that international trade was too risky to leave loosely regulated. The commissioners had long held that "headstrong, unruly traders" could *unwittingly* cause hostilities between British American and Native American communities. But they were a bit taken aback when they found Longe guilty of using the influence he garnered through trade with the Cherokees to *intentionally* incite them to go to war against the Yuchis of Chestowa, against whom he harbored a grudge.[72] In retrospect, it appears that the dispute arose when a Chestowa Yuchi man murdered a Cherokee, touching off a cycle of retribution. Longe undoubtedly benefited from the attack, for the Cherokee, who owed him money, were able to clear their debt with Yuchis they enslaved during the attack. But by all reliable accounts, Longe's direct involvement was limited to his selling the Cherokee powder and bullets. Despite this, rumors ran rampant that Longe had played a more instrumental role in the war. "Mr. Longe had some Difference with a Yuchi Indian who had pulled some of his Hair" and with another Yuchi who had defaulted on a loan a few years ago, traders recounted. To avenge these wrongs, Longe fabricated a "Governor's Order for cutting off Chestowee," thereby prompting the Cherokee to go to war. Most of the traders agreed that the "Cherokees would not have cut off the Yuchis if they had been expressly ordered to the Contrary." Despite the fact that the Cherokee Skiacasea declared that this was an intertribal dispute, and that "the War Captain of Euchase, Flint, and Caesar, and one or two more att the Middle Settlements contrived the cutting off the Euchees and kept itt very private till they came near the Town," the commissioners ruled that "Mr. Long was instrumentall in encouraging the Cherokee Indians to cut off the Yuchis." They stripped Longe of his license and recommended that the governor prosecute him.[73]

The hearsay evidence in this case suggests that Longe's alleged incitement of war between the powerful Cherokee and the Yuchi fed on the settlers' predisposition to be wary of merchants in general, and peddlers in particular. These peddlers held a precarious position in the expanding early modern market and were at the forefront of the drive to help Britain amass global resources.[74] International traders served as a repository for the anxieties bred by the balance-of-trade philosophy: trade relationships were, by nature, exploitative and potentially hostile. This fear of explosive trading relationships dovetailed with a wariness about individuals who relied on mobile property rather than real landed property. Traditionally, landholders who held a stake in a community and were required to take up arms to protect it were considered reliable community members. Merchants, on the other hand, were viewed as so greedy that their lust for money overshadowed any concern they might have for the welfare of their community or their trading partners.[75] Animosity toward movable property was most clearly directed at peddlers, who were not only landless but peripatetic. They were thus accused of being so disconnected from their home community that they had turned into foreigners.[76] In the play *The royal merchant: or, beggars bush*, performed widely in the eighteenth century, a newly returned merchant declared, "My five year's absence hath kept me a Stranger / So much to all the Occurrens of My Country."[77] Instead of categorizing them as hardworking individuals, early modern legislation, in the mainland and the colonies, "stigmatized peddlers and itinerant tradesmen as inveterate rogues" and useless vagabonds.[78] In Britain, disquiet provoked by traveling salesmen rose sharply from the mid-1670s onward, coinciding with the settlement of South Carolina.[79]

To the British, whites who traded with the Native Americans, referred to as "Indian traders," closely resembled peddlers. They were highly mobile, splitting their time between the colonies and Indian territory, often traveling up to twenty-five days at a time. They operated primarily out of doors and connected distant people to an international trade.[80] Therefore, it is not surprising that colonists imported English suspicions of peddlers and hurled them at Indian traders. Many assumed that Indian traders, like peddlers, had no sense of allegiance to anyone but themselves. As shown in the Longe case and later interpretations of the Yamasee War, Indian traders would go to any length to protect their meager economic interests. They were "people of loose disorderly lives" with "no kind of property or visible way of living or supporting themselves."[81] They had to be regulated, officials argued, because they "generally lead loose, vicious lives, to the scandal of the Christian religion, and do likewise oppress the people among whom they live, by their unjust and illegal actions."[82] The stereotype persisted throughout the colonial period. Patrick Graham invoked this prejudice when, in speaking to the Georgia President and Assistants, he attributed Cherokee aggression in the early 1750s to Indian traders. He disparaged them as "men of broken fortune" who had devised the violence "to attain some private ends, as it wou'd be the interest of such to fish in troubled waters; for if a war should ensue, they wou'd have some excuse for not being able to pay their just debts."[83]

Settlers often referred to foreigners and traders in the same breath as enemies of the British colonies.[84] Thomas Hepworth, Speaker of the South Carolina Commons House of Assembly, worried that the Creek Indians' faltering loyalty was "caus'd by the French and Spaniards and some of our own Traders."[85] Distrust of itinerant colonial merchants predated the cautionary tale of Longe, the vengeful trader. Especially wary were the proprietors, who wholeheartedly adopted the ideal of landed property. When they first learned about the Westo War, they assumed that "particular men by trade"[86] had promoted the war and had thus jeopardized the "Interest of the Planters."[87] They even wondered if their trusted agent of the monopoly, Henry Woodward, was applying "himself to war also."[88] In the proprietors' view, planters were men of peace, and traders were men of war. The fact that these traders were also supplying slaves to the plantation owners did not appear to trouble them.[89] The Longe case demonstrates how, when their assumptions that trade could be handled with simple mediation were tested, members of the House shared the same fear that trade was inherently unequal and traders potentially exploitative.

These treacherous Indian traders were particularly dangerous when they assumed a governmental role, a position traditionally reserved for disinterested, independent property owners.[90] But the truth of the matter was that oftentimes these traders were the closest thing to an ambassador the colonists had. They were expected to be the eyes and the ears of the government, and required to "keep a separate Book of Way of Journal in which should be entered any remarkable Occurrencies related to the Indians," and to "carefully observe the Number of strange Indians that may at any Time come into their Towns."[91] In times of unrest, they were called before governmental boards and probed about their observations on the ground.[92] Often, they were the only spokesmen available to deliver government talks to their towns.[93] Yet colonial officials remained uneasy about their reliance on Indian traders. Three years before the Longe case, the commissioners drafted a requirement that Indian traders given a government post must "not abuse itt by making Use therof to promote your perticular Interest with the Indians."[94] Longe's rumored misappropriation of a governor's order exacerbated the officials' anxiety. In their next draft of instructions, the commissioners ordered that traders were "not to promise or engage the word of the government or of the commissioners, or any Indian whatsoever, without a particular Order for the same."[95]

That Indian traders were entering into commercial relationships with foreigners added to their untrustworthiness. In medieval and early modern England, dealing with foreigners sparked so much apprehension that transactions had to take place in public view. As buying and selling between locals and outsiders became more common, traders found ways to circumvent these strictures. However, exchanges conducted away from the authoritarian eye continued to evoke suspicion within English communities.[96] Well into the eighteenth century, British communities controlled commercial spaces to ensure that exchanges were visible and easily regulated, even when foreigners were not involved in the transactions. In Britain, sales had to occur "in a place that is overt and open; not in a back-room, warehouse, nor behind hangings or cupboards in a shop, so that those who stand or pass by the shop cannot see it."[97] South Carolina officials similarly strove to ensure that trade was conducted transparently. Transacting business on unregistered ships in the harbor, for instance, was strictly forbidden.[98] Most trade occurred in public markets where trading times, items, and terms were regulated and weights and measures were standardized.[99] By use of these safeguards, colonial officials aimed to protect consumers from the "scheming merchant" who "was a stock figure in the early modern world."[100]

The colonists believed that Native American consumers also needed to be protected from colonial traders. Though settlers feared that traders to the Southeastern Indians would act contrary to the interests of British communities, they rarely, if ever, accused traders of exchanging their British loyalty for a Native American identity. This perception was belied by day-to-day realities, as traders formed intimate relationships with Native Americans. Traders spent at least half of the year living in Southeastern Indian communities, were fluent in Southeastern Indian languages and dialects, formed families with Southeastern Indian women, and, in the eyes of some European witnesses, little resembled their cosmopolitan brothers in dress and appearance. But they escaped the label "White Indian" and the precarious position of cultural boundary crossers in the

British Atlantic world.[101] In fact, in the Southeast, intermarriage with Native Americans increased, rather than detracted from, a trader's status.[102] The most likely explanation is that colonists, who viewed merchants within their own community cynically, did not tar Indian traders as "White Indians" because they assumed that Native Americans were wise enough to keep merchants at arm's length. Though cognizant that buyers and sellers formed at least a rudimentary relationship, the British suspected that both parties hid their motives and personalities to gain a strategic bargaining advantage. Consistent with the balance-of-trade mentality, settlers believed that trade encompassed two conflicting expectations: buyer and seller were bound by the complementary act of exchange while simultaneously concerned solely with their own interests.[103] Colonists did not fear that Native American communities would wholly absorb white traders because they believed that white traders were able to form only tenuous ties with their Native American trading partners.

Yet, as the Long episode demonstrated with chilling clarity, traders were able to finesse commercial alliances in order to convince Native Americans to do their dirty work. Settlers and officials referred to Indian traders who weaseled their way into Indian communities as "rogues" who used disguises to infiltrate a community with which they were, in fact, at odds. Indian traders impersonated well-meaning, honest friends and merchants while conspiring against the best interests of the Native American communities in which they lived.[104] Acting for the benefit of neither Southeastern Indian nor British settler communities, the nefarious Longe epitomized the trader who would do anything to pad his pocketbook while using the unregulated frontiers for cover.

It took one major war to cement the suspicion that trade across boundaries was volatile and that self-interested Indian traders were deceitful. One year after the Longe incident, the Yamasee, in conjunction with surrounding indigenous groups, waged a serious assault against the young South Carolina colony, killing nearly 400 settlers. To make sense of the calamity, settlers and colonial officials immediately blamed the "extortion and knavery of ye traders," accusing them of inciting the hostility of the surrounding Native Americans through unethical commercial practices.[105] A group of planters suggested that "the want of good government among the Indian traders might have given provocation. That trade being at present under no good regulation."[106] Mr. Crawley, who lived on the outskirts of the settlement, reported that he had seen the

Carolina traders "frequently take from them their hogs, poultry, corn and other provisions, as they wanted it, and had only paid the Indian for it, what they thought fit." Crawley further claimed that the traders forced the Native Americans to "carry their burthens, thro' the woods for little or nothing, and beat and abuse them when they scrupled it."[107] William Byrd of Virginia observed that South Carolina traders "have so abused and so imposed upon the Indians in selling them goods at exorbitant prices, and receiving their peltry at very low rates, that they have been thereby very much disgusted."[108] In other words, the traders were abiding by balance-of-trade principles on an individual rather than a national scale, a practice long acknowledged by the English as creating volcanic relationships. All strata of society, from powerful planters to colonial officials to small farmers and traders, pointed accusatory fingers in one direction: the traders.[109]

After the Yamasee War, the South Carolina General Assembly, acting on the same suppositions as the proprietors, resurrected a monopoly and settled the trade by relocating all trading activities to three forts.[110] As a representative governing body, the assembly was safe from legal censures faced by royal monopolies, though Carolina merchants still vociferously objected to being excluded from the trade.[111] The assembly paid employees a salary to exchange public goods for skins, and strictly forbade them from selling any personal property or keeping any of the deerskins they obtained.[112] They standardized prices for skins and European trade goods.[113] Their goal was to deprive traders of any incentive to profit by lying or cheating.

The revolt against the proprietary government in 1719 led to the dissolution of the public monopoly. It was fully dismantled by 1721, barely five years after the Yamasee War. The royal governor (who had more regulatory power over the Indian trade than the proprietors had) and the Lower House ensured, however, that the Indian trade was tightly regulated. Now traders could purchase and sell their own goods, but their trading locations and partners were predetermined through licenses that restricted their movement to a few towns. They could not privately negotiate the prices of their goods, which remained standardized, and they could not decide how much credit to extend to their trading partners. Throughout the remainder of the colonial period these rules remained stable, even when the structure governing the Indian trade changed.[114]

The regulations on private trade, location, price, and debt all sprang from the British notion that nonitinerant merchants who operated within stable economic networks were more likely to be trustworthy. In 1725, Indian Trade Commissioner Colonel George Chicken, who suggested that the South Carolina legislature pass a law requiring "that the traders be confined to trade in any one or two towns of their own choice," explained that such regulation would tame these "loose vagabond sort of people" and reduce competition between these traders, who would "say or do anything among the Indians for the lure of a few skins."[115] He invoked the same suspicion of peddlers as his predecessors, and concluded that the solution was to take the traveling out of the Indian trade. Domestic trade was less exploitative than international trade.

Georgia followed suit when, responding to disturbances in Southeastern Indian country, it restricted trade to authorized localities. For example, in 1764, the Georgia legislature received numerous complaints from licensed Indian traders that disorderly settlers were traipsing through Indian territories, selling stolen horses, and trading with the Native Americans "in the woods" outside of Southeastern Indian towns. These settlers were causing "quarrels and disturbances" among the Indian traders and the Southeastern Indians. The resulting act did not target trespassing, selling stolen goods, or mistreating the Indians. Instead, it specified that it was not "lawful for any person or persons to sell, truck barter or exchange with any Indian or Indians any rum or other strong liquours clothing or any other thing whatsoever privately in the woods in their hunting grounds or at cowpens in the settlements or any other place other than at stores or houses licensed for that purpose."[116] Georgia officials thus reiterated the conviction that, by circumscribing the permissible areas of trade, abuses would largely disappear.

Most traders embraced restriction on their movement, even when they ignored other regulations. Contrary to prevailing fears, most traders did not relish the opportunities afforded by the lack of imperial oversight. Like trader John Evans, many were as eager to add structure to the frontier as the officials were.[117] Evans was a resident of southern Virginia who participated in both the northern South Carolina and the southern Virginia Indian trade in the early eighteenth century.[118] He was among the minority of literate Indian traders and used this skill to record his activities. Before 1708, Evans conscientiously kept an account of his debts and credits. Travel was a staple of Evans's profession from the beginning of his career, as evidenced by entries for river ferry charges and reminders that he left his goods temporarily with his "landlord" and "landlady." But after 1708 travel became even more central to his life when he entered new territories.[119] At that point he turned to his journal to record, rerecord, and meditate about space and distances.

His journals, the best existing documents of their kind, demonstrate that movement over long expanses was the organizing principle of his life and that he had absorbed the anxieties about long-distance trade that his contemporaries voiced. To cope with his explorations through foreign territories, he devoted copious amounts of space to understanding distances. A typical selection reads:

> I went from home to Stony Creek. From thence y 11: to Magtoyim.
> Got at Nottoway skins. Thence to Meherrin river to Arthrr—
> Rananah y: 12: to y Sappones from thence to the Oconees at
> Roanoke y: 13: down y same river to weekcoano crossing y same
> going: 8: miles to sappony swamp: 4: miles to [illegible] well: 4 miles
> y small swamp: y: 14 to y cross path [illegible]: 5 miles down tholad
> creek: 20 miles crossing it: down Jonhenten River 13 mi. thence
> cross it to Tororouis: y first town of Jodany: then they had known
> of our coming: and our business: [illegible] came to lay there that
> night: y next day: 15: we went from thence 5 miles to Ticoro.
> There we left our peoinon: from thence up y country 26 miles
> Ronoto y: 16.[120]

Evans assiduously recorded the number of miles he traversed daily and where those travels led him. Despite the fact that he journeyed between many of the same towns, Evans often took different routes. He mulled over the miles traveled anew, as if each trip were an important discovery. Sometimes, at the end of the day, he computed the distances in a column, rather than in his usual narrative form:

> Tiacoro: 30: miles to
> Routa: 12 miles to
> Noreanten to Co___ha to
> Nuhanied 8 to Yoahamina: 8
> to Conmery 6: to Cottann: 10:
> Connorock = Nonoreaneack
> 6: thence to Tiacoro: 16
> Juonoach: and three villages in miles of the country

Underneath this column of computation, he rewrote the distances in a paragraph, at times using variable Native American and English place-names: "Tiacoro ye first town, and from thence to Rourta 30 miles from

thence to Nonhuna. 12 from thence to Kenhay, from thence to Wor-
suckca 8 from thence to Yoahawuney 8 from thence to Connewcartho, 6
from thence to Cottanaw 10 ffom thence to Cunnoryounh. 30 to Tiacoro
and three villages in the middle and Juneiwach."[121]

Evans's journal demonstrates that at least some Indian traders studiously pondered the question of how to traverse space. While exchange
was his livelihood, travel structured Evans's days and ordered his professional self-conception. After 1708, his records of exchange are often
haphazard and hastily jotted down. On the back of some pages, and up-
side down on others, he scribbled economic accounts: "1 doz. skins for
paint / 1 buck for shot." And beneath a different tally of the distances he
traversed during the day, he recorded: "July 19th. Received of Thomas
Evans Fifteen shillings for Col. Edwards. Daniel Wagnon." But his attention to place and distance was systematic and thorough.

Evans's connection to the space he traversed was so strong that he
eventually purchased land that he surveyed in his journal.[122] Rather than
adopting a counterculture model of society that rejected landownership
as the basis of power, many traders aspired to the accouterments of traditional elites—plantations, slaves, luxury goods, and government titles.[123]
Evans is a case in point. Despite his existence at the edge of the empire,
Evans embraced (whether intentionally or not) European methods of
conquering land. In form, his journal bears a resemblance to colonial sur-
veyors' records.[124] He reveals how the Tory conception of an empire of
land and the Whig conception of an empire of trade often intersected
in the minds of colonial traders.

Their ambitions did not stop at owning land. Those Indian traders who
were successful enough to amass property went on to hold governmental positions, and even those who did not purported to. So many traders
pretended that they officially worked for the colonial government that
the South Carolina Commons House had to explicitly forbid them to do
so.[125] Even without official titles, some Indian traders conceived of themselves (not incorrectly) as central to an imperial mission whose duty was
"to serve the Country."[126] Their goal was not to make a fortune; they
were "Duty bound" to bring the Southeastern Indians "to right Temper
and Understanding with the Government."[127] In drawing repeated attention to how they would "venture their Lives to these rumble Parts through
so many Dangers," they tapped into the language of sacrifice for the empire that American colonists used in the political pamphlets and letters
that formed settler political discourse leading up to and during Ameri-

can independence.[128] Brown, Rae, and Company noted that they had "risqued our all in the Colony, & have been no small Benefactors to it."[129] A similar willingness to "serve the Public," one Indian trader noted, had resigned him to having "been a great sufferer in my own private Affairs."[130] Lachlan McGillivray likewise noted that he had "upon all Occasions exerted himself in the Indian Nation for the publick Good even to the Neglect and Detriment to his own private Business."[131] Thus, instead of operating in an alternative system, some traders cast themselves as extensions of the empire, and believed that the work they were completing was a crucial component of colonialism. Some traders, like George Galphin, refused to trade in towns where French flags were hoisted.[132] There were even those traders who had lived their whole lives in Native American towns. But when their community's members insulted English officials, they demonstrated their allegiance to the colony by threatening to leave.[133]

Although traders fully recognized the difficulties and labor required to conduct trade throughout the Southeast, colonial officials were ambivalent about the value of this work. Elsewhere in the British Atlantic, an emerging ideology held that movable property and labor were as socially valuable as land ownership. To colonial administrators, however, peddlers carrying goods into Indian territory remained suspect as political and cultural liabilities. Not until the middle of the eighteenth century, after James Glen became governor of South Carolina, did the distance an item had to travel contribute to its price.[134] As colonists became less convinced that peaceful trade relations with the surrounding Native Americans were crucial to the colony's existence, they felt less of a need to insulate the trade from its most pernicious factor: long-distance movement. This change figured conspicuously in Glen's speeches about the prices of Indian trade goods. In 1753, in response to the Creek Indians who demanded that they purchase items for the same prices as the Cherokees, Glen told the Creek to consider "the great fatigue of carrying up goods, and besides the great fatigue they are at great expense." The Creek towns were farther away than Cherokee towns, and required crossing multiple rivers.[135] This statement stood in marked contrast to the custom of shielding the Southeastern Indian trade from fluctuations in the market and other contingencies. During much of the colonial period, white and Native American trading partners were not permitted to negotiate prices for the goods they exchanged. To do so would have allowed them to calculate an object's worth according to the myriad factors that contributed to its production and transportation. Instead, colonial officials and Indian leaders fixed prices, often at treaty negotiations, and ordered "that no man be permitted to sell for less, or exact a higher price than shall be stipulated upon any pretense whatever."[136]

Britons commonly established commercial agreements with foreign nations by diplomacy. After the late seventeenth century, Britain crafted commercial treaties with other European nations with increasing regularity.[137] In the Southeast, this practice became standard in a slow, piecemeal fashion after the Yamasee War, when the trade came under a public monopoly. As they created the public monopoly, the South Carolina Commissioners for the Indian Trade appointed factors and often deferred to them as to how to assess merchandise. The instructions they sent to each of the chief factors—William Waties for the Northward Indians (a term used to describe the Catawba and other Piedmont Indians), Bartholomew Gaillard for the Winyaw (referred to as the Wineau by the commissioners) at Santee, and William Blakeway for the Cherokee at Savano Town—differed slightly. They ordered Waties to follow the guidelines he used when he worked for Landgrave Smith's trading firm.[138] They provided Bartholomew Gaillard with a table of prices that were based on their cost to the commissioners, and told him to at least break even, if not to make a profit.[139] The factors trading with the Cherokee, on the other hand, were bound to the prices negotiated between Colonel James Moore and Charite Hagey (the Conjuror) of Tugaloo.

During the colonial period, all of these methods of price setting—through custom, profit calculation, and treaty negotiations—coexisted in the Southeast. But from the perspective of colonial officials, the trade was more successful when the terms were established in the diplomatic sphere. This was certainly true of the Cherokee trade, which significantly outperformed all other markets during the public monopoly period. In towns where the leaders did not actively support trading within the confines of the colonial regulatory system, individuals were more likely to trade with other Europeans or unlicensed traders. Unable to compete with the private trade between settlers and individual Native Americans, the public trade with the Catawba and the Winyaw struggled mightily. Although colonial officials prosecuted the few settlers they could prove were trading with neighboring tribes, these actions were futile, as Southeastern Indians routinely sought out merchants who might offer better trading terms.[140] The competition was so stiff that the Indian commissioners moved to shut down the factory at Santee due to inactivity.[141]

The custom of negotiating prices in the diplomatic realm can be traced back to Charite Hagey of Tugaloo. The price table he devised in the spring of 1716 was later adopted during treaty meetings with leaders of other powerful groups. Of these, the Chickasaw entered into formal trading relationships with South Carolina in December 1717, and the Creek Indians the following month.[142] Throughout the eighteenth century, Southeastern Indian leaders continued to use treaty meetings as the appropriate forum for negotiating prices. Despite the diplomatic setting, these talks were purely economic in nature, with leaders focused on calculating the appropriate value of goods.[143] It is also important to note, however, that not all groups that traded with the English negotiated the prices via their leader.[144]

British ambivalence about bargaining explains why officials so readily supported fixed prices. The historian Craig Muldrew describes bargaining in early modern England as "a skilled process whereby the buyer and seller explored the details of their respective needs and situations, as well as the nature of the goods and market conditions."[145] By allowing buyers and sellers to account for quality, profit, demand, and each party's economic standing, "bargaining was one of the central processes of commutative justice, whereby the final price agreed upon and contracted for was considered to be the just price."[146] But some individuals during the seventeenth and eighteenth centuries disputed the assumption that bargaining was an honest method through which individuals could determine a fair price. They reasoned that the market was confusing and unstable and that the needs and interests of individuals were not readily discernible. Without fully transparent and accurate commercial knowledge, two parties could not trust each other. In England, Quakers and other dissenting groups, as well as John Locke, encouraged merchants to set a fair price that buyers would be free to accept or reject. Haggling, dissenting groups charged, promoted insincerity and dissimulation between buyers and sellers. Instead of advancing a mutually beneficial result, the process of bargaining rewarded the one who was best able to trick the other party.[147]

Colonists believed that bargaining would benefit both parties if they stood on an equal footing of knowledge and need. Fixed prices, on the other hand, were designed to protect the vulnerable. Officials in the colonial Southeast prevented merchants and customers from bargaining in situations in which one party was at an obvious disadvantage. In early Georgia, where storekeepers operated with little competition and were the sole resource for newly arrived settlers, officials feared that merchants would use "such extortion partly by taking advantage of the peoples necessitys." They lauded storekeeper John Brownfield, who promised that he would "set up three or four retailers in Savannah and . . . make it their interest to deal reasonably by fixing moderate prices at which they shall sell."[148] Fixed prices could also protect shopkeepers. Georgia settler Mary Townsend complained that storekeeper Thomas Jones kept "a private store, and furnishes shops with goods by wholesale, whilst he undersells them by retail."[149] Settlers accused Jones of keeping "a storehouse purely to prevent other private storekeepers from selling their goods."[150]

Lack of information about the marketplace could also disadvantage a bargaining buyer. According to some historians, British consumers were fully aware of market forces and fair market values, and were thus able to create an equal playing field in the sport of bargaining. This was probably not the case for Native American consumers.[151] The records suggest that colonial traders did not inform their Native American trading partners of fluctuating market conditions across the Atlantic. Often, the traders themselves did not have a clear picture of the changing European fashions and broader transatlantic economic pressures, which raised and lowered prices (a picture that even historians struggle to piece together).[152] Whether Indian traders told their customers how much they had paid for European trade goods, what prices deerskins could fetch in Britain, how much profit traders needed to make in order to live, or what overhead costs cut into Indian traders' profit is a matter of conjecture. Without this type of information, Native Americans were not able to become informed consumers or sellers, a point that colonial officials probably realized. Further, as will be discussed in the following chapter, colonists believed that Native Americas were particularly vulnerable because they needed, instead of simply desired, European manufactures. All of these factors led colonial officials to believe that Native Americans were incapable of meeting Indian traders on an equal basis. As a result, Native Americans required the protections offered by official prices. South Carolina governor James Glen told a group of visiting Cherokee Indians that "we want to have the prices of goods settled among them so that the traders may not have it in their power to impose upon them." Glen assured the Cherokees that prices were fixed "for their wellbeing."[153]

Colonial officials also contended that setting a nationwide price restricted movement and tempered competition. The 1751 South Carolina trade regulations linked concerns about movement with price, prohibiting an Indian trader from acting "under the pretense of giving larger measure, or of selling his goods at a lower value, or under color of making presents to the Indians and in this way draw Indians from other districts into his own." Neither could the trader "countenance or even permit the Indians of another District to lay out their leather with him."[154] The lure of cheaper goods, they implied, would have the power of upsetting Southeastern Indian communities and, even worse, moving them through colonial settlements.

Both Southeastern Indian individuals and colonial traders chafed under the restrictions on price negotiations set by their leaders. There is evidence, though understandably little, that a number of buyers and sellers did not abide by official prices, choosing to conduct their own negotiations. In early 1755 a group of Cherokees approached their local trader and asked him for a lower price on some goods he had for sale, unaware that the man standing with him was a government official. Under official scrutiny, the trader knew exactly how to answer: that he could not "presume to conclude upon an Affair that so nearly concerned the Publick and Government" by determining prices.[155] It is likely that these Cherokee had successfully bargained for better prices before, or had at least heard of others successfully doing so, and were surprised by his answer.[156] Colonel George Chicken's fears that traders studiously hid their unlawful behavior were confirmed when one admitted to him that he evaded detection by never trading "in the presence of any white man for fear of his being discovered."[157]

Some traders interpreted official trade restrictions as an infringement on their rights of ownership. They maintained that the items they sold were not completely their own unless they were given the right to sell them as they saw fit. After the meeting discussed above, where the Cherokee men asked the traders for lower prices, turmoil ensued when a group of traders admitted to disagreeing with the official line they had parroted earlier. They insisted that "their goods were their own, and [they] would dispose of them or give them away as they thought proper."[158] Traders met the 1751 "Scheme for Regulating the Indian Trade" with similar resistance, telling "the Indians not to mind what was said to them by the government for their goods were their own and they would sell them how, and in what manner they pleased."[159] In 1753, agent Thomas

Bosomworth reported that Samuel Elsinore, a trader who worked among the Creek Indians, refused to follow trading instructions that banned him from selling his goods to certain settlers. Bosomworth stated that Elsinore "dares any man to touch his goods or effects," insisting that "his goods are his own property, and asketh the question whether he can't dispose of them to any British subject without incurring any guilt."[160]

Later that year, breaking with earlier officials, South Carolina governor James Glen used this same logic of property ownership to explain to the Lower Creek why he could not order all the Indian traders to lower their prices. This concept would have been particularly confusing to Southeastern Indian groups accustomed to decades of government-imposed price-fixing. Glen told the Lower Creek that "the goods are their own, and ... I have no power to compel them to give them away or part with them at your prices, and that it would be unjust in me if I had such a power to make use of it, and this you know is the case among yourselves. You can oblige no man to part with his property unless he pleases. I said I had power to send for any of the traders out of your nation that misbehaved, and punish them for it. I could prevent their going there, but I could not force them to dispose of their goods, which are their own property."[161]

Glen's proclamation rang false to his audience. Trader input on official prices was occasionally solicited but rarely explained to the Southeastern Indians.[162] When Governor Glen informed a group of Upper and Lower Creek Indians that the Indian traders could not afford to meet the prices desired by the Creek, the result was disastrous. In one of the most dramatic gestures recorded, the Creek leaders abruptly exited the area where the talks were being conducted and deliberately left the governor's gifts behind. Before leaving, Wolf King said, "No wonder that the Traders cannot afford to sell their goods at the prices we desire when they give away such quantities to their wives and women which they keep. This is the true reason."[163]

Wolf King's accusation shows that Southeastern Indians recognized the complex interplay between social and economic determination of price and that they did not appreciate that the officials pretended otherwise. By attributing rising prices in one area to an effort to offset monetary losses in another, Wolf King noted that traders were guided by economic calculations. But although market fluctuations and other economic stressors may have dictated how the traders allocated resources to strangers, the Southeastern Indians had ample reason to believe that settlers had some flexibility in setting prices for their friends. Despite regulations, Indian traders continued to form affectionate ties within their circumscribed communities and used goods to validate and rank their relationships.[164] With a hint of disbelief and horror, the naturalist William Bartram described an Indian woman who drained her love-sick trader "of all his possessions."[165]

Wolf King's displeasure also highlights the impossible situation that the trade regulations created for colonial traders and Southeastern Indians. During the colonial era, Indian traders were not entirely masters of their own goods. They were pressured to sell goods at official prices or incur penalties if they violated the practice. Their ability to extend credit to trusted Native American merchants was severely limited, if not forbidden outright. Whereas colonial merchants were free to move where they wanted and trade with whomever they pleased within the colonies, Indian traders were subject to restrictions on mobility and their choice of trading partners. By shielding Native Americans and traders from the inconsistencies of the market, colonial officials prevented them from making commercial decisions informed by an understanding of wider economic forces. Deprived of economic data, and operating in a commercial world manufactured by their leaders, Southeastern Indians had no choice but to interpret a refusal to lower prices in social terms. At the same time, colonial officials attempted to restrict social relationships between Indian traders and Southeastern Indians by outlawing the two most interactive economic practices in early modern England: price bargaining and the extension of credit. Traders were trapped between social and asocial exchange systems.

Like price negotiations, credit and debt relationships were both intimate and strained. Fears about debt sprang up regularly in the colonial period. Reflecting on the causes of the Yamasee War, South Carolina planters postulated that "the great debts due from some of the Indians to our traders being about 50,000 l. [pounds] was one cause of their insurrection," and recommended that "to prevent contests with them, it would be well if the law made there against trusting of Indians were strictly put in execution."[166] In reality, the Yamasee would not have viewed their debt, which amounted to 250 deerskins per man, as insurmountable so long as they had an ample supply of potential captives; they could sell a single slave for the equivalent of 200 deerskins, after all.[167] Yet the belief that debt caused wars persisted through the colonial period and was adopted by all strata of society. When South Carolina officials asked

Indian trader William Thomson why the Cherokees were resolved to kill the settlers in the early 1750s, "he said these Indians were so much indebted to the white people for goods, that they imagined if they killed them the debt was paid."[168]

There were colonists who thought that Native Americans either did not understand or disregarded the obligations that a debt-credit relationship entailed. But most individuals who exchanged goods with Southeastern Indians understood that debt, which is a form of delayed reciprocity, was not a foreign concept to the Native Americans. Moravian bishop August Gottlieb Spangenberg recorded his frustration when a Native American man to whom he had given a pewter pitcher as a gift kept returning with goods for repayment:

> Recently one of them came and asked for a pewter pitcher. We gave it, and shortly afterwards he brought a deer hide which had already been tanned on one side in the Indian manner, to pay for it, but we did not accept it. Then he wished to give the bands he had around his legs, but the brothers did not wish to accept this either, for they saw that he needed them himself. Therefore he went away but soon came back and brought a large piece of venison that was cut into little pieces. . . . The brothers accepted it in order not to shame him.[169]

Spangenberg and others who exchanged goods and services with the Southeastern Indians were well aware of what a delicate affair negotiating repayment agreements could be, especially across cultures. For systems of debt and credit to function properly, the parties had to decide when payment was due, the form it would take, and what would happen if creditors did not receive repayment. Even within Britain and its colonies questions remained as to each of these operations. The amount of time that elapsed before a creditor recalled a debt, for instance, varied according to location and was adjusted according to the items in question and the creditor's and debtor's relationship.[170] Whereas a creditor in seventeenth-century England expected to wait an average of eight months and twenty-five days before repayment, a debtor in eighteenth-century South Carolina could expect a twelve-month reprieve before having to balance his books.[171] Creditors were expected to be lenient in demanding repayment; three months was far too short a time to recall one's debts, and even expecting to be fully reimbursed three months after the agreed-upon due date was optimistic.[172]

When a debt was significantly overdue, British, South Carolina, Georgia, and Southeastern Indian officials all agreed that goods or services equal to the amount outstanding should be seized from the debtor. Colonial Georgia law dictated that if a creditor demonstrated that an individual owed him money, "the debtor's goods may be confiscated, appraised by a court official, and the equivalent to the amount owed given to the person who has a right to the money."[173] In the colonies most people believed that court-sanctioned confiscations were the best way to end conflicts and were more humane than imprisonment. If an individual did not have the funds needed to repay the debt, as few did in early Georgia, some averred that "there should be a Clause giving the Creditor power over his Debtor to make him labour and work out his Debt at certain times, computing a proper Number of Days Labour pound Sterling."[174] Though this proposal was not instituted, there was little leniency offered to debtors, even when inflation or a scarcity of coin prevented them from fully paying their creditors on time.[175]

Many observers reported that Southeastern Indians dutifully worked to repay their debts. Thomas Nairne claimed that the Creek Indians at Tallapoosa did not have to concern themselves with the recovery of debts because "they pay one another faithfully." Nairne described a system of ensuring that debts would be repaid that would have been familiar to the colonists—social shame—"for he [is] reckond a ridiculous person and dealing with him avoided, who does not perform his engagements." If, however, a debtor was negligent, "the creditor only goes to his house and takes the value of his debt in what he can find."[176] James Adair, who lived among the Creek and Chickasaw Indians for decades in the middle of the eighteenth century, confirmed Nairne's account. Although the Native Americans had "no compulsive power to force the debtor to pay," Adair explained, "the creditor can distrain his goods or chattels, and justly satisfy himself without the least interruption." Adair claimed that such seizures "seldom happen," for they were "very punctual in paying what they owe among themselves."[177]

Although the British and the Southeastern Indians agreed on the fundamentals of credit, disputes over specific requirements led to conflicts. At what point was a debt overdue? How did one determine value equivalency when seizing goods to make up the debt? If a debtor had no movable goods that could be confiscated, how would a creditor be compensated? With labor? By a family or town member? Misunderstandings about the debt terms led debtors to accuse creditors of theft when they confiscated goods for repayment.[178]

Adair and Nairne painted an idealized picture of Southeastern Indian debt practices, one that was difficult to sustain when the hunting was poor and currency inflation in the colonies and Britain increased the price of goods. Evidence suggests that Southeastern Indians did indeed fall into debt, sometimes so deeply that it would have taken several years of hunting to repay the deficit. And with slavery outlawed after the Yamasse War, hunting was their only option for recompense. While a debt of the equivalent of 250 deerskins seemed like nothing to a man who could clear that debt with one slave, such a debt would take a deerskin hunter at least three years, and probably more, to pay off.[179] White traders became indebted to the Indians as well. In reshaping their role within the Atlantic market economy, Southeastern Indian leaders attempted to carve out a position of debt enforcer. They policed the white traders in their town, ensured that they repaid debts owed to their town members, and learned how to frame their grievances to colonial officials by marking the goods at stake, the time the goods changed hands, and the witnesses to the event.[180] They also used various methods to ensure that their town members repaid their debts. Some leaders refused to permit their town members to "return [from hunting] till they were able to pay their debts."[181] Others seized goods directly from debtors, or a debtor's kinsman, and handed them over to white creditors.[182] And when the debts that their town members accrued seemed insurmountable, they devised debt restructuring programs.[183]

Controlling the terms of debt repayment is a form of controlling labor; even if debtors are not explicitly enslaved, the adjudicator requisitions the fruits of their labor. Thus it is not surprising that Southeastern Indian groups did not permit their leaders to hold a monopoly over debt enforcement, just as they did not allow their leaders to control their productive labor in the Atlantic trade. While individual Native American creditors were rarely stopped from seizing goods to satisfy their debts within Indian territory, Adair claimed that Creek and Chickasaw leaders had "no compulsive power to force the debtor to pay."[184] If Southeastern Indian leaders lacked compulsory power, it was not for want of trying, but rather because their people would not permit it. When the headman of his town "took away his wife and a slave for the payment of the white men for a debt due from the town," Tukena, who lived in the Creek town of Cussita, challenged the headman's authority to enforce these obligations. He appealed directly to the South Carolina Commissioners of Indian Trade.[185] Tukena was hardly an anomaly; others undoubtedly believed that they were responsible only for the debts they consented to, not those owed by others in their community, despite the rules their leaders made. The colonial officials heard these complaints and validated them, making it a matter of policy that a debtor had to consent to the terms of the debt.[186] The commissioners extended the same logic of individual consent and accountability to white traders as well. At first, they had liberally provided the traders with insurance money in case Native Americans defaulted on their loans. As 1712 drew to a close, they decided that they no longer wanted to be responsible for repaying debts contracted between individual parties. They informed the traders that if they chose to "give any trust, or credit, or contract with any Indian for the Time to come for any sum or sums of money exceeding the value of sixty skins, it shall be at the risk of such trader and the agent shall upon no account whatsoever award him above the said sum."[187] Southeastern Indian and white traders who entered into a credit and debt relationship were now solely responsible for fulfilling the terms of the agreement.

This laissez-faire attitude about debt relationships did not last long. It is no coincidence that as the Yamasee were engaging in what the settlers believed was a violent solution to their insolvency, an increasing number of the colonists were falling into debt by trying to stock their expanding rice plantations with slaves. In an attempt to keep the struggling economy afloat while paying for wars and public infrastructure projects, the South Carolina Proprietors issued a number of bills of credit. This action spurred a vocal debate in South Carolina during the year of the Yamasee War.[188] Thus, when the proprietors described the Yamasee War as a crisis caused by debt, they were at least partially projecting their own anxieties of the time.

Deliberations about debt were not merely academic. The British believed that an unsettled debt threatened a previously healthy relationship. Despite the fact that virtually everyone in early modern society carried a liability, scholars agree that debt invited anxiety and was "at once cohesive and yet subject to constant strain," a phenomenon that only increased as the market expanded and networks of credit became more complex.[189] Ludovick Grant, Indian trader and adviser to Governor Glen, explained that "any thinking Man" had to acknowledge that debt turned intimate relationships into fraught ones, not only with Native Americans, but "even among ourselves."[190] The lack of comprehensive insurance left those who extended large amounts of credit vulnerable to life-damaging loss if they were unable to recoup their money. And if too many individuals defaulted on debts, a pernicious domino effect created community-wide hysteria.[191] William Stephens recounted such a panic in Georgia in 1739 when "fatal tydings came of the bad estate of affairs throughout, by reason of such great debts incurred, and the deficiency of funds to discharge them." In response, "all credit was stopped, and the stores in a great measure applied towards payment in part of some of the creditors." The failure of the credit system reverberated throughout society, and there "began to be a visible change in peoples looks and tempers; and little stories continually flew about, to augment fears and jealousies."[192] The fear of the collapse of the credit system rent the social fabric.

This credit system ensured that commodity market operations were anything but asocial for early modern Britons. Creditors protected themselves by using one of the few tools at their disposal: denying credit to all but those who were likely to repay it. Reputation guided creditors' decisions about whether or not to lend someone money, and shame and moral sanctions pressured the debtor to pay.[193] Because of the overlap between credit and social standing, in the early modern period the term "credit" had not acquired the strictly economic definition used today. Instead, as Craig Muldrew explains, it was "extended between individual emotional agents, and it meant that you were willing to trust someone to pay you in the future."[194] The evaluative nature of credit ran even deeper. The extension of credit required a particular form of imagination: the ability to believe that one's current shortage would give way to prosperity.[195] Credit was premised on "more than simple expectations of another's capacity to pay what he had borrowed, what he had promised; they were boomtime beliefs, obliging men to credit one another with the capacity to expand and grow and become what they were not," J. G. A. Pocock explains.[196]

To label a group unworthy of credit was to make a larger claim about its productive potential. For instance, Georgia officials had particular difficulty imagining that the early inhabitants, who were brought over as part of a charitable mission, had the potential not only to subsist, but to grow. Officials tried to prevent all colonial merchants from extending lines of credit for fear that the shortsighted settlers would misinterpret the goods they received on credit as free. Official Georgia storekeeper

Thomas Causton characterized credit as that which "the idle will seek and the industrious may be tempted to," and believed that outlawing it would benefit all members of Georgia's society.[197] To satisfy the Georgia Trustees, John Brownfield promised that in his stores he would make it his "chief rule to decline the giving of credit since that was proved very hurtful to those who have received it: for they quitted all thoughts of labour about finding that goods could be had without."[198]

In South Carolina, officials prejudged Native Americans and lower-class traders to be economically unreliable and attempted to bar them from credit networks.[199] As the historian Joshua Piker cogently states, the British would allow American Indians "to fall into debt but they would never receive 'credit'—the conjunction of economic resources and personal confidence—because they were not seen as creditable."[200] Like the poor of Georgia, some colonists erroneously believed, the Southeastern Indians did not fully grasp that taking goods on credit meant that they were later obligated to pay. The colonists assumed that instead of fulfilling their rightful duty to pay for goods they consumed, Native Americans would do anything to get out of paying their debt. The Yamasee War persuaded the commissioners of this line of reasoning, and they promptly outlawed the extension of credit completely.[201] Indian traders like Theophilus Hastings objected, stating that the credit restriction, "if punctually complied with, may be of hindrance and ill consequence to the trade." The commissioners conceded that traders could extend trade "to the value of one, two, or three skins; and no further."[202]

Instead of seeking the commissioners' permission, many traders simply continued to extend credit to their Southeastern Indian trading partners regardless of official restrictions on the practice. After visiting both Upper and Lower Creek towns in 1725, Tobias Fitch reported to the South Carolina Grand Council that, despite the ban on extending credit to Native Americans, "they make as much practice of trusting the Indians as ever." He observed that there was one trader who "trusted one man as he told me himself with the care of three hundreds skins worth of goods that were all sold and trusted out." Fitch "told the traders of the breach of their instructions and they say without they do trust they cannot trade."[203] During his mission to the Cherokee in 1727 and 1728, Colonel John Herbert had to remind the traders that they were not to give goods on credit.[204] At the Cherokee town of Tunnissey (also referred to as Tanasi and Tanasee), Herbert tried another method of putting a stop to credit, bidding the leaders to tell their people "that they must not expect the white men to trust any of them for their goods except powder and bullets for that I have forbid them doing it." But much to Herbert's dismay, Southeastern Indian leaders did not control credit any more than European leaders did.[205] Both cultures sanctioned personal property ownership, allowing the owners of that property to argue that they had a right to decide what risks to take when disposing of their goods.

Ultimately, experience trumped official prescriptions. Government officials were slowly convinced that debt did not pose a problem in and of itself, but rather that the amount of debt accrued by some Indian groups could be crippling. The South Carolina and Georgia governments restricted, but did not altogether ban, the extension of credit. The restrictions varied, but were usually designed to prevent Native Americans from accumulating more debt than they could pay off in a single hunting season.[206]

The history of credit and debt regulation in South Carolina and Georgia reveals the interplay between economic assumptions and experience. Believing that economic relationships were volatile and that debt etiquette was complex and fluid, colonial officials surmised that Indian traders and Native Americans would continuously run into difficulties if they attempted to establish a system of credit. If this structure collapsed, as the colonists had witnessed in their own communities, hostility and distrust might reverberate through both colonial and Southeastern Indian societies. Thus, instead of navigating the perilous path between cultures of compensation, officials attempted to eliminate the risk of disharmony by outlawing the extension of credit. But British traders and Native Americans had been negotiating terms of credit since the late seventeenth century, and although they regularly encountered disputes, both parties were determined to retain debt and credit as part of their economic relationships.[207]

In some ways, colonial officials' proclamations against debt hurt rather than helped trade relationships. Prior to official meddling, Southeastern Indians, who proved themselves entirely willing to honor debts, quickly realized that the colonial governments would periodically deem debts null and void, thereby excusing them from their past obligations. Adair pointed out that the Southeastern Indians had "grown quite careless in discharging what they owe to the traders since the commencement of our destructive plan." Adair continued, " 'An old debt' is a proverbial expression with them, of 'nothing.' "[208] The Southeastern Indians incorporated this distrust of debt in their dealings with newcomers to their towns as well. As Reverend William Richardson noted when he moved to the Cherokee town of Chota in 1759, he was required to pay four months' rent in advance, for "their Custom is to receive payment immediately."[209] In this instance government regulations made trade relationships less, rather than more, reliable.

Southeastern Indians had to remain flexible in order to adapt to changing official policy. This was especially true in the area of leadership. The career of Charite Hagey illustrates the opportunities and limits of Southeastern Indian leaders in the British Atlantic trade. Until his death in 1719, Charite Hagey was able to shift the locus of trading activity to his Lower Cherokee town of Tugaloo.[210] Since the chief Cherokee factor, Theophilus Hastings, settled in his town, Charite Hagey often had the ear of the colonial administrators. South Carolina archives document Charite Hagey's routine appearances before trade officials. The thousands of pounds of deerskins he funneled into South Carolina from Cherokee country via the mechanism of the public monopoly attest to Charite Hagey's business acumen. At a time when other Southeastern Indian groups refused to do so, Charite Hagey was able to persuade the Cherokee in his town and beyond to trade with the appointed factors and at the established factories.

But there were limits to his and all other Southeastern Indian leaders' control over the trade. Leaders did not, as some of their chiefly ancestors may have done, act as the only conduit for foreign goods. One can envision a system in which a leader collected all the deerskins hunted and dressed in his town, purchased all the goods required for his town from the Europeans with those deerskins, and then distributed the European goods to his town members. This system did not take root in the Southeast, despite a Mississippian-era precedent of some chiefs controlling surplus labor products.[211] Some Southeastern Indian leaders were able to amass a large quantity of skins from their town members, probably using a taxing system whereby each hunter owed a percentage of the skins he procured to the town leader. Coosata King, for example, sold Theophilus Hastings a thousand deerskins on credit, which is far more than he alone could have hunted and dressed.[212] But this model did not predominate in the Southeast, either because the town leaders did not insist on it or because the town members would not tolerate it. Instead, individuals took the skins that they personally procured directly to colonial traders and factories and purchased the European goods they desired.[213]

Within the Atlantic trading system, Southeastern Indian leaders became advocates for the traders and consumers in their towns; they demanded fair treatment and access to a plethora of goods at low prices. One of Charite Hagey's visits to the Indian commissioners in early 1717 elucidates these roles. He appeared before the board to complain that John Jones, a commander at Edisto Garrison (who was not employed by the public trade), "hath cheated his People" by stealing skins, furs, and baskets from Hootleyboyaw, a warrior of Tugaloo, and Yorogotoga-kee, another Lower Cherokee man. Charite Hagey further charged that a settler stole a horse from another Cherokee man on the pretense that he would give him rum and a coat in return for borrowing it. While he was there, Charite Hagey also noted that Colonel Mackay never gave a fourth member of his town a reward for returning two horses. Charite Hagey was successful at his mission. He persuaded the commissioners to reimburse the wronged Cherokee individuals for the stolen goods and overdue payments, even as they chided him and his people for trading with nonlicensed traders. In retort, Charite Hagey expressed his doubts that the government could supply his people with all the goods they de-sired. The commissioners promised him that they would build another trading fort, and sent him away with a boat loaded with goods, which he personally inspected while in Charles Town.[214] Charite Hagey's re-quests on that January day were very similar to Tomochichi's a decade and a half later. Long afterward, Native American leaders continued to see themselves as protectors of, as one Cherokee Warrior stated, "the gen-eral good of my people."[215] Southeastern Indian leaders, seeking redress and full economic participation, gathered the complaints and demands of their town members and brought them to colonial administrators. In return, Southeastern Indian leaders regularly safeguarded the goods and bodies of the white traders who serviced their towns.[216]

Historians have debated whether Europeans tried to alter the hierar-chies of traditional Southeastern Indian political systems. By offering lesser elites, or colony-friendly leaders, an abundance of gifts and access to trade goods, Europeans afforded them the opportunity to redistrib-ute themselves to the top.[217] Colonial officials undoubtedly strove to have this power. The Indian commissioners instructed agents to "acquaint yourself with their Custom, Usage &c., giving the King and Head Men Advice in Relation to the managing their People the better to keep them in Subjection, and with Example and Arguments drawn from a Paralel with our Government, and allways as much as in you layes, keep in Favour with the Chief Men, advising and assisting them to maintain the Authority given them by this Government."[218] The commissioners aimed to provide friendly Native Americans with the items needed to consolidate their power. In addition to gifts, throughout the colonial period, government officials would dole out "commissions," or notes of official sanction, to willing and worthy Native Americans and regale them with ceremonies reserved for important diplomats.[219]

Many Southeastern Indian leaders welcomed these accouterments of power. Leaders almost always accepted gifts, and some would even return to Charles Town with their old, worn-out commissions and ask for new ones.[220] Maintaining healthy alliances with other governments became central to at least some indigenous leaders' positions, and communities would not hesitate to punish, or even kill, individuals who jeopardized those relationships.[221] But, as demonstrated by Charite Hagey's January visit to the commissioners, successful leaders were not merely puppets of colonial governments. Their position continued to be hallowed by "all the ceremonies that are used in making a head beloved man, of which there are a great many in this nation," and the political hierarchy was reinforced nightly in townhouses where the leadership had designated seats among all of the town members.[222] Their focus was primarily local, and their loyalties were to their town.[223] Charite Hagey proved this when he risked the ire of South Carolina officials by supporting his town members' decision to trade outside of the public monopoly. Instead of creating leaders, European gifts served to inform Native American communities that their leaders were acting as successful diplomats and thereby protecting their economic interests. As a group of Chickasaw explained, "Piomingo has talked Severall times to your Beloved People, and they have Promissed him grate Supplyes for the Nation, and their not Coming makes him a shamed when he speaks to his warriors, as they tel him his talks has maid them Poor."[224] When a leader was unable to secure resources for his community, he was deemed an unsuccessful leader.

But the British were unable to command absolute power over leadership positions in Southeastern Indian communities. The Scotsman Alexander Cuming described his difficulty in gathering a delegation of Cherokee to return to London with him and meet with King George II in 1730. Initially, Ouconecaw (also known as Little Carpenter and Attakullakulla at different times in his life) recounted, "not one of our people would consent to go," for the distance would keep them away from their home for too long a time. With the help of longtime trader Eleazar Wiggan, Cuming was eventually able to gather a small group of seven individuals to accompany him across the Atlantic, but they were motivated by curiosity ("they had heard much of England and wanted to see it") instead of ambition. They made it clear that their power was circumscribed; they could not, for instance, cede any of their land, but they could secure access to European manufactures. Furthermore, the delegation abided by Cherokee notions of hierarchy. Even though Cuming wanted to appoint Ouconecaw the spokesman for the group, a position that would have provided him an English title and prestigious gifts (including a red coat instead of a blue coat), he declined the honor. Ouconecaw explained that he could not betray the Cherokee practice of allowing only middle-aged men with established careers and military successes to become leaders: "I was the Youngest of the Company it would not be right, that I should be the Speaker."[225] Although the English had limited control over the process, Ouconecaw eventually did become a powerful leader of his community. His trip to England may have demonstrated to his town members that he possessed the necessary skills to protect the economic health of their community and act as their spokesman.[226]

Policing trade in the colonies was equally important. Southeastern Indian leaders, like colonial leaders, watched European traders like hawks, and demanded access to the tools with which to detect dishonesty. To solve an ongoing complaint by their town members that traders were cheating them by using unreliable scales, leaders across the Southeast insisted that "the king of each town might have the weights given them that the traders might not cheat them with false weights."[227] Treaties consistently stipulated that "there shall be Weights and Measures delivered to the Head Men of each Town, to keep a Check on the Traders."[228] Different towns requested different measurement technologies. The town of Chota, for instance, insisted that their old stilliards be returned when they were replaced with a new measuring tool. Tassittee explained that his townsmen entertained "a great many Notions of the Scales and Weights as not knowing Nothing about them. Wherefore desires the Stilliards as formerly."[229] The colonial officials did not balk at demands for specific measuring tools, as they, too, diligently ensured that calibrated weights and measures were utilized in markets.[230]

While Southeastern Indian leaders acted as spokesmen for their town members, they did not hold a monopoly on regulating trade or bringing grievances to colonial officials. Since each trader had to utilize weights and measures with a colonial seal, any individual trading with them could verify the justness of the trade. Individuals, regardless of station, could directly approach colonial officials if they felt they were wronged. Charite Hagey, for instance, was not the first to bring the aforementioned thefts at Edisto Garrison to the attention of colonial officials; the aggrieved parties approached Colonel John Barnwell to complain about John Jones's actions.[231] Colonial records attest to the fact that individual Southeastern Indians who did not hold positions of power spoke out on the same issues as their leaders: the prices of goods, the fairness of the trading system, and the actions of white traders.[232]

Providing and organizing labor for transporting goods and building forts was another area of the trade that was only loosely directed by certain Southeastern Indian leaders. As discussed earlier, by concentrating trade in designated forts and, later, specific Southeastern Indian towns, colonial officials attempted to insulate Indian-white exchanges from the potentially harmful presence of traveling traders. Traders who spent their days face to face with their business partners were best sequestered in safe communities that could regulate their behavior.[233] Commissioners could now concentrate on the minutiae of deerskin transportation. Gathering horses to transport goods, commissioning leatherworkers to create packsaddles, purchasing boats, and creating tarps to protect skins from water damage were vastly preferable tasks to worrying about whether vagabond traders would create the next war.[234] But these activities begged the question of how goods and skins would move between these forts and Charles Town and who would direct the movement.

The system regulating movement of cargo developed in a piecemeal fashion. Some groups, like the Lower Cherokee, delighted in the job of carrying manufactures and skins themselves. Others, like the Catawba, threatened to trade exclusively with the Virginians if South Carolina did not assume responsibility for shuttling the items back and forth.[235] Charite Hagey again took the lead in figuring out how best to transport goods. He was able to command a considerable amount of his town's, and the region's, labor in this enterprise, ensuring that "his People should fetch them [the European goods] from Savano Town, as likewise bring their Skins without any Promise from him of sending pack Horses, amongst them, or being paid for it."[236] Indicative of his expanding power across the region, he also determined which towns would trade at each factory, surmising that "thereby Burdeners [who transported goods] might be more easily got." He ordered that at each fort the factor should "wait some Days after the Burdeners arrive, before any of the Goods be exposed to Sale, and that you give Notice to the adjacent Towns, of the same, to prevent any Pretentions of their not knowing that the Goods were come up."[237] He also, along with other Cherokee leaders, assumed a prosecutorial role, promising to "punish the Burdeners that keep back or imbezil any of the Goods or Skins sent by them."[238] The commissioners provided Charite Hagey with an invoice for the goods sent via the burdeners so that he could confirm that none went missing. In Charles Town the commissioners also religiously checked their deerskin invoices to ensure that the white packhorsemen they hired stayed honest.[239]

Charite Hagey also used his position as leader to mobilize warriors of his town to protect the burdeners during times of war. The commissioners reported that "if Charitey Hagey of Tougeloe had not used great Diligence, he could not have procured Burdeners to bring down the Skins, before the next Spring; the Indians being informed that the Paths were way-laid by the Creek Indians; but by Means of the said Charitey Hagey (who came as far as Saludee, with a Company of Warriers to guard them) they were prevailed with, to come down now."[240] This passage reveals another important dimension of Southeastern Indian leadership during the colonial period: whereas some precontact chiefdom leaders had a measure of coercion at their disposal when structuring labor, postcontact leaders used persuasion. Ultimately, Native Americans who carried goods back and forth worked for themselves, not their leader. Only after Native American individuals said that they were "willing to carry Packs" were they "laden with goods."[241] Though an Indian trader could suggest the appropriate items with which to pay the Indian burdeners, the commissioners doled out the goods directly, ensuring that they maintained authority over transportation.[242] Indian burdeners were well aware of their right to compensation for carrying goods and skins and complained to the commissioners if they were not adequately paid for their services.[243]

Both Southeastern Indian and colonial leaders attempted to organize the transportation of goods over the vast and perilous waterways and landscapes, but difficulties abounded. They could load up specific individuals with specific goods in either Charles Town or at the fort, but they could not ensure that these arrangements would survive the duration of the journey. Although Theophilus Hastings informed the commissioners that he was sending down fifteen burdeners to carry beaver skins to Charles Town in July 1716, the commissioners were irked to find that "they divided their burthens and made up twenty-one." The commissioners rebuked Hastings and warned him that in the future he was "to agree positively with the Indians, how many burdeners are to be paid."[244] The commissioners did not hesitate to refuse the help of certain Southeastern Indian groups. After a team of fourteen Catawba burdeners arrived over a week late to Charles Town, having sold 150 of the skins along the way, the commissioners decided that the Catawba were not cut out for the transportation service. Instead they informed factor Eleazer Wiggan that they were resolved "wholly [to] make use of pack horses for that Trade, thereby not to be subject to such delays and inconveniences from the Indians."[245] Increasingly, the commissioners allotted more funds to hiring packhorse men, the majority of whom were white, so that they could exert more control over the transportation of goods.[246] Private trading firms followed their example. Although they would hire Southeastern Indian guards and scouts to accompany their packhorse trains, the bulk of their transportation fleet was composed of white employees and African or African American slaves.[247]

Monopoly employees posed their own set of problems. By limiting the social relationships that the Indian traders could develop during economic transactions, and giving them minimal control over trading terms, colonial officials turned Indian traders into "masterless men." These employees of the colony required constant supervision, for they were not driven by self-interest. Daniel Defoe advised that "he who expects his servants to obey his orders, must be always upon the spot with them to see it done," an untenable command given the vast distance that separated the colonies from Indian country.[248] Whereas Southeastern Indian leaders controlled some forms of behavior, colonial traders had little motivation to protect colonial interests. Officials noted that the lack of onsite management led Indian traders to conduct the trade carelessly. Colonel George Chicken warned that some Indian traders had "so little regard to what they do amongst [the Indians] or how they dispose of their employer's goods" that they left the majority of skins poorly tended and exposed to spoliation.[249] In response, colonial officials had to invoke the self-interest they had so studiously sought to erase. Appealing to their Indian trader employees' less altruistic instincts, officials urged them "to take the same care of [the deerskins], as if they were your own private interest."[250] In essence, unwittingly or not, the regulations instituted by colonials and Native Americans reinforced the stereotypes of the economically uninformed Native American and the careless Indian trader.

White traders did not necessarily gain more freedom when the government's control over trade receded. Many traders were under the command of larger merchants, either as employees or as debtors. The complexity of the Atlantic trade favored large trading firms that could maintain relationships with British merchants, find ships with room to transport skins, store the skins safely until the ships departed, front the money needed to purchase a year's worth of goods for Southeastern Indian consumers, and manage the fifty- to one-hundred-horse caravans to carry goods to and from Indian country.[251] Records from the early eighteenth century reveal that small traders were already amassing debt with larger merchants—so large that some merchants turned to the judicial system for legal remedies.[252] As established merchants involved in the Indian trade became wealthier and banded together to form partnerships, they were able to seize an even larger share of the trade. During the 1740s Augusta, Georgia, provided a hospitable environment for established and aspiring merchants. Recognizing the profitability of the Indian trade, they sought a place at the fringes of the Georgia Trustees and the South Carolina Commons House's seats of power. Soon 600 white men flocked to Augusta, many from South Carolina. Those best positioned formed partnerships and used their connections and skills to gain a substantial corner on the deerskin market.[253] Brown, Rae, and Company, a conglomerate of seven powerful traders that included Patrick Brown, John Rae, George Galphin, and Lachlan McGillivray, controlled 75 percent of the Creek and Chickasaw trade by 1755.[254] The smaller fry of Augusta's merchant clan were relegated to working as employees for larger businesses. Not only did they lack the capital to compete with these companies; they also were unable to secure licenses, most of which were already held by members of the more powerful firms.[255]

While trading companies lacked some crucial powers of the state—the power to arrest, for instance—there were similarities between government-run monopolies and trading firms (which were sometimes maligned as monopolies).[256] It can be argued that large trading firms were able to corner the market only to the extent that they were able to seize trading licenses issued by colonial governments. At least they believed this to be true. Brown, Rae, and Company, for example, fought against the Georgia President and Assistants who threatened to withhold trading licenses from members of their firm. Colonists had complained that Brown, Rae, and Company held a stranglehold on the Indian trade market, and Georgia officials were determined to break it. The language that Brown, Rae, and Company used to defend its standing in the trade mimicked the rhetoric used by companies who defended monopolies in other parts of the British Empire.[257] Their oversight of the trade, they urged, benefited colonial interests as much as it did their own business concerns. Because they were "the best Acquainted with Indian Affairs of any in this colony," they were able, "by our Endeavours," to keep "the Indians on good terms with this Colony as well as Carolina for some years." Their size and wealth were crucial to achieving this goal, they reasoned, citing an episode in which the Choctaw almost fled to the French when their English supplier went broke. Brown, Rae, and Company's ability to "send a Large Quantity of goods to those Indians" was the only measure that "prevented them from going back to their old Friends the French." It would be risky, they suggested, to relinquish the trade to "Raw Unexperienced people" who lacked not only the infrastructure to keep the Southeastern Indians "constantly supplyed" but also the relationships the company had built with Southeastern Indian towns.[258] Like other British enterprises, Brown, Rae, and Company relied on the central thesis that trade with foreigners was a risky affair and that it could be adroitly navigated only by wealthy and successful companies.

As the debate between Georgia's trustees, its president and assistants, and Brown, Rae, and Company suggests, colonial governments did not always look kindly on partnerships that were monopolizing the Indian trade. In the end, seemingly convinced by Brown, Rae, and Company's argument, the president and assistants allowed the trade to continue unchanged, but their hand-wringing attests to the ambivalence about monopolies during this period. On occasion, the British or colonial governments were at the helm of liberalizing commerce in America. This occurred, most famously, when the Royal Proclamation of 1763 extended to all British citizens the right to trade with any Native American, as long as the latter could post bond.

When the government demurred from regulating trade, wealthy merchants took up the challenge. At times it seemed that the fissures in the Southeastern Indian trade followed the lines between small and big Indian traders as much as between Indian traders and government officials. Established traders were all too happy to turn unlicensed traders in to the authorities and to report the indiscretions of competing licensed traders. And when the authorities suggested loosening the licensing requirements to afford more individuals the right to trade with the Southeastern Indians, it was those with licenses who sounded the loudest alarms about the menace of poor whites.[259] Many traders recognized that the arm of government could be used to prop up their business.

But even without government privileges, wealthy traders exerted enough economic pressure over the trade that they were able to prevent potential competitors from entering and excelling in the deerskin market. The degree of exclusion created by these economic realities was so prohibitive for small traders that they may just as well have been barred by legal sanctions. Thus it is not surprising that some small merchants used similar language when discussing their wealthier employers as when discussing governmental officials. Few sources capture these relationships, but historians are fortunate to have a short journal created by William, an employee of Augusta's Macartan and Campbell Company, which traded with Chickasaw and Upper Creek towns. On October 10, 1767, William set out to complete a number of tasks for his employers: delivering letters (some of which moved between colonial officials), scolding debtors, retrieving goods to sell at market, and reporting on the behavior of other traders who were employed by Macartan and Campbell.[260] Just like governmental bodies, Macartan and Campbell issued "Instructions," and William stated proudly that even in the face of adversity he was "oblig to mind my instructans" and "Darsent to go against my Instructians." William, probably mindful of the fact that his employers might read his journal, showed great deference to "Mr Macartan and Mr Camel," who were both "gentlemen," just as Indian agents and traders showed deference toward government officials in their vicinity.[261]

William conveys a lot of the chaos that made managing the Indian trade nearly impossible, both for colonial governments and for employers. Some of the disarray was caused by forces beyond human control: the traders got lost regularly, sometimes in the mist; they were waylaid by overflowing rivers; horses ran off or were stolen, leaving them scrambling to trade for more. Alcohol was a persistent problem. The traders drank regularly and heavily. Levy Taylor, for instance, dipped into the rum and got so "groggay" that he almost got himself killed. Traders encountered Southeastern Indians who also wanted rum and little else. Traders played favorites by doling it out to some but not others. Taking matters into their own hands, the thirsty Southeastern Indians stole the desired rum under cover of night, carting away some other goods in the process. But there is an air of frivolity about the thefts, and instead of becoming enemies, the traders and the Southeastern Indians partook in a cat-and-mouse game to retrieve the stolen goods.[262]

The real animosity of at least one trader, but probably more, was reserved for William's employer, Macartan and Campbell. William had been sent to enquire why "Mr Bubby dident Com down and settle with Mr Macatan," and Mr. Bubby was happy to explain. He described a system in which Macartan and Campbell would "fool him [about] his wagers as he did all the Rest of his hierling" by dwindling his wages down to zero after deducting the amount of "old pack sadles and all the horses that were Lost." During another conversation (and there were many, as Bubby kept trying to evade William, who always managed to catch up to him), Bubby insisted that if William wanted any of Macartan and Campbell's goods back he had to "Com to settle with me and pay me my Wagers," for, he later claimed, for "2 yeare" Macartan had "never pade him a single six pence." Finally, Bubby allowed William to seize "Every thing But the Dearskins and the Negrow Boy," a note that reveals that slavery had penetrated the outskirts of Georgia a mere decade and a half after it was legalized. Presumably, Bubby meant that William could repossess the European goods that Macartan and Campbell had furnished him to sell to the Southeastern Indians. William was lucky that Bubby complied willingly, for, as he acknowledged, on the frontier Macartan and Campbell had no effective way to enforce its claims. They could fire Bubby and incur a loss, or they could rely on the colonial judicial apparatus. "If any Body Transgress my Bisness," William noted, he would have to "send them down and Let the Law tak its Corse," conceivably under the banner of debt evasion. This was yet another way that expanding commerce was dependent on the colonial government.[263]

Bubby's next move suggests that traders shared a camaraderie, one that was built around a general distrust of their employers. Despite the fact that William was acting as the face of Macartan and Campbell, Bubby saw a glimmer of similitude and moved to take the young employee under his wing. Bubby, William recounted, "Called me one side to advise me as a friend Now he ses young Man." Bubby warned William that the goods he confiscated from Bubby were "moath Eaten and Rustay," and that when William went to sell them at market, as Macartan and Campbell had ordered him to do, they would "fetch nothing hardly and theay Will blame you." He suggested a strategy that would shield William. Bubby was taking a calculated risk. He ventured that the allegiance

William owed to his employers would be trumped by his sober assessment that his own self-interest required binding with his coworkers and undermining their employers. But William, perhaps naively, claimed in his journal to find this unfathomable. He wondered, "How Can the[y] Blaim me When it my orders to sel them Up at Vandue and I am oblig to mind my instructans."[264] William may not have joined with Indian trade firm employees who coped with their hardships by drinking and keeping at arm's length from their employers. But his account suggests that traders who worked in Southeastern Indian country found more common cause with each other than they did with the individuals in colonial centers who trusted them with horses, saddles, and Indian trade goods.

TRADERS TRIED TO EXERT a modicum of control over their professional lives, and at times they succeeded. All of the efforts of the companies, officials, and Indian leaders to control the sites and terms of trade were largely futile. Within the sparsely inhabited region of regulated exchange, where neither Southeastern Indian leaders nor colonial officials enjoyed hegemony, Southeastern Indians and colonists negotiated their own trading terms. Many Native Americans and British settlers eschewed the belief that personal, fluid commercial relationships were dangerous, and were eager to conduct trade outside of sanctioned settings. Peddlers continued to risk punishment by frequenting different Indian towns.[265] And Southeastern Indian customers shopped in backcountry markets, where settlers ignored the restrictions on trading with the Indians and paid even more for deerskins. Licensed traders and trading fort factors regularly complained that these "fraudulent and clandestine dealings" robbed them of the skins they had counted on securing.[266] The tug-of-war between centrally controlled economies and informal systems did not pit Native Americans against British settlers. Rather, it was ordinary Native American individuals and settlers who forged ahead toward a more modern economic model. Meanwhile, their leaders tried to hobble them with traditional notions about the dangers of free trade. Left with a circumscribed role in the arena of commodity exchange, Southeastern Indian and colonial leaders turned to gift giving as a way to achieve a measure of mastery over each other.

CHAPTER THREE

Gift Exchange

Gift exchange and commodity exchange are not as different as they might at first appear. We often think of gift giving as voluntarily initiated and reciprocated. But obligations follow gifts from hand to hand, even though these responsibilities are not expressly codified. A gift may not carry an actual price, but within any given culture, there is at least a rudimentary acceptance of the debts that accrue when one receives a gift, whether they involve bestowing a return gift at some point in the future, treating the gift with reverence, or holding the giver in higher esteem.

The introduction to this book recounted an episode in which a Cherokee man wanted to buy a gun with ten pelts but was forced by the South Carolina Commissioners of Indian Affairs to exchange the items as gifts.[1] Chapter 2 explained why this trade violated colonial policy: the Cherokee man was attempting to trade with someone other than the factor assigned to his town; he was also attempting to trade outside of a fort; and, furthermore, he was trying to bargain the price of the gun down to ten beaver skins, well below the officially established price of thirty-five deerskins. Colonial administrators and Southeastern Indian leaders proved equally vigilant when regulating price negotiation and trade relationships.

While chapter 2 sought to explain why this Cherokee man was not allowed to trade, this chapter explores the reasons he was allowed to exchange the same items as gifts. As the episode illustrates, in the Southeast the line between gift exchange and commodity exchange was blurred and contested. While the Cherokee man assumed that a transaction of guns and skins could be conducted between two strangers in the realm of commodity exchange, the English disagreed. The exchange, according to the British, was a social event that joined the Cherokee "Head Man" (as they now crowned him) and the South Carolina governor together via a gift transfer. Furthermore, the gun was not being offered against the ten skins; the gun was being bartered for the Cherokee man's labor—"the Care he took of the Burdeners." In their interpretation of the transaction, the South Carolina Commissioners highlighted two major aspects of gift exchange that differentiated it from commodity exchange in the Southeast: it was a practice controlled by leaders in both societies, and it was a mechanism through which to try to control each other's actions. Shaping the behavior of gift recipients became one way that colonial and Southeastern Indian leaders worked to secure their neighboring territories.

AS CROSS-CULTURAL TRADE permeated all levels of society, Southeastern Indian headmen and colonial officials turned to gift exchange to structure the relationships founded on trading. Gifts had the benefit of being articles of peace, unlike the commodities trade, which, the British believed, created ties that were unstable and prone to violence, an issue explored in the previous chapter.[2] Partly to insulate these trade relationships, British officials insisted that a formal peace, often consecrated with gifts, precede any business transactions. Using the strongest of terms, the South Carolina Commissioners of Indian Trade positively forbade any factor "to enter into a Trade with [unaligned Native American groups], until they have first come down hither, paid their Submissions and concluded a Peace with the Government."[3] These moments of peacemaking were peppered with gifts. When a group of Choctaws approached Major William Horton at Fort Frederica to inquire if "some English traders might be sent among them," he refused to agree to their request until they brought him a gift "of some French prisoners" to prove that their allegiance was with the English.[4]

In addition to oiling the levers of peace, gift giving proved powerful in binding people to one another in hierarchical, rather than reciprocal, configurations. It is this shadow function of gift giving that this chapter investigates.[5] For example, in bestowing a gift, the giver could demonstrate his largesse, and thus superiority, over those less fortunate. As historians have shown, the British were well practiced in using gifts to delineate social class. During events of open hospitality, such as large feasts, attendees sat according to their rank, with those of highest status receiving the choicest selections.[6] Ilana Krausman Ben-Amos explains that feasts were central to "cultivating group reciprocity as well as enhancing social standing and rank."[7] In this sense, feasts were similar to the annual Green Corn Ceremony enacted by the Southeastern Indians—a practice emphasizing both social cohesion and the elites' control of social hierarchies.

Traces of British and Southeastern Indian cosmological beliefs colored their habits of gift giving, more so than in commodity exchange.

The ideology of social reproduction discussed in chapter 1, seen most clearly in the myths and ideologies of the British and the Southeastern Indians, was perpetuated by the elites of both cultures, and it was those very individuals who also dictated the practice of gift giving. South Carolina colonists went to great lengths to ensure that the ceremonial aspects of gift giving were strictly the province of the governor. Even though South Carolina's legislature was unlike those of other colonies in its extensive control over Indian trade, its members (along with all members of society) were barred from personally handing over the gifts.[8] As shown in the episode of the Cherokee man with ten beaver skins, the legislative branch funded the gifts and orchestrated their distribution, but it was the governor who was charged with explaining to the recipient the meaning of the object bestowed.

It is no coincidence that royal governors, particularly James Glen, who envisioned themselves as using relationships with Native Americans to strengthen and expand British interests, transformed gift giving into an instrument of empire building by using cosmological principles.[9] Geopolitically, the colonial Southeast presented difficulties for administrators, and gifts provided some solutions. The area was situated on a parcel of land that was hemmed in by the Spanish to the south and French domination to the west, and Britain's control of its periphery was particularly crucial. The colonists quickly realized that their very existence depended on their ability to stay in the good graces of the neighboring Native Americans. The British also determined that they might even be able to deploy Southeastern Indians in their battles with the Spanish and French.[10] Gifts played a role in this process for the obvious reason that they cultivated goodwill and friendship. But gift giving had an insidious use as well, one that resonated with the British theory of production explored in the first chapter. If colonial officials could remake the material world of the Native Americans with gifts, would they not be the Native Americans' Maker? And would the Native Americans then not owe them the boundless allegiance that humans owe God? Instead of Christian "labourers" who were obligated to work as husbandmen in God's vineyard, these Native American laborers would be required to work for the British Empire.[11] Gifts were just the means to accomplish this goal. By plying them with specific goods, especially guns and ammunition, the British hoped to co-opt the Southeastern Indians as British agents.

Meanwhile, Southeastern Indian leaders likewise attempted to empower themselves with the gifts they gave to the British. Consistent with their use of hunting charms and the ancestral strategies of the Creek origin myth, Southeastern Indian leaders created British effigies designed to subdue British influence and prevent future harm. Southeastern Indians also used gifts of hospitality to claim jurisdiction over land. When that failed, they used theft (gift taking) to assert their territorial claims. Far from being gestures of alliance (a function fulfilled by trade), all groups used gifts in an attempt to control the terms of colonization.

GIFTS OF HOSPITALITY, primarily food and clothing, which those who inhabited the land gave to visitors, were one of the earliest forms of gifts. Sharing food and clothing created enduring bonds between two parties by making them internally and externally similar. This concept spanned and outlived the colonial period. British and Native Americans were "brothers, who are born on the same land and suck the same milk," noted Samuel Elbert in his 1777 talk to Tallasee Creek warrior Handsome Man.[12] Swapping clothing could also turn two different nations into one people. When the Creek encountered a group of Cherokee with whom they had declared peace, they, as a "token that they were quite reconciled together pulled the feathers off their own heads and put them on the heads of the Cherokee."[13] The Cherokee performed a similar ceremony as "a solemn token of reconciliation and friendship" with a group of South Carolina colonists when they "stripped themselves, and laid their clothes by parcels at the feet of some of our most considerable men, who in return must do the like to them," missionary Francis Le Jau reported.[14] Baronet Richard Everand would have preferred to consecrate his relationship with the Creek at Coweta by lying "with their Women." Instead, Chicali "took ye Baronet's Gold laced Hat off his head, putting it on his own, and gave him an Old hat in Exchange, Saying, when any of his Daughters wanted an husband he would send for him."[15] It is likely that the same sentiments linking apparel and friendship fueled the Yuchi's desire for used clothing. As noted by the German traveler Philip Georg Friedrich von Reck, "an old garment or shirt they [the Yuchi] highly value, and, when such a thing is given to them, they are eager to put it on, go about with it ostentatiously, and let themselves be seen more frequently."[16]

But in order to forge equality, the food and clothing had to be created and presented in a particular way. The preparation of food in Cherokee marriage rituals is a case in point. A man would propose a union by laying a pile of wood at the woman's door. As Alexander Longe explained, "If the young woman comes and takes of the wood and makes fire therewith and calls him in and gives him victuals to eat, the marriage is confirmed."[17] This marriage food ceremony deliberately combined male and female products and labor into a final meal. Feasts for visitors and other gestures of hospitality, on the other hand, created an unequal relationship where one party was dependent upon the other. A European visitor was vulnerable, often traveling without enough food to sustain him and, potentially, with clothes unsuitable for the environment. By giving gifts of food and clothing, Southeastern Indians could create a hierarchy of knowledge, asserting a command over the environment and customs of the land superior to that of their visitors.

Thus, in a contest over land, gifts of hospitality marked one party as the outsider and the other as the insider. Southeastern Indians and Europeans alike utilized these items to demarcate power. From the earliest days of contact and throughout the eighteenth century, Southeastern Indians gave European travelers who entered their territory provisions during their stay.[18] The peoples of the Mississippian chiefdoms encountered by Hernando de Soto and his expedition regularly presented the Spaniards with food and clothing. Only rarely did they confer prestige goods, such as pearls, on these visitors.[19] This practice outlived the collapse of the chiefdoms. Henry Woodward, who visited the Westo Indians in 1674, recorded on his first night's stay that "they presented mee diverse deare skins, setting before me sufficient of their food to satisfy at least half a dozen of their owne appetites."[20] More than eighty years later, Southeastern Indians continued to treat visitors in a similar manner. Captain Raymond Demere, who was stationed at Fort Prince George, recorded that when he arrived at the town of Keowee in 1756, the Cherokees "presented me with a great number of cakes of bread of their own make and green peas and squashes, every woman bringing something of this kind in a basket and laying it before me, notwithstanding provisions are now scarcer amongst them than ever was known."[21]

Skins, the primary form of Native American clothing prior to contact, were the first nonconsumable gifts Southeastern Indians offered their visitors. Robert Sanford told the South Carolina Lords Proprietors that the Edisto Island Indians who encountered a 1666 expedition presented the crew with skins, and later, near Parris Island, "the Cassique himself came aboard with a Canoe full of Indians presenting me with skins and bidding me welcome."[22] A few years later, John Locke noted a "Friendship with the Emperor of T——who sent a present of skins to the governor."[23]

Journeying into Cherokee territory during chilly fall weather in 1716, Governor James Moore received a warm beaver matchcoat.[24] Skins, whether intricately fashioned or simply dressed, promised to shield the visitor from the elements. Expecting that their visitor came from a distant climate, the residents wished to ensure that he was equipped to survive in their environment. Colonel John Herbert noted that while he was at Tugaloo, "Old grater face presents me with a parcel of skins telling me that I was in a cold place and that they were to make me gloves—I thanked them."[25]

When the Southeastern Indians entered new colonial settlements with victuals, they were casting these colonists as transients. During the first days of Georgia's settlement, an anonymous writer recorded that "Tomochichi Mico, Toonahowi, his nephew, and a large party of Indians came down to Mr. Oglethorpe and brought in as many deer as fed the whole colony for some days."[26] The Yuchi Indians performed similar gestures of hospitality shortly after the Salzburgers settled nearby. "A few days ago an Indian came to the neighborhood of Abercorn in a small boat, with his wife and two children," the preachers recorded. They "brought us a whole deer so that we could give large pieces to the Saltzburgers that are still here, and also to some of the other people."[27] While the Georgia settlers viewed themselves as permanent residents with a right to the land, these Yamacraw and Yuchi gifts of food proclaimed otherwise.

Given their own similar tradition of using hospitality to stratify society, the British colonists probably recognized the messages contained in the Southeastern Indian feasts. Colonial officials proved to be masters of using gifts to create their own hierarchies and consummate their own model relationships. For centuries, individuals in England both cemented and upset social hierarchies by giving and demanding gifts. Through the act of giving generous gifts, English individuals declared their superiority over the receiver. But gift giving could also be subversive. By giving a large gift to someone who was considered one's equal or superior, an individual of lower station could aspire to a new and higher position.[28]

In an effort to redress the unequal social relationship created by hospitality gifts, colonists began to make counter-gifts "to the Indians thro those Nations we shall pass," thereby turning dependent relationships into reciprocal relationships.[29] Colonists began to decline gifts of food on land they considered their own. They were determined to wine and dine Native American visitors to their colonies, just as British officials did with ambassadors of foreign countries.[30] They expressed great anxiety when they were unprepared to greet Southeastern Indian dignitaries with suitable ceremony. When planning for the Upper Creek's visit to Georgia in June 1735, "Mr. Mackay urged an enlargement of the presents," which he stressed was "one of the necessary occasions wherein he was at any price to secure the friendship of the Indians."[31] Despite the colonists' best efforts, gifts were sometimes hard to come by. The Georgia Trustees' Secretary William Stephens related a particularly awkward episode in 1739: A party of Choctaws unexpectedly paid a visit when "the Stores were never so empty," leaving the officials with few provisions to offer. After divvying up their small supply of tobacco, biscuits, wine, and pork, Stephens breathed a sigh of relief when "by good Fortune a New York Sloop coming newly up the River which had good Beer on board, Mr. Jones got two or three Casks of that, which was to be dealt out to them."[32] Newly arrived governor Henry Ellis was not so fortunate. When a group of Lower Creek Indians from Cussita came to Georgia in 1757 to congratulate him on his new position, he had to rush to the store to "buy them a little Powder and Ball," for there were no presents to be found in the public stock. He gave them a rain check for more, explaining that "he hoped soon to have more from the King his Master, and then they should have a Share of them, withal desiring that the Chain of Friendship might be continued bright and the Path straight."[33]

The British and the Southeastern Indians shared a desire to remake their visitors into citizens of their communities. In their gifts of clothing, colonial officials paid little heed to what Native Americans actually wore. Instead, officials gave them items that would help them blend in with the settlers. Not one Indian trade list or Indian trade account book contains shoes, for the Southeastern Indians despised European footwear. Nevertheless, ten "lucky" Cherokee leaders walked away from a South Carolina peace conference with a pair apiece, complete with heels and buckles.[34] Fine red coats, gold-laced hats, waistcoats, and full suits of broadcloth and silk brocade, items rarely coveted by Southeastern Indians, were favorites among British gift givers.[35] If the bestowing of gifts was a vehicle for assimilation, British leaders established the ground rules by choosing items that identified their own fashions, not those of the Southeastern Indians, as suitable for American wear.[36]

The process of assimilation did not stop with appearances. Transforming Native Americans into facilitators of British interests was the ultimate goal of colonial administrators. In 1711, Jean Baptiste Le Moyne

Bienville, French commandant of Louisiana, attested that the British had become adept at using gifts to persuade surrounding Native Americans to conduct raids on the French settlements. He blamed "the great presents that they give them both to encourage them to destroy ours as well as to insinuate to our Indians that the King our master is abandoning us."[37] Bienville understood that gift giving by British settlers served as a device to shape the actions of their Native neighbors. The British believed that, because their manufactures were comprised of their labor and identity, they were able to extend their interests into areas they could not physically inhabit. In the minds of the British, reinventing the material world of the Southeastern Indians included the use of gifts to make the Southeastern Indians beholden to their British "Makers."

This mechanism of using gifts to further one's interests was not theoretical; in the Southeast the colonists explicitly molded gift giving to Native Americans into a category that, above all else, rewarded services.[38] Bestowing presents on individuals who performed their duties ably was common within British culture. Colonial officials recorded gifts to British captains of a scout boat, captains of rangers, and other settlers who filled important roles.[39] But among themselves, reward for service was not the primary reason to give gifts. The British gave gifts to their peers to honor friendships and mark a shared history; gifts were precious items and consecrated relationships.[40] In their interactions with the Native Americans, however, British gift giving was principally aimed at compensating the Southeastern Indians for their work on behalf of the empire.

This trend is clearly seen when tracking the four main occasions on which colonial officials bestowed gifts on Native Americans: (1) to reward them for, or induce them to carry out, colonial services; (2) to commemorate peace negotiations; (3) to provide for their comfort during visits to the settlements; and (4) to honor Native American leaders. The gifts given during all of these occasions followed the general rule discussed above: they were used by the British to assimilate their neighbors and to rank their neighbors vis-à-vis themselves. But within this broad category, the expectations of the assimilated individual took different forms. As shown in Chart 1, between 1717 and 1757, colonial officials primarily gave gifts to Native Americans to persuade them to perform or reward them for performing colonial-expansion projects such as going to war against an enemy, extending and facilitating trade, or simply being good subjects.

To Leaders[d]
13%

Visitors[c]
16%

War/Service[a]
48%

Peace/Negotiation[b]
23%

CHART 1 Reasons British officials gave gifts to Southeastern Indians. September 26, 1716, *JCIT*, 113; January 26, 1717, *JCIT*, 153; January 30, 1717, *JCIT*, 155; June 29, 1717, *JCIT*, 193; September 11, 1717, *JCIT*, 206; September 25, 1717, *JCIT*, 213–14; November 9, 1717, *JCIT*, 225; December 2, 1717, *JCIT*, 236–37; June 11, 1718, *JCIT*, 291; Speech of William Bull, July 8, 1751, *DRIA*, 1:105–7; Presents Given to the Cherokee Indians, November 23, 1751, *DRIA*, 1:161–62; Cherokee Talk to the Board of Trade, September 9, 1730, CO5/4 part 2, accessed November 24, 2015, http://www.colonialamerica.amdigital.co.uk/Documents/Details/CO_5_4_Part2_014; Reck, *Von Reck's Voyage*, 39; Georgia, Trustees of, "Brief Account," 14; Georgia Trustees, November 11, 1734, *CRG*, 3:93; Georgia Trustees to Tomochichi, January 20, 1736, *CRG*, 21:70–74; May 2, 1736, *CRG*, 3:150–52; Georgia Trustees, March 17, 1734, *CRG*, 29:57; Trustee Accounts for 1739, *CRG*, 29:280; *Gentleman's Magazine*, in C. Jones, *Historical Sketch of Tomochichi*, 64; Mancall, Rosenbloom, and Weiss, "Indians and the Economy of Eighteenth-Century Carolina," 306, 307; Chicken, August 30, 1725, Council Journal #3, SCDAH; August 23, 1732, *South Carolina Council Journals*, 5.1:205; February 19, 1757, in Warren and Jones, *Georgia Governor and Council Journals*, 1:494; Salley, *Journal of John Herbert*, 25.

Note: This sample includes gifts British officials gave to Southeastern American Indians on thirty-one separate occasions. Categories are determined by the reasons expressed by British actors. Gifts that appeared in account books for future general use were not included in the chart, which takes into account only gifts known to be exchanged between specific individuals at a specific time.

[a] Giver specified that the gift was based on past or future services rendered in support of war efforts or general duties such as carrying items for the trade or delivering messages.

[b] Giver expressed that the gift confirmed alliance or peace. Usually these items were presented during formalized peace treaty meetings.

[c] Giver expressed that the gifts were to provide visitors nourishment and entertainment during their stay in the settlements or during their travels to and from the settlements.

[d] Giver stated no reason for the gift other than the recipient's status as a Native American leader.

When presenting a gift, colonists often specified the actions they were rewarding. Commodity exchange, with its standardized prices, did not provide an opportunity for routine commentary about the value of certain labor. But gift exchange, which allowed for a certain leeway in determining value equivalency, did give participants a chance to take note of the worth of their own labor and the labor of the receiver. The episode with the Cherokee man who wanted to exchange ten beaver pelts for a gun but was forced into a gift exchange, is a case in point. When the South Carolina Commissioners of Indian Trade wrote to Cherokee factor Theophilus Hastings about the event, they instructed him that "if you hear Anything of it amongst the Indians, you may make Answer it was not in Way of Trade, but a Present made for the Care he took of the Burdeners."[41] The Cherokee man had assumed that the labor that he invested in hunting, dressing, and delivering the ten pelts was worth a gun; the commissioners countered that it was the labor he invested in overseeing the transportation of goods that was valuable.

The Cherokee man was one of many who were informed that they were receiving a gift in return for a particular task that colonial officials deemed beneficial. On December 2, 1717, the Commissioners of Indian trade "ordered that a present of liquor and a gun be sent by Capt. Hatton and delivered to Cheritey Hagey of Tougeloe in the Cherokee, in consideration of his services and assistance to the Factors in managing the trade for the benefit of the publick." They sent a few more gifts to ten Cherokee headmen, "informing them that the said present was given them as a reward for their particular services, and to encourage them to assist the white men."[42] Women, too, were plied with gifts to assist the colonies. The deputy governor of South Carolina promised to give nine Cherokee women a gift of $7\frac{7}{8}$ yards of strouds cloth if they agreed to follow their warriors' camp to the war against the Yamasee.[43]

Gift givers also attempted to influence the future behavior of the recipient, often by insisting that a particular gift be used in a particular way. This illustrates how gifts remained linked to their givers even after they left their hands. These connected gifts, which the anthropologist Annette Weiner calls "inalienable possessions," had the ability to expand information about the giver far beyond his body, allowing him to extend his interests into territories he could not physically reach.[44] The gifts of guns that the British gave the Chickasaw, a headman suggested, communicated British superiority even if the warriors who held those guns were defeated. If they were to die "along side of them Guns," the headman promised, "the Guns would still remain on our Ground to shew the French how much the English loved us."[45]

Colonists could usually distinguish whether the guns, textiles, and beads that Native Americans possessed were of Spanish, French, or English origin, but they would not be able to determine if this item was a gift or a commodity. In the Southeast there was great overlap between gift goods and commodity goods, despite the fact that people who purchased items had fewer obligations than those who received items as presents. Historically, this lack of distinction is unusual, as gifts are generally physically unique, and their appearance is their primary means of impressing those who come in contact with them. The Creek leader Malatchi artfully noted these overlapping forms when, in presenting a gift to the governor, he identified it as his people's primary form of currency, or "their wealth."[46] Soon after trade was established, Malatchi recounted, "it was agreed upon that skins should be the commodity given in exchange for what they may so want. . . . As they are the most valuable thing we have, I have ordered my people to bring [them] as a present to the Governor in the name of our Nation."[47] The same could be said of most types of goods that the British used as gifts, many of which can be found on trading lists.

Because gifts and commodities often looked the same, it was incumbent on the giver to make their differences known. The distinction between southeastern gifts and commodities lay not in their appearance, but in who controlled their use. In return for goods given at a reduced cost and relabeled as "gifts," the colonists expected Native American receivers to provide their labor to the settlers by using the specific goods to further the settlers' interest. With a British gift in his hands, a Native American temporarily became a British worker, living and fighting as the gift giver desired.

The Southeastern Indians were attuned to the expectations that traveled with European gifts. A headman reported that when Governor Glen made the Cherokees a present "of axes, hoes, knives, guns, or ammunition as he frequently did, he always desired them to hunt briskly to kill plenty of Deer, that with the Skins they might buy Cloaths for their Wives, and with the Flesh that they might feed their Children, that they might grow up stout Men and good Hunters and that they might become a numerous and powerful People." The French, on the other hand, "sometimes made small Presents but their Language was very different; it was, go kill and destroy, bring us plenty of Hair, plenty of Scalps, this was their constant Cry, that it was no difficult Matter to discover who was their friend and who was not, since the one wanted their Preservation and other desired their destruction."[48] The message was clear: the recipient could not assume that a gift could be used in accordance with his own wishes. He had to await the express permission of the giver to do so, and without that permission, he was expected to use the gift to fight the benefactor's battles.

While settlers and officials most commonly gave their visitors food and clothing to incorporate them as temporary members of their community, officials consistently used gifts of weaponry to transform the Southeastern Indian receivers into British agents. Unlike cloth and tools, guns and ammunition were foreign to Native Americans at the time of European arrival. Colonial officials believed that by giving the Indians guns they had revolutionized Native American lives. As one Georgia official declared, before the white men arrived, the Southeastern Indians did not have "any arms to kill Deer, or to go to war against their enemies, or defend themselves, but only bows and arrows."[49] South Carolina governor James Wright mocked the Creek Indians who believed they could subsist without European goods, asking, "Can you make guns, gun powder, bullets, glasses, paint and cloathing, &c &c? You know you cannot make these things."[50] The British contended that in their weaponless precontact state Native Americans had lived in great poverty. In 1725, during a diplomatic mission among the Upper Creek Indians, Tobias Fitch declared, "I must tell you young men that had it not been for us they would not have known how to warr nor yet have any thing to warr." Fitch proceeded to enlighten the youngsters about their precontact state, informing them that "before we came among you there was no other weapons than bows and arrows to hunt with. You would hunt a whole day and bring nothing home at night." Fitch painted the white men's arrival as a godsend, for they taught the Indians "the use of fire armes as well to kill deer, and other provisions, as to warr against your enemies." Fitch emphasized the worth of the white man's gift of technology and the resulting obligation when he chided the Creek for having "set no greater value on us that have been such good friends to you than you do to your worst enemies" despite the fact that the British had forever bettered Creek lives.[51]

Like the sermons discussed in chapter 1, which preached that humans were permanently beholden to their Maker, the British believed that by giving the American Indians guns they had irretrievably altered their lives. According to the British, the life-changing gift of technology permanently bound the American Indians to the British. Fitch relied most readily on the language of indebtedness. In accepting this gift of revolutionizing technology, the Upper Creek owed the British allegiance. The obligation was unending, for the British would continue to view the guns as rightfully theirs, a belief bolstered by the continued contact that British gunsmiths had with Native American guns. When such guns were "rendered almost useless for want of but a very little mending," Native Americans were often able to negotiate that "there may be a workman in each Fort who can mend our guns," often on the colonial dime.[52] Archaeological excavations of Southeastern Indian towns reveal that some Native Americans worked on their own guns and produced their own ammunition.[53] More often than not, however, they were happy to delegate these tasks to the colonists. One of the pitfalls of this practice was that the colonists never fully ceded ownership of the guns manufactured by their kinsmen. The English asserted possession over European technologies, even when American Indians actually owned those items. There are a number of court cases in which English individuals were exonerated after seizing European manufactures from American Indian homes, for these actions were not considered theft.[54] The fact that many of these guns had entered Native American society as gifts instead of commodities emboldened the British to come to this conclusion.[55] These gifts of guns, which in the minds of colonists still belonged to them, could not be used, in the words of Governor Glen, to "kill the Great King George's Children."[56]

South Carolina settlers used presents of guns and ammunition to direct Indian actions very early in the history of colonization. On May 6, 1685, Caruse, a Yamasee leader, testified that "about 3 months ago the Scotts settled at Port Royall did send Caleb Westbrooke and Aratomahan a Cheiftain among them to the Yamassess to encourage them to make war on the Timecho Indians . . . which they agreeing to the Scotts furnished them with 23 fire arms in order to destroy the said Timechos."[57] In 1717, the Commissioners of Indian Trade gave Indians Caesar and Partridge presents of guns, ammunition, and cloth to carry out an expedition against the Yamasee Indians.[58] Nearly a decade later Colonel John Herbert's promise of ammunition convinced Choa:te:hee, a head warrior of great Tellico, to go to war against the Lower Creek.[59] By the middle of the eighteenth century, the Southeastern Indians understood that the sight of Europeans bearing gifts was meant to coax them into war. Pouchimatah, a

Choctaw, said to Jadart de Beauchamp "that he supposed that the goods which I had brought were intended to engage them to go to war upon their enemies and ours," and was surprised to find otherwise.[60]

The British conviction that Native Americans should use British weapons to fight British battles accorded with a Southeastern Indian belief that shared weapons of war were powerful sign of alliance. This may explain Pouchimatah's assumptions regarding interactions between the Choctaw and the Europeans. When urging the Catawba to join with them and the English against the Shawnees, for instance, Antossity Ustoneeka and Tocoe said, "I have taken up the Hatchet with my Brothers the English against their enemies and I have sent you the hatchet which I expect you will take up also and come here and strike our enemies with it."[61] Much like sharing food and clothing, sharing weapons was a potent way of confirming Southeastern Indian martial alliances.

In the colonial setting, however, these allies were not always equal. The British decreed that the gift giver was the officer in charge and that the Native Americans were merely soldiers to be commanded. This belief aroused suspicion that Native Americans who took gifts from a competing European power were enemy combatants who were working for a competing imperial power. Nathan Brownson, governor of Georgia, scolded the Creek Mad Men who "for the sake of a few trifling presents did . . . wantonly fall on our warriors in the night."[62] Later, he admonished the Creek, "we fear while you keep among you lying people, who thirst for our blood, which they dare not attempt to take themselves; nor to look us in the face, but wish by a few goods to hire you to spill your own blood in attempting to feed them with ours."[63] John Martin asked the Creek at Tallassee, "Is there any among you who would for the sake of a fine coat, shirt, or a few other trifling presents, so far forget himself, as to sacrifice his happiness, the happiness of his wives and children, and bring future misery upon this country?"[64]

Brownson's and Martin's protestations hint at the notion that, by exchanging goods for services, the Native Americans acted as mercenaries. When they were feeling especially cynical, colonial officials were prone to think of the Southeastern Indians themselves as commodities. The Georgia President and Assistants remarked that they "thought prudent to purchase them [the Creek] with large and handsome Presents."[65] And as the English and French vied over Native American allies during the French and Indian War, British captain Raymond Demere snapped,

"Indians are a commodity that are to be bought and sold, and the French will bid very high for them. And on this particular occasion if we don't bid as high we shall absolutely lose them, for Indians are but Indians and are but very little to be depended on; the highest bidder carries them off."[66] The Spanish, too, averred that Indians "become final allies of him who gives them most."[67]

Implicit in these statements was the British colonists' belief that one could not use a gift contrary to the wishes of the giver. Gifts had a mysterious power that caused the possessor, as John Martin claimed, to "forget himself." In the process of gift giving, the goals, desires, and societal obligations of the recipient were replaced by those of his patron. One was unable to take a gift and decontextualize it and use it for one's own benefit. A gift insisted on being used in one way only: as the giver intended it to be used.

The colonists employed many devices to ensure that the Southeastern Indians used their gifts as allies should. If notice was "taken of their good behavior" they received more gifts.[68] Indian agent Patrick Mackay suggested that "presents should be bestowed on the most deserving."[69] If the Southeastern Indians used their gifts contrary to the wishes of the givers, they risked seizure of those items or a forfeit of future gifts. Governor Glen informed Upper Creek leader Acorn Whistler that because the Creek made "ill use of their guns" by firing on the Cherokee, the British would not give them any more guns.[70] John Highrider threatened to ration gifts of ammunition and guns to the Choctaw and Chickasaw when they started using these items more quickly than he thought prudent.[71] After Malatchi and other visiting Creek misbehaved, Benjamin Martyn suggested that "when the Presents are deliver'd to them by the Agent, it will be proper for him to represent to them, that in Case They do any Mischief hereafter to any Inhabitants of the colony ... proper notice will be taken of it,; and those Indians, who shall be guilty, will be distinguish'd from the rest by having no Presents given to them."[72] James Glen informed the Cherokee that, because they had been faithful to King George, they would be awarded presents, but he would not "give any to the other towns which have not so well deserved them."[73] The French had similar expectations. Jadart de Beauchamp recorded how he reprimanded the chief of the Abekas for not properly using the flag he had given him. "I spoke to him about the flag which he had taken down and I told him that the flag was not for himself alone but for all the village and that he must raise it again or else I would have it taken away from him."[74]

Because colonial officials used gifts to encourage certain behaviors, they were careful to specify which actions they were rewarding. On January 12, 1763, Georgia governor James Wright informed the council that Selechee and a few other Creek Indians were headed to town with a Spanish scalp. The council was "unanimous in Sentiment that the scalp should not be received but that the Indians should be kindly used and dismissed with Presents, but not on account of the scalp."[75] On another occasion, James Glen emphasized that he was presenting the visiting Cherokee Indians with gifts not because they had agreed to the treaty terms (for the stipulations were for their own good) but because they had been "good friends to this province and to Georgia."[76]

By the mid-eighteenth century, Southeastern Indians viewed British gifts as synonymous with attempts to control their behavior. In order to assert their own intentions, some leaders stipulated that they were not acting in order to receive gifts. A Cherokee warrior clarified: "I am an old man, and don't desire any matters to be made easy for myself, that I may get a present of clothes. No, I speak for the general good of my people, and for the instruction of my young men."[77] Similarly, Judd's Friend relayed to Glen that he planned to come and visit him in the future, "but not for the sake of presents but only to renew the Friendship."[78] In a world where gifts and actions were so intertwined, Native Americans who wished to proclaim their own desires had to eschew British presents.

Other Southeastern Indians manipulated their neighbors' understanding of gift exchange for their own benefit. In the process, they pushed the British argument into unintended territory. The Cherokee leader Raven was one of many who used the language of European technological superiority to squeeze gifts out of the colonial coffers. "We are a poor people and can make nothing ourselves, nor have we anything but what we get from the white people," said Raven as he worked up to his demand for guns. "I had a dream that the enemy was in the path, and we want more guns, for with our bare hands alone we cannot do any thing against the enemy," he concluded.[79] The colonial government handed over the guns. How could they not? The Southeastern Indians were exercising the very logic crafted by the colonists themselves.

The Southeastern Indians insisted that if the British wanted to take responsibility for the beneficial effects of gun technology, they had to be held accountable for their deleterious effects as well. Warfare was, of course, a feature of precontact chiefdoms. But, as Tobias Fitch observed, before the Europeans arrived Native Americans had not "known how to warr nor yet have any thing to warr."[80] They may have known how to wage war, but not this particular kind of war. European colonizers escalated combat by asking Native American groups to ally with them as they strove for control of America. Indirectly, the settlers created new military zones by dispersing populations whom they had forced to flee into new territories. In these newly contentious regions, some groups turned to guns, either to defend themselves or to seize more territory. A ripple effect ensued as new populations were forced to flee. European colonists also financed an Indian slave trade, sparking battles between Native Americans intent on seizing bodies for English buyers.[81]

At times, the Southeastern Indians were so consumed with warfare that they lacked the time or resources for subsistence. Some colonial leaders, like James Oglethorpe, acknowledged the hardship placed on the Indian allies who "lose their Hunting and Corn season for our Defense." He insisted that the Georgia trustees "give them Food, Arms, Ammunition and some Cloathing, which they otherwise Buy with Skins which they get by hunting."[82] More often than not, Southeastern Indians had to petition for the type of compensation that Oglethorpe voluntarily bestowed. They demanded restitution from the colonists in the form of gifts, usually of the very guns and ammunition that the English had used to remake the Southeastern Indian world and advance their imperial mission. "In former Times when we either went or sent to you we had Presents of all kinds of Cloths, Duffels, Read Coats, and a great many good Things," a Chickasaw headman reminisced in 1754. But in this theater of constant warfare, he continued, "we do not desire any other then Guns and Ammunition to preserve our Lives with."[83]

Oglethorpe was able to easily discern that his neighbors were entering into a war that he was creating, but in the middle of the eighteenth century, in the "theater of constant warfare," the tangled alliances and the uncertainty of a particular battle's origin prompted Southeastern Indians to draw the connections for their English allies. It was the English colonists' obligation to furnish them with guns and ammunition because, as Killa Cunsta of the Cherokee town of Joree argued, the "French Indians" are "your Enemies and ours." The Cherokee were "not no Way acquainted with the French," and the "great King over the great Water" had promised that if they helped the English in this imperial battle, they would be supplied with the necessary tools of war.[84] It seemed only fair, they reasoned, that when they made good on their promise that the "Great King George's enemies shall be our enemies; His people and ours shall be always one, and dye together," that the colonists should make some sacrifice. But as the Native Americans were painfully aware, the colonists were often loath to give up their lives and livelihood: "We come hither naked and poor, as the worn out of the earth, but you have every thing," the Southeastern Indians protested.[85] They traced their misery back to the arrival of Europeans, and thus felt emboldened to ask for compensation. When the spokesman for a group of twelve Cherokee Indians said to Governor Glen, "We come here to see what we can get as I and my people were out hunting, we were drove down here by the Creeks," he was linking the disruption to their subsistence to the colonial presence, and demanding gifts as recompense.[86]

The colonists often complied with these requests, but not happily. Some suffered silently. Georgia official William Stephens was accommodating to the Southeastern Indians who constantly stopped by in 1742, but by June 1744 he could not contain his glee each time they departed. "Early this morning at Sun rising the Indians went off, much to my satisfaction," he recorded in his journal. Later that month he gloated about his luck when more "Indians came down this morning and by good fortune, I now had ready conveyance for them to Frederica."[87] South Carolina governor James Glen, on the other hand, could not always suppress his dislike of the Southeastern Indians' lengthy visits, and he liked even less their demands for gifts. When a group of Upper Creek Indians meandered into town in April 1752, Glen chided them for coming unannounced. The second headman of Ulchitchi cut straight to the point, asking the interpreter to tell Glen, "I am glad to see him. I want a gun if he pleases." But Glen did not please. Acorn Whistler intervened, informing Glen that there were "10 men and 2 women of our upper towns came down with us, and there were 26 of the Lower Creek, that want guns, our guns being almost gone." Glen would not budge, responding, "I am sure I saw them have a great many good guns." He asked the interpreter to inform them that "if they had sent us word that they were in want of guns we might perhaps have supplied them by way of present, but we will not permit Indians to ask for things."[88]

Ultimately, however, Glen and others acquiesced, recognizing the power of gifts to create further debts of obligation. In 1752 Ludovick Grant reported to Glen that the Southeastern Indian towns that lay on the frontier "are not capable now in Time of this general Warr to hunt to purchase Ammunition &c. merely to defend themselves from the Enemies," thereby acknowledging the Southeastern Indians' claim that the warfare sparked by colonization was disrupting their ability to subsist. On behalf of the Southeastern Indians, Grant asked for "Succour and Relief." But unlike Oglethorpe, Grant had ulterior motives. He noted that this was a moment in which gifts could be used to reinforce the Southeastern Indians' position as subjects under the colonial government, and "put them in Mind of their Obligations." He shrewdly noted, "They have always layn under to Carolina, and now are obliged to lye under for their Relief."[89] What the Southeastern Indians construed as restitution, the colonists insisted was a debt-carrying gift.

In certain contexts, both the Southeastern Indians and the British colonists recognized that the acceptance of gifts could be a statement of power rather than dependence. Merchant Samuel Everleigh informed Harman Verelst that the "Indians have been so used of late years to receive presents that they now expect it as a right belonging to them, and the English, French, and Spanish are in some measure become tributary to them."[90] The belief that they were entitled to these goods led some Southeastern Indians to simply seize them. Along with displays of hospitality, these acts of gift taking may have been another way that Southeastern Indians used gifts to stake claims to land. According to the anthropologist John Reed Swanton, the Creek Indians in the early twentieth century believed that a man's home, or "hûti," was not restricted to the locale in which he lived, but encompassed all places inhabited by those who were part of the same maternal clan. A traveler entering a town announced his clan affiliation. A man who had married into that clan was obligated to invite the traveler to his house. "Welcome home," the resident would say to the stranger, and the stranger called this house his "hûti" even if he had never set foot in the dwelling before. The visitor had a right to all within his clansman's home, for it was his.[91]

Evidence suggests that Southeastern Indians living in the eighteenth century held a similar belief. Settlers complained that visiting Indians did not respect certain boundaries, often walking straight into homes and demanding or taking the items within. The settlers at Okeechy poured their dismay with the Southeastern Indians into letters, writing about the great inconvenience caused by Native Americans who "in passing backwards and forwards commonly demand provisions, and frequently stay here eight to ten days."[92] The Salzburger settlers in Georgia recorded many instances of Southeastern Indians entering their town and treating it as their own. The settlement of Ebenezer sat on the path between Savannah and several Creek and Yuchi towns and was a magnet for Southeastern Indians traveling between the two locations. They would typically ask for "meat and beans at our place because they had no provisions with them." And even more curious, thought Reverend Johann Martin Boltzius, was the fact that some of them "do not mind asking the people for anything they may see. Even in my room an Indian was attracted by a number of things."[93] Boltzius noted that the Indians were quite aggressive "in the demands they make. On several occasions they have demanded that I give them small medicine bottles, in which they want to keep the grease they use to oil their guns."[94] Captain Raymond Demere, who operated Fort Prince George near the Cherokee town of Keowee, faced similar conflicts over boundaries. Eventually, he simply resigned himself to the fact that the Cherokee who visited the fort would claim possession of some of its contents. In his account for reimbursement he listed "1½ dozen knives taken away by the Indians at table."[95] Sometimes the Southeastern Indians asserted their rights to goods aggressively. Matthew Toole informed Governor Glen that, in the settlements abutting Cherokee land, the Cherokees would drop in on homes and "take just what they please, and if [the occupants of the home] go to hinder them they will cock their Guns at them, and tells them they will shoot them if not they will knock them down, and take what they please."[96]

It is no coincidence that the Southeastern Indians reserved their most belligerent demands for those with whom they felt most comfortable. "When they come to visit the first time they are usually very timid as long as they are sober," Boltzius observed. But "if they come back several times they get quite bold."[97] Rather than being greedy or immoral, as many colonists assumed, it is possible that this behavior signified that Southeastern Indians were proclaiming these areas as their hûti. Like gifts of hospitality, which welcomed visitors while also marking one party as an alien and the other as a resident, the Southeastern Indian practice of demanding items was a means of claiming space, of affirming solidarity, and of establishing political superiority.

Gifts did not always entail declarations of power. Sometimes they were simply articles of peace, created to preserve memories. A Cherokee leader pointed to the overlap between words and gifts when he laid a feather down on a treaty table and added, "This is our way of talking, which is the same to us, as your letters in the book, are to you; and to you, beloved men, we deliver these feathers, in confirmation of all we have said, and of our agreement to your articles."[98] The Creek Indians living in Cussita and Buzzard Roost included a physical marker of peace when they wrote to Georgia governor Patrick Telfair and included a "full token of our friendship . . . a white wing and hopes when you see this with our talks that you will be fully convinced that we are not madmen who wish to bring our women and children into trouble."[99] Using feathers, particularly from eagles, to denote an alliance was fitting on a variety of levels. As discussed in chapter 1, the Southeastern Indians carried eagle feathers to remind them that their ancestors could defeat even the strongest of enemies. As William Bartram perceived during his travels in the Southeast, eagles were the bravest of birds, for they would never flee in the face of danger.[100] Therefore, in presenting eagle feathers to confirm treaties and promises, Southeastern Indians affirmed their dedication to upholding the pact regardless of future danger.

When gifts were not available, the paper contract sufficed to confirm an alliance. As they signed a land grant, a group of Cherokee said, "In token of our speaking strait and true we have hereunto set the marks of our several towns and families to be remembered by them and their children as long as the moon doth shine by night or the sun by day continues to give warmth and heat."[101] The Southeastern Indians guarded these contracts with care. When George Pawley traveled to the Cherokee in 1746 to reassert peace, they presented him with a roll of parchment "wherein was the Articles of Commerce and Friendship Settled between the Lords of Trade & the Cherokees Chiefs in London in 1730."[102] Georgia officials revealed the power that these physical remnants of an agreement held when they insisted on burning notes of a rejected talk. When the Creek leader Malatchi gave a speech that he quickly recanted after it deeply displeased Georgia's officials, the officials threw the written record of the talk into the fire, for they knew "the Nature of Indians to be such, that if it had been kept, it would have been a sufficient reason for them to imagine, it was Approved of."[103]

In the absence of gifts, words themselves assumed a material value. "Brothers, Do not throw away this talk of your friend," Georgia governor Henry Ellis pleaded when speaking to the Creek in 1760, echoing a sentiment that was also used by Southeastern Indian orators.[104] But the multiplicity of languages and the ease with which all parties could form and then forget their words proved troubling. Cognizant of this hazard, John Martin assured a group of skeptical Creek, "I have no forked tongue, nor double mouth. I speak Truth and not lies."[105] But Martin was over-looking part of the equation. The fear of many tongues was not based simply on the possibility that the speaker might be lying. Rather, once a variety of talks existed, one was permitted to accept one colonial talk while disregarding another. Contradictory actions voided words, and incoherent words stymied certain actions. As the Creek Indian named White Lieutenant explained to James Seagrove, agent of Indian Affairs, the Okfuskees had a "friendly disposition towards our Brothers and friends the white People of Georgia," and they had "not thrown away their talks." But, he continued, "the many & great talks we daily received from different parts" ensured that "the minds of the Indians was so confused that they did not know how to act for the want of our great chief to join us together."[106]

In this colonial world of economic and diplomatic turmoil, towns looked to their headmen to plot a coherent course. As Emistesego, headman among the Upper Creek, explained to Governor Wright of Georgia in 1774, "When there was but one path it was peaceable but not so now, for there are too many paths, and that these things and the confusion in the trade have been the cause and foundation of all the evils, and which cannot be removed if the trade is carried on as it has been of late."[107] Emistesego, and many others, blamed white traders because they often claimed to speak on behalf of the government, despite the fact that their governments prohibited them from doing so. Tomochichi maligned the traders, who "caus'd great Confusion." Their "tongues are useless; some say one thing and some another," he stated.[108] The results could be dire. The historian William Ramsey, for example, argues that the Yamasee War was sparked in part by too many contradictory talks streaming through Southeastern Indian country.[109]

A gift could remedy this uncertainty by providing a clear message of intention or agreement. Unlike words that could be uttered by a governor and ignored by a settler or trader, a gift was a symbol of community consensus. Many members of the community contributed to a gift's production, attended its presentation, and displayed their responding counter-gift. Further, a gift combined action and sentiment: the work of production and the work of display interwoven with encoded intentions and desires. Perhaps words would have more closely approximated gifts if the talks of the Native Americans were accessible to the larger settler community, but they were not. Government proclamations informed settlers of boundary lines, but they did not transmit Southeastern Indian perceptions of how land was valued. By asserting a position of authority through official declarations, British and American administrators replaced Southeastern Indian logic with their own, allowing settlers to disagree with the governors instead of responding to, and thus perhaps gaining an understanding of, the mentality of the American Indians.

Gifts that bore messages were particularly suited for public presentation in the receiving community. But though a large pile of deerskins demonstrated the hunting prowess and generosity of a town, its message was hard to discern. Most of the gifts that circulated in the Southeast were stacks of skins, or other goods similarly indistinguishable from commodities. Some gifts, however, had unique attributes capable of altering the receiver. An unnamed Southeastern Indian, for example, presented a painted skin and eagle feathers to an anonymous visitor because, the recipient explained, "the feathers of the eagle were soft, and signified love; the buffalo's skin warm, and signified protection; therefore he hoped that we would love and protect their little families."[110] Three years later Scenauky, the wife of Tomochichi, hoped that once the Georgia residents ingested her gifts they would be forever transformed from the inside out. A Georgia settler recalled that she bestowed on them "a jar of milk, and another of honey: 'that we might feed them,' she said, 'with milk, for they were but children, and that we might be sweet to them.'"[111] With these offerings the Southeastern Indians hoped to persuade the British to reform themselves into being good neighbors. A buffalo could be ferocious, and an eagle could be intimidating, just as the English could be, but the Southeastern Indians proposed that the English use their power to protect rather than subdue them. The Southeastern Indians were adept at divining and manipulating the English colonists' perceptions of them. This can be seen in Scenauky's nod to the English belief that the Native Americans were childlike. If the Indians were, indeed, childlike, then the English were required to act responsibly as parents. Scenauky conveyed this sentiment with her gift of milk and honey.

Because the function of gift giving is to remind the recipient of the giver or to mark an agreement, a gift's journey is often circumscribed: it exits circulation after it is gifted.[112] A person who bequeaths a gift to another upon his death must also transmit the history of the gift if it is to retain its original meaning. At least some Southeastern Indians subscribed to this historical obligation, and were able to pinpoint the provenance of existing gifts as well as the reasons they were bestowed. "There was a person in our country with us that gave us a yellow token of warlike honor, that is left with Moytoy, of Telliko; and as warriors we received it," a Cherokee leader told colonial officials. "He came to us like a warrior from you, a man he was, his talk was upright and the token he left preserves his memory among us."[113]

The following speeches by Chickasaw headmen to Georgia officials demonstrate the importance of a gift's lineage in even greater detail. After claiming that they had come to renew the peace initiated by their predecessors, Mingastushka and Piomingo presented a British medal that was originally given to the former's uncle:

> Mingastushka: This great man of our nation who wore this medal I show you is dead—and I am his nephew and a leader—on the death of this great man, he left a daughter who took care of this medal, and she judged it was proper when I came that I should bring it that you might see it and know such a thing belonged to our family and accordingly she and her mother sent it.
>
> Piomingo: You see this, now [pointing to the medal] it was worn by our great man, he is dead, and his daughter sent it for you to see it.[114]

Not only had Mingastushka's uncle worn the British medal during his lifetime, but the communal significance of the gift outlived this display. Long after the wearer had died, the medal retained its power, for a chosen relative preserved it and then conveyed it to other Chickasaws. Whether the "great man's" daughter intended that the Georgia officials retain possession of the medal or if she wanted to show them that her people continued to preserve this gift of peace is not clear from the above speeches. But the Georgia officials considered it a gift and replied, "We are glad you remember with pleasure the virtues of your old and worthy predecessors, and we are pleased that the daughter of one of them has sent us this medal, with the reasons for so doing—in return we will give you some present for her."[115] It is noteworthy that the Georgia officials regarded the medal as an indication of this woman's esteem for her father rather than for the settlers. Sadly, in return for this history-laden object, the Anglo-Americans bestowed commonplace presents, "including the goods to purchase provisions to——dollars."[116] Such a bland description is proof enough that the gifts chosen by Georgia officials for the Chickasaw were of utilitarian rather than sentimental value. That night, while the Chickasaw were returning home, a group of Cherokees stole every last one of the gifts, a testament to the fungible nature of these items. As Piomingo said while handing the Georgia officials strands of beads, "These white beads are of little value but in our nation, where they are kept even by our children with veneration as tokens of peace and Friendship."[117] Usually a gift is prized because of the specific and nontransferable meaning it embodies. For this very reason, it often lacks objective worth to individuals outside of the relationship. In their gift-giving practices, the British often failed to honor this standard of value.

South Carolina and Georgia colonial officials did not develop or institutionalize a system of preserving Native American gifts. Thus, they lacked a way to publicly recognize the messages conveyed in those gifts. But they did acknowledge that gift giving was crucial to sustaining peace, and that refusing a gift was tantamount to declaring ill will. Traders and factors, for instance, were forbidden from turning away a present from a Native American individual.[118] But did the officials and settlers use Native American gifts as the givers wished them to be used? Did the governor wear the Chickasaw medal? Did Oglethorpe display the painted skin for all Georgians to see, so that they might remember to treat the Yamacraw with gentleness? Did the milk and honey transform the missionaries into nurturing, sweet individuals? There must have been times when gifts bestowed by Native Americans were cherished by settlers, such as the basket purportedly woven especially for New England resident Dinah Fenner by a grateful Narragansett woman who was in need of food, and which was passed down for generations.[119] Yet nowhere is there a detailed record of a repository of Native American gifts, nor mention in newspapers or diaries of the display of, or verbal comment about, Native American gifts. British settlers, it appears, did not treasure Native American gifts in the way that Native American communities cherished the colonists' offerings.

This disregard for the memories inherent in gifts became incorporated into South Carolina colonial policy. South Carolina officials informed all traders that "when any present shall be given by the Indians amounting to a value worth sending down you are then to send them to the Public Receiver for the use of the Public."[120] But "use of the Public" did not mean that all settlers would have the opportunity to examine or make use of the gifts. It meant that the gifts were immediately sold at public auction and the profits put into the public coffers. When a storekeeper informed the board that "James Moore had delivered him a beaver match coat, weighing five pounds and a half, as part of the effects of the public's first adventure to the Cherokees, in March last," they commanded "that the said storekeeper, dispose of the same to the best advantage of the publick, and pay the money into the hands of the cashier."[121] The message contained in this gift, that the Cherokees were the rightful owners of their land and knew best how to survive in it, was extinguished.

Native American gifts were quickly turned into commodities and meticulously measured. Officials created a mathematical formula for calculating the value of return gifts. Commissioners ordered that when an Indian agent received a gift from a Native American he was to return the gift to the public store, where the storekeeper would compute the gift's value and issue a return gift of half the value.[122] A worksheet shows how strictly officials adhered to the formula. The storekeeper received from the Southeastern Indians, by way of Col. Thomas Broughton, as presents:

> Coosoe Indians = 6 dressed deer skins
> Itawan = 12 dressed deer skins, 8 raw
> Catapaw = 11 dressed deerskins

He then mixed them together and computed their worth:

> Fourteen heavy, wt. 18 lbs, at 5 s per pound = £4:10
> Fifteen light, at ⅘ d per skin = £1:1:.6
> 8 small raw at ⅘ d per skin = £ 1
> the Whole amounting to seven Pounds, seven Shillings,
>   and six Pence.

Based on these figures, the commissioners ordered "that the said Storekeeper, return in our Behalf, to the said Col. Thomas Broughton, for the Use of the several Indians, the Sum of seven Pounds, seven Shillings, and six Pence, being half the value of their respective presents."[123] There is some evidence that, in Britain, exchanges of gifts between individuals were recorded in account books. Occasionally, the value of the gift bestowed would be compared to that of the gift received in return. But this mathematical precision applied to Native American gift giving appears to have been a New World innovation.[124]

The stories and sentiments behind the gifts were quickly squandered as the items were reduced to spiritless commodities. Officials shrugged off any gesture of sentiment or appreciation as to how the Southeastern Indians wished their offerings to be received and reciprocated. In fact, Native American gifts were little prized by colonial officials. By the middle of the eighteenth century, when British settlers had achieved some measure of security, colonial administrators occasionally entreated the

Southeastern Indians not to bring them gifts. James Glen asked Malatchi to "bring no skins for a present but bring horses both for the greater dispatch and to help to carry up the presents I intend to give you."[125] The colonists wanted to be gift givers, but they did not want to be recipients of Southeastern Indian gifts.

So what if colonial officials never publicly displayed the diplomatic offerings that Native Americans envisioned as a mirror of themselves? So what if private traders or travelers did not cherish the gifts they received but rather sold them to British collectors who accumulated natural and cultural artifacts for their cabinets of curiosity?[126] Because gifts were emblematic of community creativity, hiding them from view had broad repercussions. Individuals and families conducted commodity transfers, but gift exchange signaled a moment in which a headman or group of leaders presented the collaborative decisions and labors of their town or region. As discussed in chapter 1, within their communities Southeastern Indians placed great value on collaborative labor. Gifts provided an opportunity for them to demonstrate the fruits of this labor to their European neighbors. When presenting the painted skin to Georgia settlers, for example, Tomochichi was declaring his ability to command the resources of male hunters, women dressers, and Yamacraw artisans. As depicted during the Green Corn Ceremony, the Medicine Man was an exalted individual who gathered the produce from all sectors of society and then distributed that feast to restructure society. In similar fashion, Southeastern Indian gift givers were using their offerings to structure their relationship with the English as well as demonstrate their control over their community's resources. In this way they were much like the Georgia Trustees who enthusiastically memorialized Tomochichi's visit to a textile factory, and the collaborative labor he witnessed there, by gifting him the "cloth that he saw making."

Now, imagine that you are a South Carolina settler who operates a rice plantation. You have never attended a treaty meeting with a Southeastern Indian group, and you probably never will. Since your plantation sits far from the frontier, you do not pay much attention to Indian affairs (though you have heard stories about Native American barbarities). But every time you go to Charles Town—which might be an irregular event— you are confronted by a display in front of the courthouse. It is different every time you pass. Most of the time there are stacks of deerskins; sometimes the stacks are so tall and take up so much space that you wonder how you could enter the courthouse door if you were so inclined. Other times there is just a small stack or two, shoved to the side. More rarely there are objects—painted skins, woven baskets, leather garments. You cannot imagine purchasing any of these items, and you are dubious about their aesthetic merit, but they provide a welcome distraction. There is always a plaque next to the display, but, truth be told, you stop to read it only if something is particularly notable and you have time to spare. Those large stacks of skins, for instance, were hunted and dressed by some town of Creek Indians—one town! There was a pair of gloves that, if memory serves, a Cherokee king gave to the governor. You paid attention to those gloves because the day was very cold and, for one brief moment, you considered borrowing them for a bit.

In all likelihood, this scenario would never have occurred in colonial times. But it is instructive to think about how history may have unfolded differently had the English publicly displayed Native American gifts. One cannot say for sure that a settler who regularly passed stacks of deerskins would have marveled at the productive capacity of Native American groups. There is no certainty that, if Oglethorpe had simply nailed up Tomochichi's painted skin in Savannah's town center, colonists would have appreciated the creative artistry of American Indians. But at least there would have been a chance that widespread exposure to Native American arts and ideas could have elicited respect for them. Instead, most believed as Thomas Ashe did: "Manufactures, or Arts amongst them I have heard of none, only little baskets made of painted reeds and leather drest sometimes with black and red chequers coloured."[127]

MY ARGUMENT IS NOT THAT Southeastern Indians used British gifts correctly while the British used Southeastern Indian gifts incorrectly. Neither party consistently used gifts exactly as they were intended. During the moment of exchange, gifts provided a strong symbol of friendship and esteem, and in this way they fulfilled a central function of gift exchange. But once those gifts were installed in their recipient's home, their meaning and objectives were often lost. The Southeastern Indians did not blindly work for British colonial goals while sporting red coats and carrying guns. And the British did not fulfill the Southeastern Indian wish that gifts of skins, paintings, and consumables would transform them into good neighbors—whether by making them acknowledge the might of Southeastern Indian hunters and hide producers, by creating equitable contracts for oral agreements, or by treating them with kindness and generosity. Gifts, after all, could be tokens of peace, but they could also be tools of exploitation. It is not surprising that all actors scrutinized gifts and worked to disentangle them from their self-negating aspects. One is reminded of the gift of the Red Rat that the Creek Indians' ancestors bestowed on the eagle. Though presented as a gift of peace, the Red Rat was a kind of Trojan horse, designed to lead to the eagle's downfall. One wonders if the Southeastern Indians imagined that the gifts they bestowed on the Europeans might yield the same result. If the colonists had not disposed of them at public auction, perhaps the Southeastern Indian gifts, properly heeded, would have rendered the colonists as defenseless as that eagle. Perhaps, like the eagle in the origin myth, the fleeing English would have left behind goods that the Southeastern Indians could then appropriate and use to sustain themselves against future enemies. Perhaps, in the end, the British silenced the meaning of Native American offerings because they were truly aware of their latent power.

CHAPTER FOUR

Consumption of Commodities

Gift givers demanded (or at least asked) that the receiver leave the gifts in their original form. But commodities, by definition, invited buyers to alter them and appropriate them for their own use. Yet, in a cross-cultural trade, where many foreign objects were designed to be used in a particular way, how could commodities be anything other than markers of a specific relationship and tools of assimilation? For example, how could Native Americans don European cloth without looking European? How could Britons use deerskins without thinking about the Southeastern Indians who produced the skins? This chapter explores how all parties brought exotic commodities into their communities and analyzes whether those communities interpreted those goods as representative of foreign relationships. It reveals the ways in which both Britons and Southeastern Indians remanufactured foreign goods before fully integrating them into their society, thereby creating the illusion that foreign commodities were not so foreign after all. Textiles and deerskins, the two most traded items, serve as the major focus of analysis.[1]

IN RENAISSANCE EUROPE many people thought that fashion was a window into one's identity. The essence of one's garments seeped into one's soul and allowed the soul to peek out, alerting strangers to deep truths about the individual, such as his or her alliances, place in the community, and aspirations. A person who donned Spanish, Italian, or French fashion in England was not only politically suspect, but viewed as one who embodied the stereotypical vices of those countries. A man who wore breeches made from English cloth was honest and hospitable, whereas one who wore foreign velvets was consumed with pride and self-love.[2]

This pattern of thought could lead one to conclude that, by wearing Native American leathers, individuals in Britain risked charges that they were "going Native." After all, the skins exported from the Southeast to Europe flooded the market.[3] Yet Britons in deerskin breeches were saved from metamorphosing into war-hungry primitives (as they believed Native Americans to be) by a series of steps separating these American products from their American Indian producers, helping them to transcend the link between producer and product discussed in chapter 1. Upon arriving in England, North American skins joined skins from other parts of Europe, Russia, Asia, Africa, and South America.[4] Artisans dehaired, soaked, beat, stretched, cut apart, and fashioned them into shoes, gloves, hats, purses, collars, chairs, saddles, and bridles.[5] Whether they regarded them as gifts or commodities, most Britons who ultimately used such leather goods were probably unaware that the hides came from animals originally shot by a Southeastern Indian hunter, and were then dried and dressed by a Southeastern Indian woman and transported by a Southeastern Indian man.

The appearance of skins contributed to this sense of detachment. Instead of representing something novel, deerskin replaced English leather supplies that had been depleted by an eighteenth-century cattle plague.[6] The substitution was close to seamless, causing most European consumers little concern about the leather's provenance. Skins and leather never arrived embossed or gilded, and were rarely painted or dyed with decorations that would have inspired the English to hang them on their walls or fashion them into unique furniture. Unlike Indian calico, Chinese porcelain, or Venetian glass, Native American manufactures remained unmarked as foreign products or exotic luxuries.[7] British consumers remained oblivious to their alien origin while incorporating them into the usual array of domestic necessities. In Britain, before the Seven Years' War, there was little interest in Native American culture and products. The painted skins, weapons, clothing, baskets, canoes, or wampum that did traverse the Atlantic were not featured prominently in display cabinets next to other foreign curiosities.[8] Southeastern Indian deerskins simply did not foster cross-cultural awareness among the vast majority of the individuals in Britain who used them.

European consumer culture was moving away from the Renaissance conviction that an object's natal culture had a strong transformative power over its possessor. As Peter Stallybrass describes, "Clothes could be 'fashion'—detachable and discardable goods—but they were less and less likely to be fashionings, the materializations of memory, objects that worked upon and transformed the body of the wearer."[9] *Inconspicuous* consumption increasingly symbolized masculinity and power.[10] The demystification of objects grew as Europeans consumed more and more foreign goods; "paradoxically, as Europe imported goods from Asia, Africa, and the Americas in ever greater quantities, it increasingly asserted the detachment of the European subject from those goods."[11] In the colonies, a similar process ensued. The ready access to goods that entered through the port of Charles Town, and the colonists' use of these items to disrupt rather than confirm social hierarchies, meant that objects were unreliable social indicators. This disassociation between goods and identity remained the norm until activists during the era of the American Revolution reinstated conspicuous consumption (or, in many cases, conspicuous refusals to consume) as a mark of one's convictions.[12]

British settlers in South Carolina and Georgia had as little yearning for items of Southeastern Indian fabrication as their relatives across the Atlantic. While early explorers and settlers valued Native American tools, later generations believed that European bodies and instruments were more suitable for inhabiting and harvesting America. Thus, latter-day settlers had little use for Native American implements. This British American process of disregarding Native American technologies was complete by the last quarter of the seventeenth century, the same period in which the English began colonizing South Carolina.[13] The consumption patterns of southeastern colonists validate this argument. There is scant evidence that settlers in South Carolina and Georgia, even those who lived in the backcountry and traded frequently with the American Indians, utilized their technologies or manufactures.

There were some exceptions to this rule.[14] Southeastern Indian baskets, woven primarily by women using river cane, gained a small following among travelers and settlers who noted their beauty and utility (figure 3).[15] Unlike painted hides, which, as the naturalist William Bartram found, were too cumbersome for travelers to carry home, baskets were easily transportable souvenirs of a trip into Indian country.[16] Their unique patterns also caught the attention of colonists who sought items to send abroad as gifts. Theophilus Hastings, who was a prominent white trader among the Cherokee, found himself in a predicament when South Carolina instituted a trade monopoly after the Yamasee War. The new restrictions prevented him from trading privately for the baskets he had long been bestowing on his friends. Hastings sought an exemption from the South Carolina Commissioners of the Indian Trade so that he could continue acquiring Cherokee baskets, but his request was denied. The commissioners ordered that "all baskets, to be bought by the said Hastings, be for and on the account of the public, only."[17] But Hastings did not take the commissioners up on their suggestion that he create a market for Southeastern Indian baskets. Either he believed baskets to be gifts

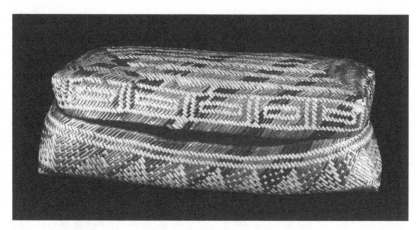

FIGURE 3 Cherokee double-weave cane basket, pre-1725. The British Museum, London, England

instead of commodities, or he could not persuade his Cherokee partners to scale up production of their baskets for the Atlantic market. Other evidence suggests the latter to be the case, which, given the laboriousness of creating a single basket, is not surprising. In 1717, John Jones, commander of the garrison at Edisto, complained that when he approached a group of Lower Cherokee men, he could persuade them to sell only one of the four painted baskets in their possession.[18]

Jones could have found many uses for the baskets at the garrison. Unlike European pots, baskets did not break, and unlike metal kettles, baskets were light. Baskets kept their form, a quality not shared by bags made of the coarse linen known as osnaburg, which planters and traders commonly used to transport rice, flour, and other foodstuffs. Still, estate inventory records indicate that only a handful of households utilized baskets.[19] One such household was that of Francis Holms, who supplied clothing, beef, and sundries for the Indian trade monopoly, and died with five Indian baskets in his possession. Rather than appearing in the inventory next to the deerskins or Indian trade items, Holms's Indian baskets were listed with iron pots, rice sieves, and sheepshearing materials. This placement implied that he used the baskets to organize farm supplies and possibly even to hold the pounds of wool listed right below them.[20]

A handful of settlers died with other Indian manufactures in their estates. Thankfully for historians, court officials found it worthwhile to itemize some of these goods instead of bracketing them under "sundries"—a term that obscures the identity of numerous Southeastern Indian products. Moses Darquier's estate included an Indian pot.[21] Cherokee "carpets," which were large woven cane mats, were among the goods of James LeBass, as well as Mr. McKenzie and Mr. Roche.[22] Thomas Bint owned an Indian lance.[23] One cannot begin to calculate the number of heirlooms and exotic items that probate recorders neglected to include.[24] For the most part, however, archaeological excavations support the probate inventories' suggestion that settlers chose not to import Native American manufactures into their communities. Native American pottery found at excavation sites of white settlements offered some possibility of cross-cultural trade. Archaeologists contend, however, that enslaved Native Americans produced this pottery and that it was not obtained through trade.[25]

The individuals that one would expect to own Southeastern Indian goods—licensed traders and deerskin exporters—did not.[26] Except for Francis Holms, the Indian trade supplier, and James LeBass, a diplomat, the individuals who owned Native American goods at their death were not registered Indian traders or government officials. Possibly, they may have been trading clandestinely. Archaeological excavations of backcountry settlements provide little or no evidence that settlers used Native American goods, invalidating the hypothesis that individuals who lived closest to Southeastern Indians and had more access to their wares were inclined to use their manufactures.[27] There are several reasons for this segregation of Native American and British material culture. The simplest explanation is that English settlers regarded their own manufactures as superior and thus saw no benefit in using anyone else's. Alternatively, individuals who lived on the boundaries of British society may have engaged in distinctive consumption patterns to set themselves apart from Native American neighbors who lived a little too close for comfort. A preference for English over Native American manufactures therefore derived from a desire to preserve an English identity.[28] Archaeological excavations provide evidence that individuals who lived in the backcountry utilized the same items as individuals who lived in the urban centers of Charles Town and Savannah. This suggests that those individuals who lived far from market centers were dedicated to maintaining a lifestyle similar to those who lived in the bosom of the colonies. Excavations at Archdale Hall in present-day Dorchester, South Carolina, for instance, revealed that the branch of the Barker family who lived in the backcountry led a material life virtually identical to that of their relatives who lived in Charles Town.[29] By reproducing the lifestyle of their urban counterparts, settlers on the borders of Southeastern Indian country created a sensory link with the people with whom they felt the strongest kinship. In this instance, manufactures really did reinforce the identity of their natal culture.

There were some exceptions to the general rule that settlers preferred European technologies. Settlers were willing to concede that Indian footwear was more appropriate to the American environment than their own. Georgia settler Francis Moore explained that "those who walk in the woods much, wear what they call Indian Boots, which are made of coarse woolen cloths, much too large for the legs, tied upon their things and hang loose to their shoes."[30] John Williams, who had three Indian baskets upon his death, also owned one pair of Indian boots.[31] Throughout the eighteenth century, Indian boots became so widely accepted as necessary for hunting, fighting, and traveling in the American backcountry that George Washington ordered them for his troops during the Seven Years' War and the American Revolution.[32] But the settlers' adoption of Indian boots did not portend a wholesale acceptance of Native American clothing. Colonists did not forgo breeches, although Southeastern Indians believed that without them it was easier to work in the backcountry.

Settlers who chose to use specific Native American goods rather than their own were few and far between. Trade with the Native Americans did not facilitate a transmission of a material culture during the colonial period. Except for a handful of baskets and Indian boots, the bulk of exports from Indian country (deerskins) were detached from their Indian producers and treated like domestic commodities.

Within Native American communities, it was more difficult to ignore the differences between indigenous and European goods. Even if European items replaced traditional goods and technologies, which many of them did, they often looked different than their indigenous counterparts. Iron knives glimmered in a way that set them apart from their indigenous copper equivalent, red strouds were brighter than indigenous milkweed-fiber textiles dyed with vegetable pigments, and European beads were shinier than the small beads produced from marine shells. If a gift is an item that represents a relationship with a particular individual or group, one could argue that all European items within Southeastern Indian communities were, in many senses, gifts, for they drew attention to the fact that they were obtained from Europeans. One could also argue that European commodities within Native American communities were, by their very nature, instruments of assimilation that brought Native Americans into a European realm of material culture. This chapter will argue, alternatively, that although Southeastern Indian groups had access to the same items utilized by English settlers, and were given repeated opportunities to learn how to use European technologies as Europeans did, they developed a body of cultural preferences that remained distinct from that of their European neighbors. The process of dividing European manufactures from European producers was twofold: first, Southeastern Indians purchased goods according to their own tastes, and second, they remanufactured many of the goods according to their own fashion.

Historians have acknowledged that Southeastern Indians were highly selective consumers of European goods. "Indians were eager customers, not slaves to imported fashion," James Merrell concluded in his 1989 study of the Catawba.[33] Kathleen Braund concurred, stating that the Creek were "very specific about what they needed and wanted in exchange for their deerskins."[34] But the evidence supporting these claims is episodic. In trying to systematically reconstruct Southeastern Indian tastes, scholars are left with a frustrating gap in the sources. The most robust and accessible body of British sources, the South Carolina *Journals of the Commissioners of the Indian Trade* (1710–18) and the *Documents Relating to Indian Affairs* (1750–65), frequently mention account books that governmental boards collected from traders working for the public Indian trade. Unfortunately, these account books remain missing. Scholars of the Hudson's Bay region have been able to use the Hudson's Bay Company's copious financial records to understand the purchasing habits of the Cree, Assiniboine, Chipewyan, and other nearby Native Americans, revealing a population of savvy shoppers who understood the market system. Southeastern Indians, however, have received no similar treatment.[35] To uncover Southeastern Indian consumer behavior, this chapter will turn away from diplomatic records, which emphasize gift exchange, and analyze purchases for the Indian trade. Until scholars discover account books that document what Native Americans bought, when, and in what quantities, the orders placed by white individuals trading with the Native Americans provide the clearest picture of Native American tastes. White Indian traders, whose livelihoods were dependent on understanding which items their Native American customers desired, studied Native American consumption practices and made their purchases accordingly.[36] Their purchases suggest that Southeastern Indian individuals were fluent in the practice of commodity exchange.

COMMODITY AND GIFT EXCHANGE are often distinguished by identifying the party who selects the item that changes hands. In a commodity exchange, the customer chooses the item transacted, whereas in a gift exchange the giver determines the object to be bestowed. Thus, by giving gifts, an individual can shape the material culture and corresponding social structure of the recipient. Moreover, as discussed in chapter 3, the giver can continue to exert control over how those gifts are used. Commodities, on the other hand, allow consumers to exercise their preferences by choosing one item over another. An individual who completes a commodity exchange retains complete control over that object and how it will be used (within the framework of his or her society's social norms and sumptuary laws).[37] This autonomy can become complicated if merchants restrict their customers' access to certain goods, thereby limiting consumer choice. Therefore, when creating a picture of Southeastern Indian taste and consumer behavior, it is essential to ascertain the pool of items available to Native American customers for purchase by asking if South Carolina and Georgia traders presented Southeastern Indians with a wide array of goods. Or, alternatively, did colonists limit the contours of taste formation by restricting the items Southeastern Indians could see, purchase, or even steal?

In the colonial Southeast, the former scenario was the norm; British officials and traders did everything they could to cater to Native American demands. Rather than trying to control Southeastern Indian material culture through the use of objects, as they did with gifts, colonists expressed no desire to limit the types of British manufactures available to Native Americans. Even when the trade was put under a government monopoly, officials gave government-employed Indian traders considerable leeway. Not only were traders encouraged to introduce a wide variety of goods that would appeal to their clients, but they could "have any Goods there without Limitation."[38] Colonial administrators regarded Native Americans as valuable customers who would enrich Britain by providing it with raw materials (skins and furs) in exchange for British manufactures. Georgia official William Stephens asserted that the deerskin trade was very advantageous to England because the Indians purchased woolens and iron.[39] The sale of a single broad hoe, for example, turned a considerable profit. Although strouds, a woolen textile popular in the Indian trade, fetched only £2 for every £1 spent, the officials believed that woolens were one of the most promising areas of trade.[40] Sir William Keith lauded the colonies, which "consume above 1/6 part of the woolen manufactures exportation from Britain, which is the chief staple of England."[41] American Indians joined settlers in this profitable consumption of wool.[42] A Georgia promotional writer extolled the benefit of the Indian trade to England, exclaiming that it "takes off a great Quantity of our woolen manufacture."[43]

South Carolina governor William Bull was eager to win over the Choctaw in 1738. He hoped that these estimated 1,600 individuals would enlarge and extend "the trade for skins and furs, which may in a little time require double the quantity of British goods such as duffels, strouds, broadcloth, guns, powder, bullets &c to supply that numerous people."[44] Bull's inclusion of broadcloth in his list, considered by the British to be one of the most high-quality woolens,[45] reveals that officials did not intend to define Native Americans as a lower class. The South Carolina Slave Act of 1735 prohibited slaves and indentured servants from wearing broadcloth, and stipulated that their clothing could be constructed only from negro cloth plains, duffel, coarse kersey, osnaburg, blue linen, checked linen, and, if costing less than ten shillings a yard, coarse garlix, calico, checked cottons, and checked linen.[46] The Native American trade was not bound by such restrictions, and encompassed many of the textiles commonly available in South Carolina and Georgia during the colonial period, including those withheld from slaves and servants (see appendix).

Though Native Americans purchased a variety of woolens, linens, cottons, and silks throughout the eighteenth century, promoters of colonization largely ignored all textiles except for wool. Unlike the other textiles, which were produced outside of Britain, woolen fabrics exported to America were manufactured in Britain and best stimulated its economy.[47] Historians have reinforced the link between Native Americans and wool, focusing almost exclusively on Native American consumption of strouds and duffels.[48] Yet there is a discrepancy between colonists' (and historians') expectations about Southeastern Indian textile consumption and the products they chose to purchase. This suggests that Native Americans, and not colonists, controlled the commodities that entered their communities.

It is true that strouds and other woolens, especially when they were the only available textiles for sale, generally sold out. In 1674, Henry

Woodward, the first English trader to venture deep into Southeastern Indian territory, could offer his customers only two pieces of red duffel and two pieces of blue duffel, which totaled approximately fifty to sixty yards of each color. His supply quickly ran out, and when he submitted an additional order of items in 1675, he included a piece more of each color.[49] Georgia merchants were able to supply their neighbors with only limited supplies of cloth goods in the first years of colonization, but according to settlers, the neighboring Yuchi quickly adopted the available woolens.[50] Similarly, "strouds and other equivalents" were all that the Indian trader John Buckles needed to carry to the Chickasaw Indian territory to receive, in exchange, eighty horse-loads of leather.[51]

But Native Americans did not, if given the choice, purchase only woolen fabric. The experienced trader Theophilus Hastings, who would later become a factor for the Cherokee trade, expected his customers to buy roughly equal amounts of wool and linen when he made his textile purchases in June 1714. His receipt contained only slightly more wool than other fabrics—48.7 percent wool (726 yards) as compared to 44.6 percent linen (665 yards) and 6.6 percent cotton (99 yards).[52] Nearly fifty years later, the Cherokee still demanded ready access to linens. At Fort Prince George, the Directors of the Cherokee Trade stocked at least ten different varieties of linen.[53] The factory ran out of linen regularly, prompting the directors to place advertisements in the *South Carolina Gazette* soliciting proposals from merchants who had linen to sell.[54] They demanded linen in more of their orders than they did duffel or stroud. Like the Cherokee, other Southeastern Indians had a penchant for linen as well. Savannah merchant Thomas Raspberry lost his sole Indian trader client in 1760, one whose customers were primarily Creek Indians. Raspberry wrote to his suppliers in Britain and requested that they cut his linen order in half because he no longer needed items for the Indian trade.[55]

The desire for linen may be linked to seasonal subsistence patterns. After the winter hunt, Southeastern Indians had a large supply of expendable deerskins, which had to be sold quickly to avoid rot and damage from rain or insects. Lightweight linens were more popular during the spring and summer months, corresponding with the time when deerskin hunters had the most disposable income. Whereas the Directors of the Cherokee Trade sought to replenish their supply of woolens in their fall orders, in their spring and summer orders they requested linen.[56]

Hunting and agricultural seasons dictated Southeastern Indian demand for utility items as well. Native Americans consciously chose to invest in instruments that would maximize their future profits. When preparing for their winter hunt, the Cherokee who frequented Fort Prince George demanded such a large quantity of bullets and gunpowder that the Directors of the Cherokee Trade had to request a loan of four hundredweight of gunpowder from the public magazine.[57] But it took a half-century for traders and officials to understand seasonal cycles, and this confusion hindered the early trade. In December 1716, William Waties, who was the factor at Wineau Bay, expressed concern that the Waccamaw were buying little else but ammunition.[58] In reality, the shift in buying habits resulted from the fact that the Waccamaw were preparing for the upcoming winter hunt and were strategically investing their skins in the much-needed tools that would facilitate their success as hunters. Waties was similarly unfamiliar with the Southeastern Indians' agricultural patterns. At the end of December, Waties returned two dozen hoes that he was unable to sell, giving the Indian trade commissioners the impression that they had sent an inappropriate type of tool.[59] In reality, the hoes were one of the last items the Waccamaw wanted to spend their deerskins on in the dead of winter. In response, the commissioners sent a different set of hoes to the factory, this time enlisting the aid of a Native American named Westoe in choosing the correct variety. To keep Waties from becoming equally finicky about the gunpowder they sent for the trade, they assured him that it was to his assistant "Mr. Hughes's liking, as also to Westoes."[60] Instead of storing the hoes until planting season, Waties again sent them back.[61] If Waties had been patient, he would have found, as the Cherokee factor Charlesworth Glover discovered, that the hoes would have flown off the shelf in the spring. In April, the commissioners apologized to Glover for being able to send him only fourteen dozen hoes because of a waylaid boat, and promised to send him more when possible.[62] Southeastern Indians responded to the traders' ineptitude in stocking goods by learning how to rework European manufactures to serve other purposes.[63]

Utilitarian concerns alone did not dictate Southeastern Indian buying habits. The warm, weatherproof qualities of deerskin could not be copied by any variety of woolen or linen fabric. An examination of the textiles Southeastern Indians chose to purchase suggests an intent to supplement rather than replicate deerskin's warmth and durability. Despite their popularity among Native Americans, duffel and stroud were considered by many colonists to be low-quality woolens. South Carolina merchant Robert Raper scolded an exporter for sending him Indian trade blankets instead of the striped blankets made out of the linen plains that he had ordered for his slaves. Raper surmised that the undersized, cheaply constructed Indian trade blankets would be "good for nothing at the end of three years."[64] But Southeastern Indians largely rejected the plains, or negro cloth, that Raper deemed durable and cost-effective, as well as the similar waterproof woolen half thicks.[65] Theophilus Hastings did not purchase a single piece of plains or half-thicks for the Cherokee trade when he placed a substantial order of textiles in June 1714.[66] At Fort Prince George, plains were included on the official price list but did not sell in ample enough quantities to require subsequent orders. Plains fared better with the Creek Indians, who bought enough of the textile to merit mention on their official price lists.[67] Yet at George Galphin's Silver Bluff store in Georgia, individuals who traded with the Creek purchased only eight yards of plains from 1767 to 1772, compared to the 126 duffel blankets and over 400 yards of strouds purchased by these same individuals.[68]

Southeastern Indian consumers were selective when purchasing linen as well, as illustrated by their tepid reaction to osnaburg. A coarse, unbleached hemp or linen cloth, osnaburg was popular among settlers and plantation owners for slave clothing, trousers, sacks, and bags. In April, May, and June 1727, Charles Town merchants Alexander Nisbet and John Blackwood, whose clientele was composed primarily of plantation owners, sold over 300 yards of osnaburg, more than any other textile they offered.[69] Osnaburg, along with the linen garlix, also comprised the majority of listings in Robert Nisbet's cashbook entries in June 1722 and March 1723.[70] Theophilus Hastings purchased 213 yards of osnaburg for the Indian trade in 1714, or 32 percent of the total amount of linen he acquired.[71] But Southeastern Indians did not consistently demand osnaburg. It was not listed on any of the official price lists. At Galphin's Silver Bluff store in Georgia, where osnaburg was the only linen on the shelves, Southeastern Indians and Indian traders steered clear of linen altogether and funneled their skins into woolens. While most of the Southeastern Indians and Indian traders purchased osnaburg at least once, quantities were so low that, from 1767 to 1772, they amounted to only thirty-four yards, representing only 3.6 percent of the total amount of textiles purchased by Native American or Indian traders at Silver Bluff during that period. The Directors of the Cherokee Trade sent osnaburg and garlix to Fort Prince George in one of their first shipments, but they avoided the linen when they made their later selections, possibly on the advice of the factor, Edward Wilkinson. While Southeastern Indians liked many varieties of linen, they found little reason to spend their hard-earned skins on the coarse and uncomfortable osnaburg. The colonists, too, avoided this textile when constructing their own clothing.

Outwitting the expectation of the British, Cherokees frequenting Fort Prince George purchased so much flannel that the fort had to restock its shelves.[72] The fact that colonists did not immediately market flannel to the Southeastern Indians comes as little surprise. Early modern flannel was soft and spongy and much lighter than the cloth that bears that name today (the cloth we call flannel more closely resembles stroud).[73] Unlike woolen broadcloth, which was produced using an extra step that hardened and tightened the woolens, flannel was not weatherproof or considered suitable for outerwear. In Britain, it was most often used in undergarments.[74] The Cherokee fondness for flannel further indicates that their taste in cloth was not entirely based on utilitarian qualities. As will be discussed more fully later, flannel provided the Cherokee with a perfect inside layer for their matchcoats. Similarly, the nonutilitarian qualities of luster, shine, and a striped design attracted Southeastern Indian individuals to calimanco, or poor man's silk.[75] Theophilus Hastings purchased 150 yards to sell during the summer of 1714, or 20.7 percent of the total amount of woolens he acquired for the trade. Likewise, the Directors of the Cherokee Trade chose to include calimanco in their initial shipment to Fort Prince George.[76] Abundantly supplied with the most durable covering of them all, skins, the Southeastern Indians turned to European textiles that offered qualities not inherent in skins: lightness, softness, and unique variety of textures and colors.

Native American consumer preferences strongly affected trade. The Southeastern Indians consumed more linen than the colonists originally expected, and were more than ready to reject linens and woolens that did not strike their fancy. Those working most directly with Native Americans, like Theophilus Hastings, quickly responded to changes in Native American taste. At times, however, colonial administrators lacked direct knowledge about Native American preferences. In Charles Town, colonial officials in charge of stocking public trading forts had to make assumptions about Native American tastes when traders failed to provide them with complete orders. Some relied on past experience when assembling a trade inventory. Others made choices by drawing on their own assumptions about the type of people who would ultimately consume the product. Despite the Southeastern Indians' lack of enthusiasm for plains and half thicks, colonial officials continued to include them in their gifts to the Native Americans and sent large quantities to the trading forts. These actions demonstrate that although the colonists did not consciously try to promote a population that resembled their lower strata of society, they assumed that cheap woolens, the sort worn by their slaves and servants, would be most suitable to the trade.[77] Southeastern Indians, however, were not shy about rejecting this vision of their material culture; they insisted that they have complete control over what their skins and furs would be used for. That Native American consumers, and not colonists, dictated which objects entered their communities, makes these items commodities, not gifts.

A second major difference between gifts and commodities is the extent to which the object remains connected to its giver. As discussed in chapter 3, gifts ideally remain physically unaltered and invoke their originator, whereas commodities may be refigured in any way desired by their owners. In the Southeast, Native Americans worked studiously to domesticate the commodities they purchased and to integrate them into their society. By the time Southeastern Indians were finished refashioning the textiles and clothing they purchased, these items were so far removed from their culture of origin as to make them almost unrecognizable to Europeans. The normally eloquent William Bartram, who journeyed through the Southeast in the 1770s, stumbled over his description of Native American dress, underscoring how foreign it appeared to him: "Sometimes a ruffled shirt of fine linen, next the skin, and a flap, which covers their lower parts, this garment somewhat resembles the ancient Roman breeches, or the kelt of the Highlanders; it usually consists of a piece of blue cloth, about eighteen inches wide, this they pass between their thighs, and both ends being taken up and drawn through a belt round their waist, the end falls down, once before, and the other behind, not quite to the knee; this flap is usually plaited and indented at the ends, and ornamented with beads, tinsel lace & c."[78] James Adair, who also wrestled with describing Southeastern Indian dress, resorted to images that would be familiar to British readers, thus likening Native American clothing to a Roman toga.[79] But try as they might to compare Southeastern Indian dress with ancient European fashion, both Adair and Bartram could not find the exact equivalent.

Merchants, too, acknowledged the distinctive nature of the Indian trade. Savannah trader Thomas Raspberry looked to his suppliers for

guidance about which items were suitable, pleading that "as the forego-
ing are calculated for the Indian Trade I must beg you to acquaint yourself of the right sorts of those articles that are now expected for the
purpose, particularly in respect to the Beads."[80] Raspberry then asked his
wool suppliers from Bristol to make sure the strouds he ordered were
"wormed in the same manner as those that are now usually sent out here
for the Indian Trade."[81] Charles Town merchant Robert Pringle, who
devoted only a small amount of his business to the Indian trade, was
equally cautious when choosing textiles. Though he permitted his supplier to purchase most of the items on his Indian trade list, such as duffel
blankets, from London, he insisted that the strouds come from Bristol,
preferably from the "Same person that Samuel Everleigh has his, which
are Esteem'd the best & are most Saleable."[82] Discerning merchants knew
that Native Americans were not adopting European fashions, but were
using specific textiles in unique ways.

It was not for lack of example that the Southeastern Indians chose to
use trade items in vastly different ways than their European neighbors.
They had ample opportunity to witness the settlers utilizing these items
during treaty meetings, or when they visited colonial towns to transport
goods, as well as to receive instructions from the traders in their towns.
Yet, despite the fact that Southeastern Indians had occasion to experiment with various forms of clothing, they declined to wear many of the
European fashions. An English trader who spent much of his life among
the Creek Indians informed the inquisitive Salzburgers that, like the Yuchi, the Creek "will not accept European dress."[83]

Except for shirts and the occasional coat or pair of gloves, Southeastern Indians chose to purchase yards of textiles and to fashion their own
clothing. They used much of the European fabric they acquired to construct matchcoats, which were approximately two yards long.[84] A series
of drawings by the German traveler Philip Georg Friedrich von Reck depicts the Yuchi Indians he visited at Mount Pleasant in 1733 and 1734.
The Yuchi had settled at this site around 1728 at the encouragement of
South Carolina officials. Mount Pleasant had the benefit of being lo-
cated along a trade path, giving the Yuchi access to English goods, including textiles.[85] In von Reck's drawing, some of the Yuchis wore
matchcoats made of animal skin, while others sported coats assembled
from European cloth.

Instead of embracing novelty items stamped with a prescribed European function, Southeastern Indians quickly reclaimed and refashioned

FIGURE 4 Von Reck, Indian King and Queen Uchi, Senkaitschi, 1736.
Royal Library, Copenhagen, Denmark

European textiles. In von Reck's rendering, the Yuchi king wears a match-coat made from a buffalo skin, while the queen's matchcoat is a converted woolen blanket purchased from Charles Town (figure 4).[86]

A second drawing by von Reck (figure 5) reinforces this interchangeability but also underlines a difference. While the leather matchcoat to the left is painted with objects and stripes of different colors throughout, the woolen matchcoat on the right is plain white with a simple red border around the edges. As von Reck points out, in the British colonies this blanket would be used to cover a horse, not a human. The British blanket has not been altered in form, though it is being put to an indigenous use. Archaeologists at the Mount Pleasant, Georgia, site inhabited by the Yuchi observed by von Reck did not unearth beads or other forms of textile adornment, suggesting that von Reck's rendering was accurate.[87]

The unaltered blanket signals a significant change that occurred in Southeastern Indian consumption practices during the eighteenth century. As the Southeastern Indian women—and the cloth workers were primarily women[88]—became more comfortable with needles, thread, and different sorts of textiles and ribbons, they began reworking and

FIGURE 5 Von Reck, Indians going a-hunting, 1736. Royal Library,
Copenhagen, Denmark

decorating European textiles. They took the same care as they did with
the leather blankets in von Reck's illustrations. Emphasis on this process of refashioning points out the new skills developed by Native
Americans as a result of the European trade. In this light, the view that
trade led to atrophy of Native American creative abilities appears in-
valid.[89] At Fort Prince George, Cherokee customers repeatedly exhausted
the store's supply of haberdashery used to adorn textiles. All but one of
the directors' advertisements requesting items for the Cherokee trade included ribbons, thread, and/or needles.[90]

Fort Prince George opened for the Indian trade in 1762. That same
year, a delegation of Cherokee Indians led by Ostenaco of Tomotley, visited London. They were accompanied by Henry Timberlake, who had
lived at Tomotley for three months in 1761–62. The delegation's purpose
was to strengthen the fragile truce forged with Britain after the devas-
tating Cherokee War.[91] As Timberlake recounted, his first concern after

FIGURE 6 Francis Parsons, *Cunne Shote*, 1762. Gilcrease Museum, Tulsa, Oklahoma

arriving in London was to equip the Cherokee with new clothes "after the mode of their own country."[92] Timberlake was intent on replicating standard Cherokee fashion, later ridiculing a purchase made for the Cherokee by the royal messenger, Nathan Carrington, assigned by Lord Egremont (Charles Wyndham) to fulfill the Cherokees' requests.[93] Timberlake, scornful of several items of clothing listed on a receipt, insisted that Carrington "must absolutely be obliged to wear them himself, since the Indians will not." He explained, "Ah! dear Sir, you were short sighted here; two yards and three-quarters make a match-coat and leggons, five yards will not make two." He derided Carrington's choice of the quality of wool and the color, as well as the "Vellum lace broad and narrow: Was it for button holes for a Cherokee mantle? Sure Ostenaco never once had the ridiculous fancy of putting useless, and solely ornamental, buttons upon a matchcoat."[94] Timberlake refused this clothing and took great care in providing the Cherokee visitors with garb they would find familiar. Thanks to Timberlake, we can be confident that the clothing worn by the visitors as they sat for their portraits in London accurately depicts mid-eighteenth-century Cherokee fashion.[95]

The two portraits of the Cherokee visitors, one painted by Francis Parsons (figure 6) and the other by Joshua Reynolds (figure 7), show

FIGURE 7 Joshua Reynolds, *Scyacust Ukah*, 1762. Gilcrease Museum, Tulsa, Oklahoma

Cherokee leaders Cunneshote and Osteneco (Seyucust Ukah) wearing ruffled shirts cuffed by silver arm bands, necklaces, and richly textured matchcoats.[96] Unlike the plain woolen blankets the Yuchi wore in von Reck's drawings, the Cherokee delegation sported intricately decorated matchcoats. These matchcoats were double-layered, revealing how the Cherokee used the flannel they purchased at Fort Prince George. The soft and delicate flannel would have been ideal for the inside of the matchcoats, while sturdy stroud or duffel provided a weatherproof exterior. The two layers of wool were held together by a wide piece of caddis or ribbon, which bordered the entire matchcoat. Cunneshote's matchcoat also included a gold braid near his left shoulder. Unlike anything featured in English fashion, this braid was a transplant from furniture or window draperies. In addition to the coat's trim, Osteneco incorporated golden ribbon into the inside of his coat, transforming the solid-colored interior, possibly flannel, into a beautiful striped lining. Around his neck he wore a sash, probably constructed from a strip of wool and embellished with beads worked into line and diamond patterns. Both men used gartering or ribbon to anchor the large silver gorgets and other metal ornaments worn around their necks. In addition, they used cinched ribbon around their wrists to keep their sleeves in place.

Osteneco's sash, which features a repeated diamond pattern, suggests that Southeastern Indians incorporated sacred motifs into their bodily adornment. In Southeastern Indian iconography, the diamond, usually drawn with crystal quartz, represented the rattlesnake, or the mythical figure Uktena, whose forehead was emblazoned with a diamond. Rattlesnakes inhabited the Under World, a place of both danger and fertility, and were known for their resentment of humans. A human who could harness the power of the snake could keep illness and witchcraft at bay; these chosen few possessed prophetic power.[97] In seeking to channel Ukena in this foreign land, Osteneco was projecting an image of ferocity and shielding himself from the diseases and bad fortune that had befallen other Native Americans who had journeyed across the Atlantic.

The paintings leave no doubt as to the Cherokees' penchant for ribbon, lace, and decorative tape. The fact that the Directors of Cherokee Trade had to constantly restock their haberdashery supply implies that individuals from all strata of society, and not only the Cherokee leaders, transformed European fabrics and shirts into Southeastern Indian products. Not every matchcoat could sustain the number of golden stripes sewn onto Osteneco's coat. Yet the amount of haberdashery purchased from Fort Prince George indicates that much of the cloth and clothing that Cherokee individuals purchased from the Europeans underwent extensive refashioning before adorning the shoulders of their owners.

Southeastern Indians' desire for specific European manufactures changed over time, depending, in part, on how Native American communities evaluated the social associations of particular objects. The histories of blue cloth and beads reveal some changes in taste. Henry Woodward had no problem selling the blue cloth he purchased in 1674. But during the eighteenth century, some evidence indicates that Southeastern Indian purchases of blue textiles declined at specific moments in time. Public trading factors repeatedly had to send yards of blue material back to Charles Town unsold.[98] Individual traders caught on quickly. Theophilus Hastings, for one, did not specify a desire for blue cloth in his 1714 order, though he did request other colors and patterns.[99] At Galphin's Silver Bluff store only one customer, John Mathins, purchased wool specified as blue in December 1767. It is unclear whether he intended to sell this wool to a Native American client. All other purchases related to the Indian trade omitted blue woolens.[100]

At the same time that Native American purchases of blue textiles appear to have declined, colonial officials increasingly compensated their

Native American employees with blue woolens, suggesting that the two trends are related. Native Americans who provided services for the public trade worked primarily as "burdeners" who carried skins and goods between the colonies and Indian country. They received compensation in the form of clothing, creating a livery system.[101] The commissioners and directors of the Indian trade chose the type of goods used for wages, making the payment akin to a gift; many times their choices ran contrary to the desires of their workers and the advice of the trade factors. One of the first instances of compensating burdeners working for the public trade with textiles occurred in June 1716. Theophilus Hastings, by then the factor for the Cherokee trade, instructed the commissioners to give each man who carried the accompanying 473 beaver skins "a quarter of a yard of strouds; and those you load back you must give each a pair of half thicks or cotton stockings."[102] Supplier Elias Foissin, who filled the order, chose blue strouds for the burdeners.[103] Instead of half thicks or cotton stockings, the commissioners gave the returning burdeners each a duffel matchcoat.[104] Oftentimes, the factors' requests were imprecise, leaving the commissioners to determine the specific variety of payment. When Hastings requested that the commissioners compensate the two Indians who accompanied him to town with a coat or blanket, the commissioners chose white duffel matchcoats.[105] Increasingly, the commissioners chose to pay burdeners and oarsmen with blue duffel.[106]

Southeastern Indians had their own ideas of what their efforts were worth, and they did not always include staples like food and clothing. Reverend Johann Martin Boltzius of Georgia recorded that a man, probably a neighboring Yuchi, found and returned one of the Salzburgers' stray horses. In return, he expected rum. Boltzius reported, "When we gave him some food and some money for his troubles, he was displeased and said he had been cheated because he had troubled himself with the horse in the belief that he would get rum." The Yuchi man also told the Salzburgers that he knew the location of some of their cows and oxen, but this time he would not agree to deliver them until he was assured of adequate compensation. Boltzius noted that in order to "persuade him to show this place to our people and to help bring the animals back, I had to promise him money in advance. He likes twelve individual half pence better than a silver shilling, particularly when the former were newly coined and shiny."[107] The Yuchi man's preference for several shiny coins instead of one dull coin indicates that he did not plan on using the coins as currency. Most likely, they represented prestige items that, when displayed, marked his prowess in obtaining goods from the Europeans.[108] There is evidence that the Cherokee also valued coins as items of conspicuous consumption rather than as money. Archaeologists have found British coins at Cherokee village sites that were probably used for ornamentation.[109]

Like the coins, it is possible that blue wool, used by the commissioners and directors to pay Indian employees, marked Southeastern Indian individuals as laborers for the British. As an item develops a history and an association with a particular task or relationship, its value registers the significance of that task instead of its utility.[110] If working for the British was an esteemed role, it would have been inappropriate for those who had not earned the right to wear blue to don the treasured cloth. If it was a detested role, who would want to be associated with it by wearing blue duffel? In 1734, Boltzius observed of the Yuchi, "they account labouring and working for hire to be a slavery." If Boltzius's observations about the Yuchi apply to other Southeastern Indians, and they made no moral distinction between paid labor for the colonists and slavery, they would steer clear of blue woolens as symbols of lowly status.

The history of blue cloth reveals that some commodities waxed and waned in value according to the relationships they invoked. The history of beads raises the possibility that some items moved through commodity markets, whereas others were prized as gifts. According to letters written to the South Carolina Proprietors in 1670 and 1672, settlers did not trade yards of cloth for provisions or deerskins around St. Helena and Port Royal. Instead, Native Americans desired beads, and sometimes brass rings, tobacco, and old clothes. In these preferences, Southeastern Indians acted similarly to other groups across the globe that initially incorporated foreign items into their communities as prestige, rather than utilitarian, objects.[111] When Henry Woodward stocked his trading good supplies in 1674 for neighboring groups, such as the Kiawah, he chose a large quantity of adornment and ceremonial items: 252 pounds of beads, 1,296 bells, 144 Jew's harps, seventy-two looking glasses, seventy-two tin shoes, and seventy-two kettles (which indigenous groups usually used for scrap metal to create jewelry and beads). Textiles were poorly represented in his inventory, in both variety and quantity. Woodward carried some utilitarian items: two barrels of musket shot, four barrels of gunpowder, nineteen fowling pieces, 360 knives, and 348 hatchets. He had to adjust his offerings after he opened up trade with the highly militarized Westo in late 1674, for they most desired guns and ammunition. When

Woodward restocked his inventory in 1675 he included more gunpowder, musket shot, hatchets, and knives. He also added new items to his wares: wire, steels, and pistols.[112] Woodward did not need to order any more beads or bells. He had learned that they were not as sought-after by the Westo as he had anticipated.

Southeastern Indians continued to purchase beads, jewelry, and ornaments during the colonial period, but not in the amounts that Woodward expected. Textiles and silver quietly surpassed beads in Native American preferences. Theophilus Hastings bought a large quantity of silver buttons, 1,152 to be exact, in June 1714, along with 1,490 yards of textiles.[113] The buttons, like beads, were probably used to create jewelry.[114] By 1762, nothing could compete with textiles and haberdashery in the Cherokee commodities trade. The directors only once advertised a request for beads during their operation of the factory at Fort Prince George. When the factory shut down they had an ample supply of beads remaining.[115] At Galphin's Silver Bluff store, none of the Southeastern Indians who patronized the shop purchased the available beads, framed looking glasses, ear bobs, or combs. Indian traders who frequented the store appeared oblivious to these trends. They invested in twenty bushels (approximately 140 strands) of beads, thirty-six framed looking glasses, and forty-eight pairs of silver ear bobs.[116] Like the Cherokee, the Creek Indian patrons of Galphin's Silver Bluff store only occasionally bought items of adornment and ceremony in the second half of the eighteenth century. When they did so, they purchased very small quantities. In comparison, their acquisitions of textiles from Silver Bluff numbered nearly 1,000 yards.

Why did beads fail to live up to the potential envisioned by Henry Woodward? One reason may be that the English had difficulty supplying the Southeastern Indians with the beads they desired. The beads offered by the English in the late seventeenth century and the eighteenth century were of relatively poor quality. They were vastly inferior to the multilayered artisanal Venetian beads offered by the Spanish in the mid-sixteenth to early seventeenth centuries, and the Native Americans knew it.[117] Southeastern Indians were more dissatisfied with beads than with any other British trade items. Savannah merchant Thomas Raspberry, who was attempting to construct an inventory for the Creek Indian trade, was particularly anxious about ensuring that his British suppliers chose the appropriate beads for the Southeastern Indian trade.[118] Although the British invested a great deal of energy in trying to provide

Southeastern Indians with suitable beads, their efforts often fell short. In 1717, Catawba factor Eleazer Wiggan sent the commissioners a sample of beads that the Catawba fancied. The commissioners worked studiously to replicate them for some time before they dropped the matter completely.[119] The Cherokee Indians were as finicky about their beads as their Catawba and Creek neighbors. According to Edward Wilkinson, the Cherokee who traded at Fort Prince George were generally satisfied with the terms of trade "except in the price of the article of wampum." The directors informed Wilkinson that the wampum they sent up was purple and "double the value of the white," but the Cherokee disagreed.[120] They provided Wilkinson with a sample of the small white beads they preferred, probably prompting the single advertisement in the *South Carolina Gazette* for beads, but there is no indication that the correct items were obtained.[121] Had the directors more quickly supplied the desired beads, perhaps the bead category would have comprised a more substantial proportion of the sales.

It is also possible that Southeastern Indians categorized beads, buckles, ear bobs, looking glasses, and paint, which colonial officials regularly gave as gifts, as symbols of diplomatic relationships with the Europeans. Therefore, such items could retain their value only if acquired as gifts. When viewed as commodities, these articles may have lost their ability to represent important relationships. Von Reck posited that Southeastern Indians kept certain goods out of the realm of commodity exchange. He noted that in return for decorative items the Yuchi Indians presented "game which they themselves shoot," whereas they traded hides and furs for rice, rum, and woolen cloth.[122] This observation suggests that Native Americans instituted a circulation system for commodities that was separate from gifts. Deerskins moved against cloth and metal commodities, whereas meat and hospitality items moved against sentimental goods such as beads. According to this theory, the numerous beads that have been discovered at archaeological sites made their way into Southeastern Indian communities as gifts.[123]

An alternate theory suggests that individuals stopped purchasing beads because their ability to confer economic status and indicate hunting prowess diminished. That beads were inexpensive may have contributed to this decline. In the early years of contact, beads were expensive and could be acquired only in exchange for a significant amount of labor. During this time, beads were esteemed as powerful symbols denoting one's success as a hunter and trader. In 1716, in order to purchase a mere two strands of beads, a hunter had to kill and dress one deer. By the middle of the eighteenth century, beads plummeted in value, allowing a hunter to obtain five strings for a single skin.[124] Inexpensive items accessible to anyone who was able to shoot a single deer no longer had the cachet to signify success. Thus it is not surprising that archaeologists have found that in mortuary assemblages, silver, not beads, became the predominant prestige item after 1750.[125] In the diplomatic realm, however, beads could retain their symbolism when accepted as gifts. The history of beads and blue cloth suggests that, in the Southeast, multiple modes of exchange coexisted. As different goods took on different meanings, they moved into different circuits of exchange.

Relationships between buyers and sellers changed along with other registers of value. At Fort Prince George, South Carolina, colonial officials began to take on a different view of their Southeastern Indian customers. Whereas previous directors of the trade bent over backward to supply the Southeastern Indians with their hearts' desires, the new Directors of the Cherokee Trade were critical of the Cherokees' choices. "The fineness and costliness of the goods [demanded by the Cherokee] seem to us inconsistent with the indigent circumstances of the Indians," they wrote to Wilkinson, the factor, in November 1762. They urged him "not to send for superfluities, that the Indians can't, or are unable to buy, or pay for."[126] What accounts for this change in attitude, from catering to the tastes of their Native American clientele to criticizing their purchasing decisions? One explanation is that the Cherokees, who had sustained significant population losses during the Cherokee War of 1759–61, were no longer respected as a formidable foe.[127] Thus, an air of paternalism crept into official discussions concerning them. Furthermore, unlike previous traders who garnered a sizable profit from the Indian trade, the Fort Prince George directors priced many of their items at cost. They had acted on the belief that, after the end of the Cherokee War, supplying the Cherokee with cheap goods would secure their loyalty. The directors informed the factor, "We have reduced the prices as low as possible.... Neither do we expect any profit by carrying on the trade, upon the easy terms we have reduced it to, for the benefit of our Cherokee friends, who we hope will not desire that we should become losers thereby."[128] There were some items, particularly strouds, which they priced "a great deal cheaper, to comply with the usual custom."[129] Because the directors were losing money in the trade, they categorized these items as gifts rather than commodities.[130] Unlike commodities, in these gift-like exchanges, the giver and not the receiver controlled the nature and use of gifts. As gift givers, the directors were at liberty to comment on the Cherokee consumption patterns in ways they never had before. Complaining that the Cherokee were purchasing beyond their means or station was a new kind of refrain, one that broke with earlier traditions of giving the Native Americans full consumer choice.

For the Southeastern Indians, steeped in a tradition of commodity exchange, there was little chance that they would give up the role of consumers and allow their material culture to be dominated by European gift givers. They continued to demand "superfluities," purchasing stroud, flannel, and linens instead of plains, and investing their deerskins in nonutilitarian haberdashery. That the directors ultimately bowed to Cherokee pressure by supplying them with the goods they desired is evidenced in the inventory of items that was left unsold after the fort was shut in 1764: "strouds, striped duffields, headed shags, calimancoes, flannels, guns, checks and other linens, handkerchiefs, hoes, hatchets, vermillion, wampum, cutlery, silver trinkets, and a variety of other articles suitable for the said trade."[131] Many of these items were believed by the directors to be too expensive for the Cherokee. Clearly, however, their opinions did not dictate their choice of which goods to stock.

Furthermore, to compensate for their decreased power to demand lower prices, the Cherokee began inflating the value of their currency, deerskins. Unlike previous price tables that calculated goods against the number of deerskins, the Fort Prince George table calculated price based on the weight of the deerskins offered. This form of measurement persuaded the Cherokee Indians to trade deerskins that were "encumbered with hoofs and snouts," possibly because this added to the skins' weight and allowed them to purchase more goods.[132] The directors bemoaned the number of hooved and snouted deerskins sent from the fort, a trend that correlated with the Cherokee complaints about overpriced items.[133] While the British colonists moved toward a system of exchange that conflated gifts and commodities, the Southeastern Indians acted like hard-nosed negotiators.

THE CREATIVE EFFORT that the Southeastern Indians invested in the textiles they purchased, and the extent to which the clothing came to bear such little resemblance to European fashions, affirms a theory of textile commodification. British craftsmen dissociated southeastern leather from the Native Americans who hunted and dressed the skins long before English consumers encountered them. So, too, did Southeastern Indians cut, sew, shape, and ultimately transform European textiles and clothing, just as they reshaped glass, metal, and other European technologies.[134] In doing so, the Southeastern Indians ensured that by the time they wore these textiles, they no longer invoked European weavers, dyers, or transporters.

The British interpreted the Indians' rejection of European fashion in a myriad of ways. Some, like the early South Carolina Indian commissioners, paid little heed to the ideological implications of Native American taste. Others were incensed. When a group of Indians plundered Theodore Gaillard's mill house, nearby settler John Grendon remarked with surprise that they "left some china cups and saucers." He interpreted their leaving behind the valuable goods as a willful sign of disrespect.[135] This reaction makes sense. As argued in chapter 2, wearing the same clothes, eating the same food, and living on the same land were some of the means by which the English and the Southeastern Indians established affinity and solidarity. Cloth, British officials decreed, would unify all of the king's subjects, British and Native American alike.[136] But for the most part, textiles utterly failed to transform Native Americans into British subjects. Instead of forging an external likeness, textiles became instruments by which the British and Southeastern Indians maintained their identities as separate peoples.

If wearing the same clothes was a mark of friendship, misappropriating items was a mark of warfare. Goods seized from enemies were ceremoniously displayed in public spaces and on warriors' bodies, becoming some of the most prized possessions in Southeastern Indian society. The allegory was so potent that, before peace could be reaffirmed, these war trophies had to be destroyed.[137] A man who wore a piece of stroud as a matchcoat was hardly declaring war on the English, but he was declaring his independence from a people who so clearly connected production with ownership. By transforming the fabric, the Southeastern Indians had wrested control of the product from the producer.

Conclusion

The Life of a Deerskin

Spring 1759, Savannah, Georgia

Indian trader Ulrick Tobler of South Carolina had a casual yet long-standing business relationship with Thomas Raspberry of Savannah, Georgia. They exchanged a few things here and there: a German almanac, some tallow, a few yards of woolens.[1] Their business dealings intensified in 1758 when Raspberry asked Tobler if he would be able to procure cattle hides for a friend of his, a tanner in Bristol.[2] Tobler told him that cattle hides were hard to come by, but he could more than adequately supply him with deerskins. His friend, the tanner, Tobler promised, would be pleased with the quality and would scarcely know the difference. In return, Tobler asked if any of the tanner's Bristol partners could furnish him with Bristol strouds.[3] Having just landed the large Indian trading account of the firm Harris and Habersham, Raspberry was confident that he could supply Ulrick and his own son, John Tobler, with all their Indian trading needs.[4] Raspberry expanded beyond Bristol and split his business between Josiah Smith of Charles Town, Devonshire Reeve & Lloyd of Bristol, and William Thomson of London, ordering duffel, strouds, caddis, calico, and damask.[5] Raspberry began collecting skins and indigo to export to William Thomson four months in advance. In April 1759, Raspberry sent Thomson a shipment of 330 skins weighing 474 pounds, asking that the skins be carried on his credit when they arrived.[6] Raspberry also delivered skins to exporter Martin Campbell of South Carolina.[7] Ulrick informed Raspberry that his Creek Indian clients were satisfied with the Bristol stroud and that he would consider ordering a larger variety for a future shipment.[8]

Summer 1759, London

William Thomson in London received the 330 Creek deerskins, and just in time. No sooner had the *Henrietta Rains* docked and Captain Tubbs unloaded the skins than Thomson's creditors came knocking.[9] Among them was leather dealer John Mitchell, who fairly swooned over the half-dressed deerskins, claiming that the Creek skins were of much better quality than the Cherokee skins Thomson had pawned off on him last summer.[10] He and his three scrawny apprentices hauled off as many skins as they could carry and promised to be back for the rest the following day.

Back at his warehouse, Mitchell took inventory of the skins and contacted William Oldfield, his largest customer specializing in light leather crafts, to see if he had the time and space to manufacture a majority of the skins. Oldfield jumped at the chance and sent a couple of employees to select one hundred skins. He was thrilled to see that all the hair had been removed from the skins, saving him considerable time, and immediately began soaking twenty of them in train oil. Every hour or so he and his employees would remove the skins, beat them, and soak them again, until finally, by the end of the night, they removed the skins and let them dry in the open air. He put twenty more skins in oil to soak overnight.

Five days later, Oldfield determined that the leather was ready to be manufactured into goods. Not having enough employees to produce all of it, and in need of some money, Oldfield decided to keep forty of the skins for himself. He sold twenty of these to another leather craftsman nearby. Since Oldfield lacked the nerve to sell the last twenty skins back to Mitchell for a profit, he sold them to a different leather dealer. He set to tracing patterns on the leather he retained, cutting along the lines, stretching the leather, hardening some pieces, softening others, and finally sewing all the appropriate pieces together. After a few weeks, he had fashioned the stack of Creek skins into leather breeches, gloves, and hats. While his customers were fond of the products, scarcely anyone inquired into the origin of the skins. With the French and Indian War raging in America, Mitchell preferred to keep the provenance of the leather to himself.

Summer 1759, South Carolina

Ulrich Tobler died, leaving his son, John, in charge of the trading operation. Perhaps signals got crossed, or Raspberry did not trust John. Despite John's letters pleading with Raspberry to continue supplying him with strouds, and to even throw in some linens, Raspberry canceled all orders placed on the Toblers' account without informing John of his decision.[11] Because of the precarious position of the Creek Indians during the French and Indian War, it would be best not to stock up for a trade that could be cut short at any moment.[12]

December 10, 1760, Creek Hunting Land

It was getting late, and Tobler's Friend had had little luck on his hunt.[13] His gun was on its last legs. The British officials, uneasy that the Creek were on the brink of aligning with their Cherokee enemies, ordered their traders to withhold any guns or ammunition from the trade and called back the gunsmith that they had provided gratis.[14] Tobler's Friend gnawed on the side of a bullet, hoping it would counteract the faulty swerve of the gun, but it did little to help his shot.[15] He was just about to return to his hunting camp when he heard a branch crack in the distance. To his great luck, it was a large buck standing in range. Tobler's Friend took a breath and clutched his hunting pouch. Surely, now that the buck was in range, the horn from the Horned Serpent would draw the buck even closer. Not willing to waste the opportunity by using his gun, Tobler's Friend quietly reached for an arrow.[16] His first one missed, but with the help of three more the buck was brought down.

Tobler's Friend had not ventured far from the camp and was able to make it back, deer in tow, shortly after nightfall. His wife was stirring hominy over the fire, which was doing double duty in smoking six of the skins he had been able to procure since they set up camp.[17] His wife seemed pleased, but tired. She had spent the day soaking two skins that were sufficiently dried, and dehairing and pounding five skins from a couple of weeks ago.[18] After a quick bite they gutted and skinned the newest deer. Then they retired to sleep.

At daybreak, Robert Goudy came snooping around to see if Tobler's Friend had any raw skins he wanted to sell in exchange for some rum or bullets.[19] Tobler's Friend scanned the distance to make sure he was not being watched by anyone who could report to his leader or a colonial agent that he had conducted business with an unlicensed trader. Normally, he would refuse the trade, for he could get more in exchange for dressed skins from his main licensed trader, Ulrick Tobler. On the other hand, due to the ban on weapons he knew it was unlikely Tobler would have bullets.[20] Further, his wife had more than enough to keep her busy with dressing the remaining skins, and it might be beneficial to unload some of the raw skins.[21] He tested the water, seeing how much he could get for the newly scraped skin and three of the minimally dried skins. After a few minutes of haggling they settled on 150 bullets and three swigs of rum. Both parties left happy, Tobler's Friend because he had re-stocked his bullet supply, and Goudy because he now had accumulated enough skins to justify a trip to Galphin's Silver Bluff store. He had not visited Silver Bluff in several months and, as an unlicensed trader, could get away with unloading thirty skins without raising eyebrows.[22]

January 10, 1760

Tobler's Friend and his wife packed up their hunting camp and loaded their two horses with thirty dressed skins. It was dangerous to stay in the woods with too many deerskins, particularly in times of unrest when foreign Indians were prowling about Creek hunting grounds. Besides, thirty skins was an ample bounty and would be more than enough to pro-cure the European items they wanted. Tobler's Friend was nervous about the trip back to town. It was only a five-day journey, but a few people had stopped by his camp over the past week to warn him that a Creek Indian had been attacked by a group of interloping Native Americans who were streaming in from the north. The victim had survived, but the thieves made off with most of his goods and skins. Tobler's Friend was relieved to see a couple of families from his town on the trail in the distance. Together, they were sure to make it back safely.

Along the way they were stopped by a man who claimed he was a Georgia official looking for a group of Young Angry Men who had invaded the home of a white settler family two nights prior. They murdered the husband, but the wife survived. They would be carry-ing blanketing, bridles, and a pair of boots. Tobler's Friend had seen a group with those items pass his camp the previous night, but he kept quiet. He knew that the house that had been attacked was settled over the treaty line.

January 25, 1760

Tobler's Friend waited patiently for Ulrick Tobler to come to town to trade. Tobler's Friend was one of the first in his town to befriend Ulrick twenty years ago and had carried the name since. When Ulrick's son John arrived, and told him the news about his father's death,

Tobler's Friend was stricken. He retreated into his house and emerged with a string of purple beads. He recalled how years ago, before John was born, Ulrick ventured into town with one horse, bearing a few items for sale. No one in town wanted any of Ulrick's substandard wares: green plains, narrow and rickety hoes, brass kettles that were far too small. After five days, Tobler's Friend took pity on him and gave him a skin for a strand of oddly shaped, ugly beads, the same strand he was now holding. Tobler's Friend joked that what was once a nuisance item that he could not unload on any of his friends would now forever remind him of his long friendship with Ulrick.

John replied that his father had always spoken highly of him and the generosity he bestowed. Then John promised Tobler's Friend that he would continue to offer his town quality European textiles, haberdashery, and metal goods. Noticing that Tobler's Friend was suspiciously eyeing his three horses (a small caravan by any count), John hastened to assure him that, although one of his suppliers in Savannah had defaulted, he would soon return with more than enough goods. Tobler's Friend looked disappointed as he examined the duffel and stroud. The linens were plains, and therefore of little interest. John offered to make it up to Tobler's Friend, who had been such a loyal customer, by throwing in two yards of duffel blanketing. Before, Tobler's Friend would have spent all of his skins on Ulrick's merchandise; now he could find only fifteen skins' worth of goods that he wanted. He spent ten skins on four yards of strouds (enough for two matchcoats), two skins on a white shirt, one skin on twelve yards of red caddis, one skin on a knife, and the remaining skin on needles and thread. Luckily, all of the skins were in Tobler's Friend's house and not in plain view, so John would not notice the slight.

Tobler's Friend was unsure what to do next. The other two traders who regularly frequented the town had already come and gone while he was waiting for Ulrick. He could ride a day out of town and hope to find an unlicensed trader with goods that he wanted, or he could take the five-day trip to the nearest trading fort. Or he could wait for a few weeks until the traders returned. All his skins were dressed and would not decay. Hardly in desperate need of any of the goods, and unwilling to attempt a perilous crossing through Indian country, Tobler's Friend decided to wait until the traders returned.

WHEN TRACING THE LIVES of objects as they wove their way across the Atlantic and into and out of Southeastern Indian country, one major point rises to the surface: the movement of these goods, in these quantities, over these vast distances required that the numerous individuals who transacted these items had to be able to draw on a range of exchange models. Goods had to pass between the hands of strangers; goods had to pass between the hands of friends. Thomas Raspberry's relationship with William Thomason, for example, was long-lasting and required a great deal of trust; Raspberry had to trust that Thomason would honor the credit owed on the deerskins he shipped, and he had to trust that Thomason would choose and send goods suitable for the Indian trade. Raspberry's relationship with John Ulrich, on the other hand, was more ephemeral; he was willing to end this relationship at a moment's notice. Likewise, the Creek Indian, Tobler's Friend, participated in commodity exchanges with unlicensed traders whom he might never see again. Ulrich Tobler and Tobler's Friend, on the other hand, developed a durable exchange relationship akin to Raspberry and Thomason's, one that was able to pass gifts as well as commodities. My study has shown that gifting hands were not always Indian hands, and trading hands were not always European hands.

Viewing transactions in this way revises the current historiographical consensus, which holds that Native Americans understood only gift exchange and that Europeans operated according to the tenets of commodity exchange.[23] This book has demonstrated otherwise, showing that British settlers and Southeastern Indians approached one another with a repertoire of social and asocial exchanges. Native Americans did have a robust culture of gift exchange, but they also traded with strangers and were market-minded; the British gave and received gifts to develop and shape social relationships, even as they bought and sold commodities. Because each group was fluent in a variety of exchange models, it was quite easy for them to draw on the tools needed to trade goods across cultures. This variety, and their ability to find enough common ground in their commercial cultures, allowed Southeastern Indians and British settlers to transact the thousands upon thousands of deals that moved such vast quantities of goods back and forth across the Atlantic Ocean.

But this book was not just dedicated to resurrecting their similarities. Although they shared many beliefs, the British and the Southeastern Indians (or, as I suggest, an elite subset of those societies) chose to value certain actions over others. In conducting a sustained comparative analysis of British and Southeastern Indian cultures of production, exchange, and consumption, this book was able to identify those differences. In the realm of production, both the British and the Southeastern Indians had long traditions of expecting individuals to invest their labor in the health of a community instead of toward their personal aggrandizement. But in both societies in the eighteenth century, some individuals and families began laboring in smaller units that were more isolated from the community center, such as Tobler's Friend and his wife, who set up their own deer-dressing station, and the early Georgia settlers who harvested their crops as nuclear family units. The cultural reactions to this similar phenomenon differentiated Southeastern Indians and British colonists. The colonial literature lauded individual labor and furthermore argued that a white man who invested his labor (be it intellectual, managerial, or physical) in an item retained control over that item until he forfeited that authority. During the eighteenth century, Southeastern Indians, by contrast, recounted myths and practiced rituals that divested products of individual human labor. They emphasized communal labor, ancestral knowledge, and religious leaders' power over the social structure, just as Tobler's Friend did when he clutched his hunting pouch before he fired a shot. These myths and rituals do not exhaust the range of beliefs that were present in the Southeast; they represent the belief system that was publicly cultivated by the Southeastern Indian political and spiritual leaders. Their choice in perpetuating these beliefs over others, I have argued, allowed Southeastern Indians to restore social harmony in an Atlantic economy that had fragmented them into smaller economic units and driven their households further from the town square.

Because British colonists and Southeastern Indians rarely employed each other, these differing ideologies of labor went largely unrecorded in the colonial records available to scholars. They did shine through, however, when individuals presented their manufactures to each other and explained how they were created and how they expected them to be used. During commodity exchanges, neither party particularly cared whether his or her customers acknowledged these labor investments unless doing so might elevate an item's price. But gifts were another matter. Gifts, by their very definition, made demands of their recipients that were political, social, and emotional, and these demands were often predicated on how each group valued the labor invested in these gifts. When colonial officials gifted guns and ammunition, they viewed those items as repositories of their superior technological abilities. They believed that they were remaking the world of the Southeastern Indians for the better and that, in return, the Southeastern Indians were obligated to use these arms to further British interests. These gifts, in the eyes of the British, were inalienable possessions that could never be severed from their natal British culture. Southeastern Indians bestowed gifts of hospitality and art, redolent of a hard-earned knowledge of their environment and their community-wide labor. With these gifts, they hoped to remind the British that the latter were temporary visitors who must abide by the customs of the land and act as protectors, not aggressors. When these encoded messages went unheard, some Southeastern Indians asserted their claims to the land through gift taking, or theft. Gifts became a primary mechanism through which all parties staked claims to geographical and social space in the Southeast.

Many of these messages were received, even if they were not heeded. Following from this book's major argument that Southeastern Indian and British American cultures of production, exchange, and consumption allowed for a good deal of overlap is the argument that we should not view the history of the Southeast as a story of irreversible incompatibility. It is a story of how a variety of opportunities narrowed into a series of choices made by colonial officials, Native American leaders, common consumers, and merchants. Sometimes these choices stemmed from cultural assumptions: Southeastern Indians simply did not understand why they owed the white Maker allegiance. Sometimes these choices were instinctive reactions to deeply felt fears: For the British, the Indian trade summoned up worries about trade's disruptive effect on established social relationships and class systems, despite the fact that an alternate, liberal notion of political economy was taking shape. Choices are never limitless, but they are often plentiful. Though the Southeastern Indians and British Americans had the tools to do otherwise, the majority of them became adept at ignoring the messages inscribed in gifts and prescribed in commodities. Colonial officials sold gifts of paintings originally intended for a specific individual to the highest bidder. Native Americans cherished foreign-made medals, designed as markers of subjugation, as symbols of friendship and equality.

While gift exchange was the primary battleground for intergroup struggles in the Southeast, commodity exchange became the source of contention for intragroup tensions within both societies. Debates ensued about how to evaluate individuals whose livelihoods were dependent on cross-cultural trade. Indian traders faced the largest uphill battle in gaining respect. British officials and merchants in powerful trading firms held fast to beliefs that arose from the logic of mercantilism. They feared that unmonitored traveling traders, through social relationships forged by commodity exchange, would induce their Native American trade partners to pledge their allegiance to individual traders rather than the British Empire. To neutralize the harmful potential of Indian traders, leaders and wealthy merchants attempted to contain these traders in stable networks and environments within Southeastern Indian towns. They also prevented trading partners from determining the prices of their goods or the amount of debt they extended. Such measures were meant to prevent cross-cultural economic relationships from overlapping with social relationships. Indian traders reacted in several different ways. Most learned the discourse of trade regulation and were able to repeat it at the first sight of a colonial official. Though they covered their tracks well, there is ample evidence that, away from official oversight, many individuals constructed a middle ground and a frontier economy by locating tools in their repertoires that were easily communicable across cultures.[24] Some traders in this group bound together and consciously considered themselves at odds with the governments or trading firms that employed them, a stance adopted by Mr. Bubby and his coworkers employed by Macartan and Campbell. Other Indian traders, however, worked assiduously to prove their allegiance to the colonies. They described themselves as imperial agents and explicitly invoked state power (through forged public commissions or invocations of regulations), aspired to become elite members of colonial society, and toed the colonial line when interacting with Southeastern Indians. Only those individuals who were able to secure the traditional apparatus of power—land—were able to evade the stereotypes imposed upon Indian traders.

The Atlantic trade's impact on social structures in Southeastern Indian societies can be measured by tracking the status of individuals who were actively engaged in the trade, either as producers, consumers, or traders. We know from the extensive research performed by historians that Southeastern Indians began investing unprecedented amounts of labor in hunting and dressing deerskins in the eighteenth century. Hunting seasons became longer, and each town's energy shifted from performing other tasks, even subsistence food production, to harvesting skins for the trade.[25] Warfare undertaken to protect and expand hunting grounds also consumed more and more of each town's labor and the headmen's energies.[26] In this sense, even though the British were directly employing only a handful of Southeastern Indians, the Atlantic market exerted an indirect, yet insidious, control over a town's labor. A potent example of this trend is the anxiety triggered in Southeastern Indian societies when European markets shifted from desiring a wide variety of skins and pelts to purchasing only deerskins in the early eighteenth century.[27]

One might imagine that when Southeastern Indian towns became integrated into the Atlantic economy, an individual's status in society would become dependent on his or her success in the Atlantic trade. If this were the case, a man or woman who was able to purchase the greatest number of European goods, display them conspicuously, and thus exhibit his or her success at producing items for the Atlantic market would be the most respected member in society. This would have made Europeans the ultimate arbiters of social rank, for it would be their market values that determined how these goods were apportioned. European authority would have surreptitiously penetrated multiple areas of Indian society, creating a more total and invasive form of authority than that held by Southeastern Indian headmen.

But this did not happen. European drawings and descriptions of Southeastern Indians reveal that they did not use European textiles to mark themselves as employees for the trade or to distinguish their social rank. Many European travelers noted that it was impossible to differentiate between different sorts of Native Americans based on the clothing they wore. Southeastern Indians incorporated European clothing and textiles into traditional styles rather than using these items to ostentatiously mark their European connection.

The status of women also suggests that laboring for European goods did not translate into social prestige. While men hunted the deer, women in Creek societies dressed the skins. The quality of dressing, a very difficult task, determined the price of a skin as much as, if not more than, its size. Thus it is notable that women, whose labor was indispensable to the trade with Europeans, did not gain political power or social prestige during this era. Evidently, one's economic relationship with the Europeans was not the primary determinant of one's place in society.

It is possible that European observers were not knowledgeable enough about Southeastern Indian culture to notice how subtleties of dress or adornment may have corresponded with different social positions. The tracking of Creek and Cherokee cloth purchases in chapter 4, for instance, revealed a drop in purchases of blue textiles at the very same time that South Carolina officials began compensating Native Americans who transported goods for the trade with blue cloth. Blue cloth may have become so emblematic of working for the colonial government that individuals who did not perform this type of labor were deterred from wearing blue. This subtle distinction as to who was and who was not wearing blue, and why, would have escaped the notice of a casual observer. A similar social difference may explain why one of the hunters in the von Reck illustration wears a European blanket and the other a painted skin (Figure 5). But until future scholars decode the meanings of dress that were inscrutable to European observers, we are left to conclude that Native Americans' social rank, as worn on their body, was not dependent on their economic relationships with Europeans. Despite the fact that the desire for European goods altered Southeastern Indian productive priorities, European goods—the fruits of this labor—did not differentiate individuals in Southeastern society.

The separation of social rank from the Atlantic market may have been consciously constructed. Not registering European commodities as markers of social worth was one such mechanism. The myths and rituals discussed in chapter 1 provided another strategy. By regularly reminding themselves that their communities were structured according to the instructions laid out by their ancestors, rooted in nature, and guarded by their religious and secular leaders, Southeastern Indians were able to retain a significant amount of control over their societies.

The extent to which the Southeastern Indians benefited by preserving the integrity of their societies cannot be overstated. There were likely hunters and traders who were particularly successful. In turn, they may have wished to institute an alternative hierarchy of social status based on performance in the Atlantic trade. In 1725, the Creek leader Brims complained that by allowing inappropriate individuals to amass European goods, the English made "Captains and great Men" of those "who had no right to command, which made great confusion in their nation."[28] Apparently, there were individuals who strove to use European goods to enhance their social standing, and segments of society that were willing to entertain the notion that acquiring European goods made one eligible for a leadership position.

But, as this book argues, the social upheaval feared by Brims was mitigated by the expansive and fluid role of Southeastern Indian headmen. Instead of having to significantly readjust their role in the economy after contact, Southeastern Indian leaders were able to draw on aspects of their precontact responsibilities to navigate the obstacles of the Atlantic trade. This argument diverges from that of some scholars who held that the Atlantic trade greatly disrupted Southeastern Indian social structures.

Richard White, who analyzed the Choctaw in his famous 1983 book *The Roots of Dependency*, made such an argument. Though the interventions of ethnohistorians have complicated the notion of dependency to the point of near-extinction, remnants of White's social structure theory live on, as does the word "dependent" when casually describing the use of European goods.[29] White, consistent with the archaeological consensus of the time at which he was writing *The Roots of Dependency*, postulated that prior to European arrival, a chief's power stemmed from his ability to monopolize the flow of foreign goods into his community. He distributed these goods to particular members of his community, asserting his power through allocation, not accumulation. After contact, foreign goods continued to hold a central place in the power structure of the groups descended from the chiefdoms. This is why, as White explains, Southeastern Indian leaders so quickly welcomed Europeans and their European goods. These items were a new form of foreign prestige that chiefs could use to maintain their positions of authority. But these very goods led to the unraveling of many leaders' positions of power, for the Europeans bestowed goods on individuals who were not strictly entitled to them. White concluded that Southeastern Indian social structure became dependent on European goods, to the detriment of indigenous societies.[30]

This book contends, to the contrary, that there is scant evidence that Southeastern Indian leaders during the colonial period attempted to maintain autocratic control over the European goods that entered their borders, or that individuals assumed that leaders should have autocratic control. One would expect that, if Southeastern Indian individuals were raised in a culture in which goods entered their towns only via their leaders, and only leaders had the right to act as portals for these goods, they would not attempt to acquire these goods themselves. If they did, there would be mechanisms in place to punish them. But this did not occur. Englishmen on the very first Barbadian ships that arrived at the South Carolina coast in the 1660s and 1670s described hordes of Native Americans (not leaders) eager to exchange goods directly with them.[31] This behavior continued unabated. Southeastern Indian hunters and dressers readily approached traders and settlers directly with their goods, bypassing their leaders.

The absence of prohibitions against individual trading is explained by recent archaeological findings. These discoveries show that not all pre-contact Mississippian chiefdoms were rigid hierarchies in which chiefs drew their power from their control over prestige goods. Some chiefs, operating in a corporate model, did not set themselves apart from their townsmen in what they wore or ate, did not siphon off labor surpluses, and used symbols of commonality instead of prestige goods to mark their political position. Political and social power was regularly legitimated by a chief's or a ruling elite group's relationship with the supernatural, and his/her/their ability to keep their town or region safe, fed, and internally peaceful.[32] Thus, after contact, when headmen made it their top priority to secure the fairest trading terms for their townsmen, they were not giving up on their dream of having exclusive control over the trade; rather, they were perpetuating the *mico*'s obligation to mediate with outsiders. Engagement with the Atlantic trade did not necessitate a revolutionary restructuring of Southeastern Indian society.

THE STORY COMES full circle, returning, in a crucial way, to before White published *The Roots of Dependency*. White explained that he was motivated to construct his argument as a corrective to the dominant histories of his time, which focused too heavily on warfare and too lightly on culture.[33] Like White's book, this book is a study of cultural history. But it is not a history that permits us to explain the fissures between Southeastern Indians and colonists by pinpointing cultural differences. Rather, the economic practices and ideologies of Southeastern Indians and British colonists were expansive enough to allow for cooperation and collaboration. Therefore, this book concludes by suggesting that shifts in power, rather than shifts in culture, better explain the mounting tensions between Southeastern Indians and colonists. As the British became more comfortable in their economic and physical position in the Southeast, they no longer had to rely on the tools of persuasion honed through economic exchange. Although victories in the French and Indian War bolstered British confidence, their feelings of self-assurance predated these events. In James Glen's speeches of the early 1750s, one clearly hears how the British sense of security, sparked by a diversification in crops and a multiplication of their numbers, influenced their perception of the Native Americans. Native Americans were not described as creative producers or equal economic partners. No longer relying on the language they had spent nearly a century attuning to their Native American interlocutors, the British colonists invoked alternate frameworks that cast the Native Americans as dependent and inept. When language no longer worked as a tool of persuasion, settlers and Native Americans used force. Settlers encroached on land that was not theirs, and Native Americans destroyed settlers' property and lives. Already in the eighteenth century there were hints of the dynamics that would lead to the coerced migrations of the 1830s. These dislocations grew out of the politics of force, not a chronicle of a defeated or defunct Southeastern Indian culture. To borrow a phrase used by the subaltern studies theorist Ranajit Guha, the history of the colonial Southeast was one of "dominance without hegemony."[34]

Textiles in the Colonial Southeast

Textiles in the Colonial Southeast

	Approved for slaves and indentured servants, 1735[a]	Purchased by Theophilus Hastings to sell to the Cherokee, 1714[b]	Appears on Southeastern Indian price lists, 1716–51[c]	Available for sale at Fort Prince George, 1762–63[d]
Linen				
Bedbunt				
Blue linen	X			
Buckham				
Cambrick				X
Canvas				
Check	X			X
Crocus				
Diaper				
Dowlas				
Garlix	X	X		X
Holland		X		X
Irish linen				X
Lawns				
Osnabrig	X	X	X	X
Silesias				
Striped linen				X
Tandem				
Tickling				
White linen				X
Wool				
Broadcloth				

(*continued*)

Textiles in the Colonial Southeast (continued)

	Approved for slaves and indentured servants, 1735[a]	Purchased by Theophilus Hastings to sell to the Cherokee, 1714[b]	Appears on Southeastern Indian price lists, 1716–51[c]	Available for sale at Fort Prince George, 1762–63[d]
Bunting				
Calimanco				X
Camplets				
Cloth			X	X
Crape				
Damasks				
Duffel blanket	X		X	X
Drugget		X		
Flannel			X	X
Half thicks			X	
Kersey serge	X			
Plains	X		X	X
Rug		X		
Sagathy		X		
Shalloons				
Stroud			X	X
Stuff		X		
Tammy				
Velvet				
Cotton*				
Calico	X		X	X
Chintz				
Dimity				
Fustians				
Ginghams				
Muslin		X		

(continued)

	Approved for slaves and indentured servants, 1735[a]	Purchased by Theophilus Hastings to sell to the Cherokee, 1714[b]	Appears on Southeastern Indian price lists, 1716–51[c]	Available for sale at Fort Prince George, 1762–63[d]
Romall		X		
Thicksett				X
Silk				
Alamode				
Damask				
Drouget				
Persian				
Satin				
Silk handkerchief				X
Tobine				

Sources: Daybook kept by John Blackwood and Alexander Nisbet, GD237/1/151, National Archives of Scotland; Cash book of Robert Nisbet, GD237/1/150, National Archives of Scotland; Advertisement of Goods Lately Imported by Yeomans and Escott, August 12, 1732, *South Carolina Gazette*; Advertisement of Goods to Be Sold by Isaac Chardon, September 9, 1732, *South Carolina Gazette*; Advertisement of Goods Just Imported by Jenys and Baker, September 30, 1732, *South Carolina Gazette*; Advertisement of Goods Just Imported by Morel and Telfair, May 26, 1763, *Georgia Gazette*; Advertisement of Goods Just Imported by Johnson and Wylly, December 1, 1763, *Georgia Gazette*; Michie, "Charleston Textile Imports, 1738–1742," 20–39; Staples, "'Useful, Ornamental or Necessary'"; Baumgarten, *What Clothes Reveal*; Montgomery, *Textiles in America*; Queen, *Textiles for Colonial Clothing*.

[a] Slave Act, 1735, South Carolina, in Cooper and McCord, *Statutes at Large*, 7:396.

[b] THJR.

[c] Table of Goods and Prices for the Indian Trade, April 30, 1716, *JCIT*, 89; A Schedule of the Stated Prices of the Goods, as They Are to Be Disposed of to the Indians in Barter, August 11, 1716, *JCIT*, 104; Prices of the Goods Negotiated with the Creek Indians, June 3, 1718, *JCIT*, 281; Talk to the Creek Indians, July 8, 1721, in South Carolina, General Assembly, "Report of the Committee," 59; Oglethorpe and Lower Creek Indians, "Oglethorpe's Treaty," 14–15; Georgia Treaty with the Yamacraw, May 18, 1733, as quoted in C. Jones, *Historical Sketch of Tomochichi*, 35; List of the Prices of Goods for the Cherokee Trade, November 1, 1751, *DRIA*, 1:146–47.

[d] Public Cherokee Trade, Account Book, Goods Sold and Delivered out of the Fort Prince George Factory, August 31, 1762–September 29, 1763.

(*continued*)

Textiles in the Colonial Southeast (continued)

Note: This appendix does not provide an exhaustive accounting of every textile type sold in colonial South Carolina and Georgia, but is rather a list that represents the most commonly available textiles compiled from the sources listed above. This table includes textiles that Southeastern Indians purchased. For a more comprehensive list of all items that entered Southeastern Indian towns in the eighteenth century as gifts and commodities, see Waselkov, "Eighteenth-Century Anglo-Indian Trade."

* Cotton cloth was not produced in Britain during the colonial period. Many of the textiles referred to as "cotton" by British and American merchants were woolens and linens processed to resemble cotton. Only textiles manufactured from cotton fibers are included under "cotton" in this list.

Notes

Abbreviations

BPRO-SC   William Noel Sainsbury, ed. *Records in the British Public Record Office Relating to South Carolina, 1663–1782.* 36 vols. London, 1860–1919.

CO 5   Colonial Office 5. The National Archives, Kew, Britain. Digital access through www.colonialamerica.amdigital.co.uk.

CRG   Allen D. Candler, Kenneth Coleman, and Milton Ready, eds. *The Colonial Records of the State of Georgia.* 32 vols. Atlanta, 1904–16; Athens, 1974–79. Unpublished vols. 33–39. Microfilm. Georgia Department of Archives and History, Atlanta, Ga.

DRIA, 1:   William L. McDowell Jr., ed. *Documents Relating to Indian Affairs, May 21, 1750–August 7, 1754* [vol. 1]. Columbia, S.C., 1992 [1958].

DRIA, 2:   William L. McDowell Jr., ed. *Documents Relating to Indian Affairs, 1754–1765* [vol. 2]. Columbia, S.C., 1992 [1970].

GDAH   Georgia Department of Archives and History, Atlanta, Ga.

GHS   Georgia Historical Society, Savannah, Ga.

GSB   George Galphin account books, Silver Bluff, 1767–72. MS 269. Georgia Historical Society, Savannah, Ga.

HWA   Henry Woodward, Accounts as Indian Agent of the First Earl of Shaftesbury, 1674–78, P900101, South Carolina Department of Archives and History, Columbia, S.C.

JCHA   A. S. Salley, ed. *Journals of the Commons House of Assembly (1692–1735).* Columbia, S.C., 1907–47.

JCIT   William L. McDowell Jr., ed. *Journals of the Commissioners of the Indian Trade: September 20, 1710–August 29, 1718.* Columbia, S.C.: Department of Archives and History, 1992 [1955].

KRC   Keith Read Collection, Hargrett Rare Book and Manuscript Library, University of Georgia Libraries. Available online at Galileo Digital Library of Georgia, Southeastern Native American Documents, 1730–1842.

LOC   Library of Congress, Washington, D.C.

SCDAH   South Carolina Department of Archives and History, Columbia, S.C.

SCIAA   South Carolina Institute of Archaeology and Anthropology, Columbia, S.C.

SCL   South Caroliniana Library, University of South Carolina, Columbia, S.C.

TCC   Telamon Cuyler Collection, Hargrett Rare Book and Manuscript
            Library, University of Georgia Libraries. Available online at
            Galileo Digital Library of Georgia, Southeastern Native American
            Documents, 1730–1842.
THJR   Samuell Wragg, Jacob Satur and Joseph Wragg vs. Theophilus
            Hastings, Judgment Roll, 1719, S136002, Box 014A, Item 0211,
            South Carolina Department of Archives and History,
            Columbia, S.C.

Introduction

1. It is difficult to determine whether the storekeeper would have lost money on this sale. We know that the gun eventually gifted to the Cherokee man cost the South Carolina Commissioners of the Indian Trade 3 pounds and 15 shillings; July 23, 1716, *JCIT*, 83. But it is hard to determine how much the commissioners earned from these ten beaver skins, as the value of beaver skin was much more variable in colonial South Carolina than deerskin, and depended to a greater extent on the weight and condition of the beaver skins; see Commissioners to Capt. Bartholomew Gaillard, October 2, 1716, *JCIT*, 116. The specific qualities of the skins the Cherokee man offered were not recorded. Still, it is probable that this Cherokee man was looking for a bargain. By default, beaver skins were usually counted as a single deerskin, and at this time a gun cost the Cherokee thirty-five skins, much more than the ten he offered; see *JCIT*, 89.

2. Commissioners to Jos. Thomas, July 14, 1716, *JCIT*, 79; Commissioners to Theophilus Hastings, July 24, 1716, *JCIT*, 84.

3. Snyder, *Slavery in Indian Country*, 55–56. For similar arguments, see Hall, *Zamumo's Gifts*, 63–64, 82; Hatley, *Dividing Paths*, 44; Piker, *Okfuskee*, 159; Saunt, *New Order of Things*, 40; R. White, *Roots of Dependency*, 59; Merrell, "'Our Bonds of Peace,'" 279. For this view of Native Americans as gifters in other parts of North America, see Calloway, *New Worlds for All*, 43–44. For recent studies that run contrary to this trend and analyze the market behavior of Southeastern Native Americans, see Hanh, "The Mother of Necessity." William Ramsey also argues that eventually the market system led to a loss of Native American control over the trade, but he roots the cause in economic rather than cultural factors; *Yamasee War*, 57–78.

4. Bosher, "Huguenot Merchants," 77–102; Minchinton, "Merchants in England in the Eighteenth Century," 23–24; Glaisyer, "Networking," 464–68; Kagan and Morgan, *Atlantic Diasporas*; Muldrew, *Economy of Obligation*, 125–47. See also Wrightson, *Earthly Necessities*, 300–303; Glaisyer, *Culture of Commerce*, 38–42.

5. Anthropologists working in a wide range of geographical locations and in various time periods have demonstrated that it is more viable to begin cultural research from the assumption that individuals are fluent in a diversity of economic approaches rather than with the belief that a people in any space or time utilize only one mode of exchange: Appadurai, *Social Life of Things*; Thomas, *Entangled*

Objects; Akin and Robbins, *Money and Modernity*, 10; Parry and Bloch, *Money and the Morality of Exchange*, 19–30; Humphrey and Hugh-Jones, *Barter, Exchange, and Value*, 5.

6. My methodology is influenced by David Graeber's suggestion, "What if one did try to create a theory of value starting from the assumption that what is ultimately being evaluated are not things, but actions?"; *Toward an Anthropological Theory of Value*, 49.

7. In 2002, Patricia Albers pointed to a historical disinterest, if not a disbelief, in a Native American productive culture, a gap that this book rectifies; Albers, "Labor and Exchange." Although the historian Daniel Usner has begun to fill this void, his interest largely lies outside of the colonial period; Usner, *Indian Work*.

8. Appadurai, *Social Life of Things*, 13–16; Akin and Robbins, *Money and Modernity*, 10; Parry and Bloch, *Money and the Morality of Exchange*, 8–9; J. Davis, *Exchange*, 41–42; Gell, "Inter-tribal Commodity Barter," 144; Munn, *Fame of Gawa*; Weiner, *Inalienable Possessions*; Mauss, *The Gift*.

9. Waselkov and Braund, *William Bartram on the Southeastern Indians*, 151.

10. M. Morris, *Bringing of Wonder*, 75; Braund, *Deerskins and Duffels*, 130–31; Pressly, *Rim of the Caribbean*, 197. For exceptions to this historiography, see Merrell, *Indians' New World*, 33. Historians have elucidated the creativity with which Native Americans in other areas engaged with goods; see Richter, *Before the Revolution*, 130, 141; Ray and Freeman, *"Give Us Good Measure"*; Ray, "Indians as Consumers in the Eighteenth Century"; Carlos and Lewis, *Commerce by a Frozen Sea*. More so than the history of textiles and tools, the history of guns and alcohol requires that we seriously consider the role of dependency; see Silverman, *Thundersticks*; Mancall, *Deadly Medicine*; Ishii, *Bad Fruits*.

11. For other historians who have argued that in order to understand the ideology of the center you must look at the colonies and/or frontier regions, see Newell, "Putting the 'Political' Back in Political Economy"; Koot, "Balancing Center and Periphery"; Harmon, O'Neill, and Rosier, "Interwoven Economic Histories."

12. Pincus, *1688*, 370–85; R. Davis, "English Foreign Trade,"162; Glaisyer, *Culture of Commerce*, 1–2; Magnusson, *Mercantilism*, 9–10; Finkelstein, *Harmony and the Balance*, 179, 247–53; Wrightson, *Earthly Necessities*, 249–55; Pincus, "Rethinking Mercantilism," 12–14, 17–23; Lieberman, "Property, Commerce, and the Common Law," 145–47.

13. Some argue that these categories were not neatly packaged in Britain or other parts of the British Atlantic either; Matson, "Imperial Political Economy," 36–38.

14. Conversations between Thomas Stephens and Earl of Egmont, October 13, 1739, *CRG*, 5: 236–37; Tailfer, "A True and Historical Narrative," 42–44; Henry Parker and 120 residents of Savannah, Georgia, to the Trustees of Georgia, December 9, 1738, in Reese, *Clamorous Malcontents*, 244; Martyn, "Impartial Enqiry into the State and Utility of the Province of Georgia, 1741," in Reese, *Clamorous Malcontents*, 130–32.

15. Ethridge and Shuck-Hall, *Mapping the Mississippian Shatter Zone*, 7–8; Jenkins, "Tracing the Origins of the Early Creeks," 191–95.

16. On the history of Mississippian chiefdom scholarship, see Butler and Welch, *Leadership and Polity in Mississippian Society*, 1–7, 10–12; Payne, "Foundations of Leadership in Mississippian Chiefdoms," 91–92; Anderson and Sassman, "Mississippian Complexity and Contact Coalescence," 152–190; Blitz," New Perspectives," 1–39.

17. A. King, "Leadership Strategies"; Beck, "Persuasive Politics," 20–24; Payne, "Foundations of Leadership in Mississippian Chiefdoms," 91–93, 102–6; Myers, "Leadership at the Edge," 158–59; Gougeon, "Different but the Same," 185–90; Welch, "Interpreting Anomalous Rural Mississippian Settlements," 216–19, 230–31; Cobb, "Mississippian Chiefdoms"; Anderson and Sassman, "Mississippian Complexity and Contact Coalescence," 173; Blitz, "New Perspectives," 4–7, 17–18, 20; Ethridge, "Introduction: Mapping the Mississippian Shatter Zone," in Ethridge and Shuck-Hall, *Mapping the Mississippian Shatter Zone*, 3–7.

18. A. King, "Leadership Strategies"; Beck, "Persuasive Politics," 24–28, 35; G. Wilson, Marcoux, and Koldehoff, "Square Pegs in Round Holes," 43–44, 50–51, 64–65; Payne, "Foundations of Leadership," 104–6; Schroeder, "Walls as Symbols," 134–35; Myers, "Leadership at the Edge," 159, 172; Gougeon, "Different but the Same," 178–81, 189–90; Anderson and Sassman, "Mississippian Complexity and Contact Coalescence," 162–63, 167–68, 173–77; Blitz, "New Perspectives," 4–6, 10, 17, 20, 22–23.

19. Ethridge, "Introduction: Mapping the Mississippian Shatter Zone," 9.

20. Ibid., 1–2, 8–10, 20–26, 32–42. All of the essays in Ethridge and Shuck-Hall, *Mapping the Mississippi Shatter Zone*, address this process in great detail; Ethridge, *From Chicaza to Chickasaw*; Marcoux, *Pox, Empire, Shackles, and Hides*, 65–106; Beck, *Chiefdoms, Collapse, and Coalescence*. The exceptions to this trend are the chiefdoms of the Natchez and Tensaw on the lower Mississippi River, which were able to survive beyond the era of colonization.

21. Knight, "Formation of the Creeks"; Hahn, *Invention of the Creek Nation*, 1–47; Jenkins, "Tracing the Origins of the Early Creeks," 188–249; Browne, "'Carying Awaye Their Corne,'" 109–11; Waselkov and Smith, "Upper Creek Archaeology," 242–64; Worth, "Lower Creeks," 265–98. A similar coalescence occurred with the predecessors of the Cherokee, who were probably survivors of the South Appalachian chiefdoms, although the process is less fully understood; Marcoux, *Pox, Empire, Shackles, and Hides*, 5–9, 141–42; Ethridge, "European Invasion and the Transformation of the Indians of Tennessee," 15–16.

22. While tribe-specific studies have long been the norm, recently scholars have argued that the groups of the Southeast shared a regional identity due to their shared experiences as descendants from Mississippian chiefdoms; Waselkov and Dumas, "Cultural Revitalization"; Snyder, *Slavery in Indian Country*, 10.

23. On the ethnic diversity in the British colonial Southeast, see Weir, "'Shaftesbury's Darling'"; Roberts and Beamish, "Venturing Out." Paul Pressley argues that early Georgia was made up of three distinct centers with three distinct goals; *Rim of the Caribbean*, 12–31. On the practice and validity of treating the southeastern region as a whole, see Gallay, *Formation of a Planter Elite*, 1–6.

24. Wesson, "Prestige Goods," 110–25; Ethridge, *From Chicaza to Chickasaw*, 17–18, 40, 61. On the difficulty encountered by leaders in other areas of America in controlling prestige goods, see Richter, *Before the Revolution*, 127–28.

25. While writing this book, I was influenced by Gell, "Newcomers to the World of Goods."

26. Barber, *Generation of Plays*, 7.

27. Stahl, "Colonial Entanglements," 834.

28. Graeber, *Toward an Anthropological Theory of Value*, 49.

29. This view is consistent with the argument made by the new borderland history; see Hämäläinen and Truett, "On Borderlands."

30. A. King, "Creek Chiefdoms," 221–26; Saunt, *New Order of Things*, 24.

31. Wesson, "Prestige Goods," 117–25; Anderson and Sassman, "Mississippian Complexity and Contact Coalescence,"187.

32. LaCombe, "'A Continuall and Dayly Table,'" 669–87.

33. Hewitt, "State in the Planters' Service."

34. Roper, *Conceiving Carolina*, 51–67, 86.

35. Sweet, *William Stephens*, 56, 61.

36. Ibid., 48.

37. Sylvia Frey demonstrates that after the American Revolution southerners emphasized that ownership of property (in the form of African slaves) was the premier freedom that they were entitled to; Frey, "Liberty, Equality, and Slavery." This book shows the colonial roots of this argument and how it was made in reference to Native American slaves and labor before it was made in reference to African slaves.

38. Tortora, *Carolina in Crisis*, 172–74; Pressly, *Rim of the Caribbean*, 198.

Chapter One

1. For an itinerary of the Yamacraws' visit to England, see Vaughan, *Transatlantic Encounters*, 150–60; Sweet, *Negotiating for Georgia*, 40–60. Neither of these secondary sources mentions the Godalming textile factory visit, probably because the parts of the visit that did not occur in London were not covered by the press. While the correspondence about the tour refers only to "cloth," the type of woolens created in Godalming at this time were kerseys; Cox, *Magna Britannia et Hibernia*, 397.

2. Mancall, Rosenbloom, and Weiss, "Indians and the Economy of Eighteenth-Century Carolina," 312.

3. While traders and Georgia officials did, at times, commission settlers to sew shirts for the trade, the textiles used for the Indian trade were primarily produced in Europe and not in America; see November 30, 1717, and May 23, 1718, *JCIT*, 235, 276. On shirts purchased from Martha Chevas, Jane Dick, William Calwell, Darrix Jarritt, Ann Cossle, and Mr. Stewart, see GSB, 27, 30, 34, 35, 38, 39, 44, 56, 60, 67. On the Board of Trade's attempt to guard textile industrial secrets, see R. Morris, *Government and Labor in Early America*, 23.

4. R. Morris, *Government and Labor in Early America*, 11–12.

5. Harman Verelst to Thomas Causton, March 17, 1734/5, *CRG*, 29:57.

6. Harman Verelst to Thomas Causton, August 11, 1737, in Davies, *Calendar of State Papers*, vol. 43, available online at *http://www.british-history.ac.uk/cal-state -papers/colonial/america-west-indies/vol43*.

7. Axtell, *Invasion Within*, 10; Gaudio, *Engraving the Savage*, xix. Joyce Chaplin claims that the disregard of Native American technologies occurred only after the English became secure in their colonial position; *Subject Matter*, 71–75, 220–42. For an examination of the persistence of this view of Native Americans through the twentieth century, see Usner, *Indian Work*, 8–14.

8. Hentschell, *Culture of Cloth*, 75–101; Kupperman, *Indians and English*, 49–50; Bickham, *Savages within the Empire*, 90–92; William Bull to Lords Commissioners of Trade and Plantations, July 20, 1738, *CRG*, 22.1:213–14; Patrick Mackay to the Georgia Trustees, March 28, 1735, in M. Lane, *General Oglethorpe's Georgia*, 148; William Stephens, "A State of the Province of Georgia, Attested upon Oath in the Court of Savannah, November 10, 1740," *CRG*, 2:72; "A Description of the Golden Islands, with an Account of the Undertaking Now on Foot for Making a Settlement There," in Reese, *Most Delightful Country*, 43; Thomas Coster, To the Kings Most Excellent Majesty, 1734, Duke University, Special Collections Library, Durham, NC.

9. September 3, 1768, in Warren and Jones, *Georgia Governor and Council Journals*, 2:25. See also "Governor Glen's Talk to the Cherokees, November 13, 1751," *DRIA*, 1:158.

10. Native Americans sometimes mimicked the derogatory stereotypes Europeans created for them, such as the poor, naked Indian, usually as a strategy to obtain goods. There are a couple of similar instances in which Native Americans can be seen identifying the English as technologically superior, though I interpret these rare instances as strategically employed rather than earnestly felt. See Longe, "Small Postscript," 18, 28; Proceedings of the Council concerning Indian Affairs, July 7, 1753, *DRIA*, 1:453.

11. "Mr. Ingham's Journal," in Reese, *Our First Visit in America*, 175; Sweet, *Negotiating for Georgia*, 57–60; Vaughan, *Transatlantic Encounters*, 160–62.

12. For Tomochichi's trade requests, see Sweet, *Negotiating for Georgia*, 54.

13. For kersey in the Indian trade, see Becker, "Match Coats and the Military," 161.

14. Yirush, "'Since We Came Out of This Ground.'"

15. Reck, *Von Reck's Voyage*, 113, 117. The two symbols closest to the woman's wrist are most likely the looped-square pattern that represented the Middle World throughout Southeastern Indian iconography during the post-Mississippian era; Waselkov and Dumas, "Cultural Revitalization," 10. The sinuous line in the upper right-hand corner of von Reck's sketch is another one of the woman's tattoos, which appears below her breasts. It can be seen in final form in his illustration "The Georgia Indians in Their Natural Habitat," which again shows the looped squares and arrows on her arm; *Von Reck's Voyage*, 111. The sinuous line might represent the Beneath World; personal communication, Gregory Waselkov, October 13, 2014.

16. On the historiography of Native American production, see Usner, *Indian Work*; Albers, "Labor and Exchange." Although historians have started to recreate the mechanics, if not the meaning, of Southeastern Indian skin and fur production for the Atlantic market, there is still a gap in our understanding of the meanings of different types of labor in Native American societies. Kathryn Holland Braund, in her book *Deerskin and Duffels*, devotes a chapter to the Creeks as producers for a trade economy. Joshua Piker has provided an exhaustive study of changes in hunting patterns in the Creek town of Okfuskee; *Okfuskee*, 77–88. I am influenced here by the anthropologist Marilyn Strathern's question, Whose labor is most valued in an object's life? Strathern argues that all products materialize the labor invested by multiple parties. But although many people contribute to the manufacture of an item, observers assign a hierarchy of value to the labor of various producers, based on either their status or their role in the object's creation or presentation. Thus some producers impart more value to an object than other individuals involved in the same process. In Melanesia, Strathern's site of study, women invest a substantial amount of energy in pig rearing. Yet during a pig exchange ceremony, each woman's investment in producing the adult pig is eclipsed by the male, who presents the pig to a recipient. Once it enters into exchange, a pig no longer represents female labor, but is a product of a man's power to engage in exchange and thus produce social relationships; Strathern, *Gender of the Gift*. I am indebted to Alfred Gell's explication of Strathern's work, "Strathernograms."

17. Ramsey, *Yamasee War*, 61–68; Snyder, *Slavery in Indian Country*, 77–78; Gallay, *Indian Slave Trade*, 338–39.

18. Wesson, *Households and Hegemony*, 139.

19. L. Johnson, "Stone Tools."

20. Native Americans in many areas were able to maintain control over the production of skins; Tanner, *Bringing Home the Animals*, 2–3.

21. Malatchi to Governor Glen, May 12, 1754, *DRIA*, 1:500; Malatchi to Governor Glen, May 7, 1754, *DRIA*, 1:507; Piker, *Okfuskee*, 75–108.

22. Wesson, *Households and Hegemony*, 141; Waselkov and Smith, "Upper Creek Archaeology," 257.

23. Piker, *Okfuskee*, 75–82, 148–61; Braund, *Deerskins and Duffles*, 65–68. For towns leaving together, see Ludwick Grant to Governor Glen, *DRIA*, 1:367; Proceedings of the Council concerning Indian Affairs, May 28, 1753, *DRIA*, 1:390; Malatchi to Governor Glen, May 12, 1754, *DRIA*, 1:500; Malatchi to Governor Glen, May 7, 1754, *DRIA*, 1:507. For hunting camp sizes and coordination, see Affidavit of James Beamer, July 12, 1751, *DRIA*, 1:26; John Fouquet to Governor Glen, October 4, 1751, *DRIA*, 1:124; Colonel LeJeau to Governor Glen, September 29, 1751, *DRIA*, 1:130; Samuel Hollinshed to Moses Thomson, Esq, December 28, 1751, *DRIA*, 1:216; Talk of Twelve Cherokees to Governor Glen, April 1, 1752, *DRIA*, 1:227; Lud. Grant to Governor Glen, May 3, 1752, *DRIA*, 1:261; John Buckles to Governor Glen, March 15, 1754, *DRIA*, 1:501; Deposition of William Horton, April 13, 1736, CO 5/654, part 1, accessed November 20, 2015, http://www.colonialamerica.amdigital.co.uk/Documents/Details/CO_5_654_Part1_017. On

towns attempting to stay close together, see A Conference with the Indians, *DRIA*, 1:163. On nuclear families hunting together, see John Fairchild to Governor Glen, December 23, 1751, *DRIA*, 1:155; A Conference with the Indians, *DRIA*, 1:163.

24. Wesson, *Households and Hegemony*, 112–13, 124, 140–43, 158; Hatley, "Three Lives of Keowee," 247; Anderson and Sassman, "Mississippian Complexity and Contact Coalescence," 187; Waselkov and Smith, "Upper Creek Archaeology," 257.

25. Beck, *Chiefdoms, Collapse, and Coalescence*, 196–97, 236–37, 264.

26. Ibid., 118–19.

27. A. Moore, *Nairne's Muskhogean Journals*, 48; Hatley, "Cherokee Women Farmers," 305, 317; LeMaster, *Brothers Born of One Mother*, 137–38.

28. Braund, *Deerskins and Duffels*, 68. Most of the deerskins traded were dressed until the 1760s; ibid., 68–69; Piker, *Okfuskee*, 149–52. Note that Cherokee women did not have as much of a participatory role in deerskin dressing; Perdue, *Cherokee Women*, 70–71.

29. February 29, 1764, *CRG*, 18:588–98.

30. On women's demand for specific trade goods, see chapter 4; LeMaster, *Brothers Born of One Mother*, 120–24. Women and children did occasionally bring skins to traders; Talk of the Raven, May 14, 1751, *DRIA*, 1:75; Michelle LeMaster has unearthed a variety of ways women participated in the trade but notes that their trading activities were not acknowledged by British officials; *Brothers Born of One Mother*, 131.

31. LeMaster, *Brothers Born of One Mother*, 155–58; Barker, "'Much Blood and Treasure,'" 149–67; Braund, *Deerskins and Duffels*, 36, 78, 83–86; Hatley, *Dividing Paths*, 52–63; Perdue, "'Sprightly Lover,'" 165–78; Piker, *Okfuskee*, 166–76. For the central role of women in the fur trade in other areas, see Van Kirk, "'The Custom of the Country,'" 481–518.

32. Proceedings of the Council concerning Indian Affairs, July 7, 1753, *DRIA*, 1:452. See also John Buckles to Governor Glen, June 26, 1764, *DRIA*, 1:512; Thomas Bosomworth to Governor Glen, June 4, 1753, *DRIA*, 1:408.

33. Governor Glen to the Catawba King and Head Men, May 9, 1754, *DRIA*, 1:499. For the emphasis on the male providing for his family in British ideology, see Waddell, *God, Duty and Community*, 89–90.

34. LeMaster, *Brothers Born of One Mother*, 124–27.

35. Chickasaw Indian Talk, July 13, 1736, CO 5/654, part 1, 86, accessed November 25, 2015, http://www.colonialamerica.amdigital.co.uk/Documents/Details/CO_5_654_Part1_029.

36. Chickasaw Headmen and Warriors Talk to Governor Glen, June 26, 1764, *DRIA*, 1:512. See also Petition of the Chickasaw Head Men, August 23, 1753, *DRIA*, 1:458; LeMaster, *Brothers Born of One Mother*, 124.

37. Salley, *Journal of Colonel John Herbert*, 24. See also Adair, *History of the American Indians*, 275, 397–99; Waselkov and Braund, *William Bartram on the Southeastern Indians*, 127, 152; A. Moore, *Nairne's Muskhogean Journals*, 34; Longe, "Small Postscript," 30, 36, 40; September 22, 1763, *Georgia Gazette*; Piker, *Okfuskee*, 115–18, 143; Perdue, *Cherokee Women*, 72–73.

38. To Daniel Clark or John Pettyerow, March 10, 1751, *DRIA*, 1:10.

39. Journal of John Buckles, July 1752, *DRIA*, 1:382; Examination of James Beamer by the Governor and Council, *DRIA*, 1:517.

40. Hatley, "Cherokee Women Farmers," 305–35.

41. Piker, *Okfuskee*, 143; Hatley, "Cherokee Women Farmers," 320; LeMaster, *Brothers Born of One Mother*, 133; Tortora, *Carolina in Crisis*, 39. For southeastern colonists' distaste for maize, see Edelson, *Plantation Enterprise*, 69–70.

42. Journal of John Buckles, July, 1752, *DRIA*, 1:382.

43. On a chief's role in food production, see Wesson, *Households and Hegemony*, 62–63, 112, 135. On post-Mississippian symbolism and revitalization, see Waselkov and Dumas, "Cultural Revitalization," 25, 36, 49.

44. In the 1830s John Howard Payne recorded, among other things, the Cherokee Corn Mother Myth that this chapter analyzes. Payne's informant, who communicated with Payne through two interpreters, was Sick A Towah, whom Payne identified as "one of the most aged men in the nation," suggesting he first heard this myth during the middle of the eighteenth century, within the time frame of this book. Payne took great pains to record Sick A Towah's myth accurately. The Newberry Library in Chicago has Payne's final draft of the myth as well as the notes he took while listening to Sick A Towah, filled with crossed out portions where he paused the story for clarification. While much of the story appeared to flow from Sick A Towah with ease, there were some gaps that Payne noted. The myth has chants that are not translated, for instance. And regarding an episode toward the end of the myth, Payne recorded: "I questioned Sickatower regarding the particulars of the Instructions given by the Father to his Sons; but regarding these he was silent. I understood from other sources that these instructions are held very sacred among them, and only imparted with great solemnie to the young men when initiated into the greater mysteries of their religion; and then under engagements of secrecy. These portions relating to the chase are said to be especially curious; and it is remarkable that preparatory to everything undertaken among the Indians, there is inculcated from them a religious rite" (Payne Papers, 2:202–3, Newberry Library, Chicago). The missionary Reverend D. S. Butricks also spoke of the hesitancy of the Cherokee to readily reveal their "ancient religion, customs, and traditions" to white Americans in a letter to Payne written in 1840. Much of the knowledge had been lost over the generations, Butricks concluded, while other types of knowledge were known only by, and were guarded by, an elite group of Cherokee individuals who would not betray their station by divulging the secrets (December 29, 1840, Payne Papers, vol. 4, no. 4). The tenuous position of the Cherokee within America in 1835, and the use of depictions of their culture to argue against their removal, was a third reason for Cherokee guardedness. In an 1835 letter Payne asked John Ross, as well as "All the aged and wise Antiquarians of the Cherokee Nation," to cooperate with Reverend Butricks and promised that "his object will not in the slightest degree affect the private or political rights and interests of the Cherokee people" (September 15, 1835, Payne Papers, vol. 4, no. 6). Butricks excused the Cherokees for not completely trusting Ross's words, which they did not, according to Butricks's letters written five years later. While there were obstacles in accurately recording Cherokee myths in 1835,

it appears that in Sick A Towah Payne found a knowledgeable Cherokee source who was willing to share most, even if not all, parts of the Corn Myth with him. While a more nuanced reading may have been possible using the version of the myth that Cherokee shared among themselves, there is no indication that Cherokee informants willfully distorted the information they shared with Payne.

The earliest complete recordings of the Creek myths were collected and recorded by the anthropologist John R. Swanton (1873–1958). Swanton's informants were born in the early to middle nineteenth century and therefore were not alive during the period covered by this chapter. Swanton collected four versions of the Corn Mother myth, all of which are compatible with the analysis offered in this chapter. Grantham, *Creation Myths*, 241–53, 277–78. While myths sometimes tell more about the culture that tells the story than about the people from which the myth is said to be handed down, the consistency of Swanton's four versions and the fact that the myth reveals a philosophy about production that is consistent with the origin myths and rituals recorded during the colonial period have persuaded me to include the Corn Mother myth in this exploration of colonial period Creek Indian culture.

45. Payne Papers, 2:43.

46. Grantham, *Creation Myths*, 251.

47. Payne Papers, 2:43.

48. Grantham, *Creation Myths*, 243. See also Payne Papers, 2:44.

49. Payne Papers, 2:44.

50. Ibid.; Grantham, *Creation Myths*, 244.

51. Grantham, *Creation Myths*, 244.

52. Payne Papers, 2:45.

53. Ibid.

54. Grantham, *Creation Myths*, 246.

55. Adair, *History of the American Indians*, 164; Accounts of Reverend Butricks, Payne Papers, vol. 4, no. 8:117; Bell, "Separate People," 333–34; Galloway, "Where Have All the Menstrual Huts Gone?," 203; Lemaster, *Brothers Born of One Mother*, 162.

56. Adair, *History of the American Indians*,164; Reck, *Von Reck's Voyage*, 48; Hahn, *Mary Musgrove*, 10; LeMaster, *Brothers Born of One Mother*, 163.

57. Wesson, *Households and Hegemony*, 24–26; LeMaster, *Brothers Born of One Mother*.

58. Grantham, *Creation Myths*, 242.

59. Ibid., 244.

60. Payne Papers, 2:49.

61. Waselkov and Braund, *William Bartram on the Southeastern Indians*, 40.

62. Swanton, *Creek Religion and Medicine*, 494.

63. Reck, *Von Reck's Voyage*, 46; Adair, *History of the American Indians*, 257; Hahn, *Mary Musgrove*, 3.

64. Adair, *History of the American Indians*, 376–78; Longe, "Small Postscript," 44.

65. Adair, *History of the American Indians*, 389. See also LeMaster, *Brothers Born of One Mother*, 55–56.

66. Adair, *History of the American Indians*, 391.

67. Longe, "Small Postscript," 46.

68. LeMaster, *Brothers Born of One Mother*, 52–55, 67–68, 74.

69. Adair, *History of the American Indians*, 390–91. See also LeMaster, *Brothers Born of One Mother*, 51–53.

70. "Notes and Documents: Some Ancient Georgia Lore," 192–93 (hereafter cited as "Some Ancient Georgia Lore"); Jones and Peucher, " 'We Have Come to Georgia with Pure Intentions,' " 91. The historian Steven Hahn examines the myth as Chigelly and Antiche's assertion of hegemony over the Creek people in "Cussita Migration Legend."

71. Hahn, "Cussita Migration Legend"; Nabokov, *Forest of Time*, 36–37.

72. "Some Ancient Georgia Lore," 194.

73. Ibid., 195.

74. For the Southeastern Indians' critique of British materialism, see Shoemaker, *Strange Likeness*, 50–58.

75. "Some Ancient Georgia Lore," 194.

76. Ibid., 195.

77. Malatchi to Governor Glen, May 12, 1754, *DRIA*, 1:500. See also Journal of John Buckles, *DRIA*, 1:510.

78. Journal of Thomas Bosomworth, August 1752, *DRIA*, 1:275; Talk of the Cherokee Emperor and Others, April 27, 1752, *DRIA*, 1:256; Talk of Governor Glen to the Cherokee Indians, November 20, 1751, *DRIA*, 1:185.

79. Waselkov and Dumas, "Cultural Revitalization," 49.

80. We now know that the Yuchi and Creek were two separate peoples; see Jackson, *Yuchi Indian Histories*. But both groups participated in the celebration of the Green Corn Ceremony. During this time in Georgia, the Creek and Yuchi sometimes joined to form towns and thus shared in the same rituals; see Jackson, *Yuchi Ceremonial Life*, 13–20, 28–29. The Green Corn Ceremony was a particularly convergent ritual, for the Yuchi claimed that this ceremony originated with them and that the Creek adopted it during cohabitation. The anthropologist Bill Grantham concluded that although the Creek and Yuchi Green Corn Ceremonies may differ in the amount of emphasis placed on certain elements, the rituals were essentially the same; *Creation Myths*, 74, 80–82. For this reason, and because of the identical structure of the Green Corn Ceremony that they describe, I refer to Philip Georg Friedrich von Reck's brief description of a 1736 Yuchi Green Corn Ceremony to confirm and supplement James Adair's reconstruction of the Creek Green Corn Ceremony that he observed between 1744 and 1775. Adair does not pinpoint which particular group he is discussing when he describes the Green Corn Ceremony. Adair spent much time among the Chickasaw, but there is no other mention in available sources that the Chickasaw celebrated the Green Corn Ceremony. John R. Swanton speculates that Adair is describing either the Coosa, Abihka, or Okfuskee; Swanton, *Creek Religion and Medicine*, 590. According to the account of Alexander Longe, who lived among the Cherokee for over fifteen years in the early 1700s, the Cherokee celebrated an annual Green Corn Ceremony during the colonial period as well. The preeminent Cherokee historian Theda

Perdue's reproduction of the Cherokee Green Corn Ceremony is consistent with the Creek and Yuchi Green Corn Ceremony; Perdue, *Cherokee Women*, 26–27. These similarities among the Creek, Yuchi, and Cherokee Green Corn Ceremonies are striking: they all lasted for four days; demanded a purging ritual with a black drink on the first night, followed by a fast; and required the separation of men from women. Like the Creek and Yuchi Green Corn Ceremony, the Cherokee Green Corn Ceremony concluded with a priestly lecture, a feast of new corn, and a river bath. Spanning only a page, Longe's description is far less detailed than Adair's account of the Creek Green Corn Ceremony, and thus does not provide as much room for analysis. Although I will cite Longe when his assessment concurs with Adair's and von Reck's accounts, the following analysis is primarily based on the Creek Green Corn Ceremony. Longe, "Small Postscript," 15–16. Benjamin Hawkins also described the Green Corn Ceremony that he witnessed in the Creek town of Cussita in 1798–99 (beyond the chronological scope of this book). Because he is witnessing this ceremony after Creek society is reformulating after the Seven Years' War and the American Revolution, I will note how his observations concur with and deviate from the colonial versions, but his description will not serve as a central source; "Sketch of Creek Country," in Hawkins, *Collected Works*, 75s–78s.

81. Grantham, *Creation Myths*, 80–82.

82. Ibid. For a discussion of Three Worlds, see Waselkov and Dumas, "Cultural Revitalization," 8–14; Snyder, *Slavery in Indian Country*, 16.

83. On purging, see Adair, *History of the American Indians*, 146; Hawkins, "Sketch of Creek Country," 76s. Longe noted that the Cherokee drank a purging drink made from root physics during their Green Corn Ceremony as well; "Small Postscript," 16.

84. Reck, *Von Reck's Voyage*, 49; Longe, "Small Postscript," 14, 16; Adair, *History of the American Indians*, 143, 146. Note that Hawkins, who is describing an eight-day ceremony, describes women entering and exiting the square through the second day. On the role of Beloved Women in Creek society, see Braund, *Deerskins and Duffels*, 22–23.

85. Adair, *History of the American Indians*, 143, 145, 146, 148, 150. Here Longe's rendition of the Cherokee ceremony differs from Adair's account of the Creek Green Corn Ceremony. Longe claims that for this first feast the women bring the food directly to the priest; "Small Postscript," 22. The division of female food producers from male consumers was not a central feature of other Southeastern Indian rituals and celebrations. Although archaeological evidence reveals that pits used for food processing were placed near the townhouse so that women could prepare food for other public feasts, eyewitnesses describe women preparing food in their homes for the Green Corn Ceremony, thereby suggesting that the decision to hide the process of food production was deliberate and central to this particular ceremony; VanDerwarker and Detwiler, "Gendered Practice in Cherokee Foodways," 28; Adair, *History of the American Indians*, 143, 145, 148; Longe, "Small Postscript," 20. Hawkins does not note where the women prepared the food; "Sketch of Creek Country," 76s.

86. Adair, *History of the American Indians*, 149.

87. Ibid., 151.

88. Journal of Thomas Bosomworth, 1752, *DRIA*, 1:272.

89. Adair, *History of the American Indians*, 150–51. Longe accentuated the fact that these sermons were a crucial part of the Cherokee Green Corn Ceremony; "Small Postscript," 15. Hawkins does not mention that there was a public lecture in his account.

90. "In a language . . ." quoted in C. Jones and Hicks, "Manners and Customs of the Cherokees," 24, presented in *Digital Library of Georgia: Southeastern Native American Documents, 1730–1832*, accessed March 13, 2015. In some Mississippian chiefdoms, chiefs also used their relationship with the supernatural to legitimate their position of power; Gougeon, "Different but the Same," 180.

91. Adair, *History of the American Indians*, 147.

92. Ibid., 143. "Famished multitude" quoted in Adair, *History of the American Indians*, 148.

93. Wesson, *Households and Hegemony*, 51–53.

94. Adair, *History of the American Indians*, 130.

95. Ibid., 149; Reck, *Von Reck's Voyage*, 49.

96. Locke, *Second Treatise of Government*, 20.

97. For public property, see Longe, "Small Postscript," 16, 46; Deposition of John Pettyerow before the Governor, October 8, 1751, *DRIA*, 1:16.

98. Muller, *Mississippian Political Economy*, 264–69; Saunt, *New Order of Things*, 40–41; A. Moore, *Nairne's Muskhogean Journals*, 46–7, 55; Piker, *Okfuskee*, 79, 115–17.

99. Longe, "Small Postscript," 26.

100. "Travel Diary of the Two Pastors Messrs. Boltzius and Gronau," in G. Jones, *Detailed Reports on the Salzburger Emigrants*, 2:5; see also 257. See also Cumming, *Discoveries of John Lederer*, 14.

101. Adair, *History of the American Indians*, 208.

102. Waselkov and Dumas, "Cultural Revitalization."

103. Longe, "Small Postscript," 22, 24. Note that none of the other accounts of the Green Corn Ceremony describes the headman being treated as such. Other travelers noted seeing a crown in other contexts: Reck, *Von Reck's Voyage*, 44; "Journal of Alexander Cuming, 1730," in S. Williams, *Early Travels*, 126.

104. Wesson, *Households and Hegemony*, 112–13.

105. VanDerwarker, Marcoux, and Hollenbach, "Farming and Foraging at the Crossroads."

106. Brewer and Baillie, "Journal of George's Pawley's 1746 Agency," 19; James Glen to the President and Assistants of Georgia, October 15, 1750, *CRG*, 26:62–63; Hatley, "Three Lives of Keowee," 248.

107. Hatley, "Cherokee Women Farmers," 323. On gender in diplomatic settings—both the continued role of women and the pressure by Europeans to treat only with men, see LeMaster, *Brothers Born of One Mother*, 15–50.

108. For example, Michael Taussig posits that indigenous Colombian sugarcane cutters made deals with the devil in an attempt to control new forms of capitalism

that dictated success and failure; Taussig, *Devil and Commodity Fetishism*; J. G. A. Pocock notes that in the early modern period, the British created myths about time and destiny when attempting to understand invisible money in the form of credit and debt; *Virtue, Commerce, and History*, 98–100, 112–15.

109. Appleby, *Economic Thought*, 28–29.

110. Ibid., 52–72.

111. Waddell, *God, Duty and Community*, 15–21; Neeson, *Commoners*, 5–9; Ben-Amos, *Culture of Giving*, 2–4.

112. Mokyr, *Enlightened Economy*, 24; Waddell, *God, Duty and Community*, 85–93.

113. Waddell, *God, Duty and Community*, 27–35; Neeson, *Commoners*, 18–30.

114. Morgan, *Nature of Riches*, 3. From the first publication of the weekly *South Carolina Gazette* on January 8, 1732, until April 29, 1732, *The Nature of Riches* was one of two or three pamphlets that the local printer advertised for sale.

115. Morgan, *Nature of Riches*, 4.

116. Ibid.

117. Chaplin, *Anxious Pursuit*, 118.

118. "Daily Register of the Two Pastors, Mr. Boltzius and Mr. Gronau," in G. Jones, *Detailed Reports on the Salzburger Emigrants*, 2:99.

119. Ibid., 3:148.

120. Ibid., 151, 165.

121. "State of the Province of Georgia, 1742," in Reese, *Clamorous Malcontents*, 12–13.

122. Armitage, "John Locke," 602–27; Hallmark, "John Locke," 9–36.

123. Arneil, *John Locke and America*, 124.

124. Chaplin, *Anxious Pursuit*, 108; E. Bateman, *Sermon Preach'd . . . 1740–41*, 10.

125. Locke, *Second Treatise*, 20.

126. Markley, "'Land Enough,'" 830.

127. Hundert, "Making of Homo Faber," 8. See also N. Wood, *John Locke*, 53.

128. Beginning in February 1731 and continuing through 1750, the Georgia Trustees gathered annually at London and Westminster churches to listen to eminent Anglican ministers deliver a sermon about Georgia; see Spalding, "Some Sermons," 343; Sweet, "'Excellency and Advantage of Doing Good.'" For the religious dimensions of Georgia's founding, see L. Lane, "Gender, Labor, and Virtue," 31–32.

129. Burton, *Sermon Preach'd . . . 1732*, 3, 6; Watts, *Sermon Preach'd . . . 1735*, 6, 13; Ridley, *Sermon Preach'd . . . 1746*, 3. For the argument that man must act according to the wishes of his "Maker" and "Creator," see also January 20 and January 30, 1759, in Richardson, "Diary," 33, 46.

130. Harrison, *Hobbes, Locke, and Confusion's Masterpiece*, 232.

131. T. Wilson, *Knowledge and Practice of Christianity*, 2. For a discussion of the economic language embedded in Christianity, see Stallybrass, "Value of Culture."

132. In early modern England, "labour" could refer to both mental and physical exertion; *Oxford English Dictionary*.

133. Greene, *Imperatives*, 115.

134. Ibid., 115–16; Swingen, "Labor: Employment, Colonial Servitude, and Slavery," 48–50.

135. Martyn, "An Account, Shewing the Progress of the Colony of Georgia in America from It's First Establishment, 1742," in Reese, *Clamorous Malcontents*, 145. For the restrictions in place in Georgia, see McIlvenna, *Short Life of Free Georgia*, 13.

136. S. Smith, *Sermon Preach'd . . . 1731*, 21.

137. P. Gordon, "An Account of the First Settling of the Colony of Georgia," KRC, Document KRC080, 3–4.

138. Edelson, *Plantation Enterprise*, 24.

139. Montgomery, "A Discourse concerning the Design'd Establishment of a New Colony," in Reese, *Most Delightful Country*, 21.

140. S. Smith, *Sermon Preach'd*, 23–24.

141. Watts, *Sermon Preach'd . . . 1731*, 4–5.

142. E. Bateman, *Sermon Preach'd . . . 1740–41*, 3.

143. "Charter of Georgia," 1732, http://avalon.law.yale.edu/18th_century/ga01 .asp, accessed January 31, 2016.

144. Ashcraft, "Lockean Ideas," 50. For the struggle for resources in early Georgia, see McIlvenna, *Short Life of Free Georgia*, 51, 53.

145. Martyn, "An Account, Shewing the Progress of the Colony of Georgia," 149.

146. "A State of the Province of Georgia, 1742," 11. For the trustees' ambivalence about the inhabitants, see McIlvenna, *Short Life of Free Georgia*, 13, 25.

147. J. Butler, "Agrarianism and Capitalism in Early Georgia," 12–16.

148. McIlvenna, *Short Life of Free Georgia*, 36–38.

149. Benjamin Martyn to Bailiffs and Recorder of Savannah, November 28, 1734, CRG, 29:41.

150. For the debate about whether one could survive in Georgia using one's labor alone, see Conversation between Thomas Stephens and Earl of Egmont, October 13, 1739, CRG, 5:236–37. See also Tailfer et al., "True and Historical Narrative," 42–44; Henry Parker and 120 residents of Savannah, Georgia, to the Trustees of Georgia, December 9, 1738, in Reese, *Clamorous Malcontents*, 244; Martyn, "An Impartial Enquiry into the State and Utility of the Province of Georgia, 1741," in Reese, *Clamorous Malcontents*, 125–80; Bruce, *Sermon Preach'd . . . 1743*, 41; Cozma, "John Martin Boltzius"; B. Wood, *Slavery in Colonial Georgia*, 59–73.

151. McIlvenna, *Short Life of Free Georgia*, 52–54, 71–72, 86–110.

152. Chaplin, *Anxious Pursuit*, 52–53, 67.

153. Ibid., 80, 85–87.

154. Stewart, "Letters . . . to William Dunlop," 7.

155. P. Gordon, "An Account of the First Settling of the Colony of Georgia," 71.
The Georgia Trustees explicitly disagreed that managing labor was as valuable as performing labor; Martyn, "An Account, Shewing the Progress of the Colony of Georgia," 190.

156. Edelson, *Plantation Enterprise*, 8. See also ibid., 6, 14, 33–52, 55–58; Chaplin, *Anxious Pursuit*, 67–68, 122–24. For a wider British-Atlantic account of "improvement" and the environment, see Jonsson, "Natural History and Improvement."

157. Edelson, *Plantation Enterprise*, 41.

158. Chaplin, *Anxious Pursuit*, 40–41. For the Malcontents' argument, see Tailfer et al., "True and Historical Narrative," iv.

159. Benjamin Martyn to James Oglethorpe, April 4, 1733, *CRG*, 29:10.

160. Trenchard and Gordon, "An Enquiry into the Nature and Extent of Liberty; with Its Loveliness and Advantages, and the Vile Effects of Slavery," No. 62, Saturday, January 20, 1721, in Hamowy, *Cato's Letters*, 1:427.

161. Proceedings of the Council concerning Indian Affairs, June 2, 1753, *DRIA*, 1:407.

162. Trenchard and Gordon, "Property the First Principle of Power: The Errors of Our Princes Who Attended Not to This," No. 84, Saturday, July 7, 1722, in Hamowy, *Cato's Letters*, 2:607–8.

Chapter Two

1. Muller, *Mississippian Political Economy*, 49–50, 253, 284.

2. For a summary of this argument and the literature on which it is based, see Wesson, *Households and Hegemony*, 33–40.

3. For traditional Southeastern Indian leader control over trade, see Hall, *Zamumo's Gifts*, 2–7, 67, 87; Snyder, *Slavery in Indian Country*, 26–27, 35, 41; R. White, *Roots of Dependency*, 52–53, 74–75, 80; Ramsey, *Yamasee War*, 79–97; Piker, *Okfuskee*, 138–40; Brewer and Baillie, "Journal of George Pawley's 1746 Agency," 18; Lower Creek to Governor Reynolds, October 13, 1756, *DRIA*, 1:239.

4. King, "Leadership Strategies," 73–90; Beck, "Persuasive Politics," 24–28, 35; G. Wilson, Marcoux, and Koldehoff, "Square Pegs in Round Holes," 43–44, 50–51, 64–65; Payne, "Foundations of Leadership in Mississippian Chiefdoms," 104–6; Schroeder, "Walls as Symbols," 134–35; Myers, "Leadership at the Edge," 159, 172; Gougeon, "Different but the Same," 178–81, 189–90; Anderson and Sassman, "Mississippian Complexity and Contact Coalescence," 162–63, 167–68, 173–77; Blitz, "New Perspectives," 4–6, 10, 17, 20, 22–23.

5. "The Great King over the Great Water," Talk of the Headmen of the Lower Creek of Pallochocola to the Georgia Governor, May 15, 1763, *CRG*, 9:74. See also To the Headmen of the Cherokee Indians, South Carolina Council and Governor, July 11, 1721, Records of the Grand Council and Proprietors' Council, Green Copy, SCDAH, 136; Cherokee of Hiwasee, Stecoe, Tuccoigia, Toxoway Talk to Governor James Glen of South Carolina, November 14, 1751, *DRIA*, 1:197. Malatchi's comment is taken from Speeches by James Glen and King Malatchi, the Redcoat King, the Wolf King, the Otassee King, and the Other Chiefs, Headmen, and Warriors Present, of the Upper and Lower Creeks, in Number about 100, Charles Town, SC, May 28, 1753, James Glen Papers, SCL. See also Tlahlo (Chehaws), Oakalpetchie (Oakmulges), Youlialie (Oucatchees), Toposokoie (Palochucho-

les) Talk to Georgia Governor James Oglethorpe, October 13, 1738, SC Miscellaneous Records, vol. 80, WPA transcript, SCDAH, 784; "Articles of Friendship and Commerce, Proposed by the Lords Commissioners for Trade and Plantations, to the Deputies of the Cherokee Nation in South Carolina, by His Majesty's Order, on Monday the 7th Day of September 1730," appendix to South Carolina, General Assembly, "Report of the Committee."

6. Talk between Governor James Glen and the Cherokee at Saluda, July 2, 1755, James Glen Papers, SCL. See also Cherokee Talk to the Board of Trade, September 9, 1730, CO 5/4 part 2, accessed November 24, 2015, http://www.colonialamerica .amdigital.co.uk/Documents/Details/CO_5_4_Part2_014; Jepe Mico Talk, September 7, 1775, *CRG*, 38.2:17.

7. Proceedings of the Council concerning Indian Affairs, July 7, 1753, *DRIA*, 1: 452.

8. Magnusson, *Mercantilism*, 9; Finkelstein, *Harmony and the Balance*, 179, 247–53; Wrightson, *Earthly Necessities*, 249–55; Pincus, "Rethinking Mercantilism," 12–14, 17–23; Swingen, "Labor: Employment, Colonial Servitude, and Slavery," 56–57; Edelson, *Plantation Enterprise,* 35. For a historiography of mercantilism, see Stern and Wennerlind, *Mercantilism Reimagined*, 3–9.

9. The immigrants to Carolina, including those who first lived in Barbados, New England, and Virginia, were primarily of English ancestry; Weir, "'Shaftesbury's Darling,'" 392.

10. "Proposealls of Several Gentlemen of Barbadoes, August 12, 1663," in Cheves, *Shaftesbury Papers*, 11. See also Nairne, "A Description of Carolina" [1710?], manuscript of published edition, Codex Eng. 10, at John Carter Brown Library, Providence, R.I., unnumbered pages between 12 and 13; Edelson, *Plantation Enterprise*, 13–16; Hall, *Zamumo's Gifts*, 84. For the claim that the proprietors based their dominion over Carolina on an agriculturist argument, see Armitage, "John Locke," 617–18; Roper, *Conceiving Carolina*, 19–28.

11. Sirmans, *Colonial South Carolina*, 10–11; Edelson, *Plantation Enterprise*, 35–38.

12. For a solid historiography of early modern property, see Lieberman, "Property, Commerce, and the Common Law," 145–47. For the standard landed property argument, see Pocock, *Virtue, Commerce, and History*, 68. For the growing importance of commerce and the spread of arguments that lauded mobile property in the latter seventeenth century, see Pincus, *1688*, 370–85; R. Davis, "English Foreign Trade," 162; Glaisyer, *Culture of Commerce*, 1–2; Magnusson, *Mercantilism*, 10.

13. For slave and deerskin export numbers, see Gallay, *Indian Slave Trade*, 294–308; Mancall, Rosenbloom, and Weiss, "Indians and the Economy of Eighteenth-Century Carolina," 312. Deerskin traders in early Georgia, many of whom who had moved from South Carolina, also amassed more money than agriculturalists, but it was the financial support offered by Parliament that kept Georgia afloat in the early years. Deerskin was central to Georgia becoming economically sound after the Trustee period; Pressly, *Rim of the Caribbean*, 18–19, 24–27, 193, 199–200.

14. On the centrality of merchants and the market in colonial South Carolina, see Coclanis, "Hydra Head," 1–18.

15. Koot, "Balancing Center and Periphery," 41–46; Newell, "Putting the 'Political' Back in Political Economy"; Harmon, O'Neill, and Rosier, "Interwoven Economic Histories."

16. Laws, Statutes, and Ordinances for the Governance of Georgia, CO 5/681, accessed November 25, 2015, http://www.colonialamerica.amdigital.co.uk /Documents/Details/CO_5_681_003.

17. Historians base this assumption on the belief that gift exchange was the only form of exchange that precontact Native Americans understood. See Snyder, *Slavery in Indian Country*, 55–56. Tom Hatley writes that in Cherokee society "accumulation of wealth was overridden by routines of gift-giving, and . . . consumption was more important than accumulation"; Hatley, *Dividing Paths*, 48. Joshua Piker argues that the Creek town Okfuskee was "centered on intellectual and social constructs that did not mesh easily with market-oriented behaviors"; *Okfuskee*, 159. For earlier works that claim that Native Americans utilized only inalienable forms of exchange, see Saunt, *New Order of Things*, 40; R. White, *Roots of Dependency*, 59. Kathryn Braund stands contrary to this trend, elucidating a long-standing intertribal trade where goods were exchanged for economic purposes; *Deerskins and Duffels*, 27, 63.

18. On precontact trade networks, see Myers, "Leadership at the Edge," 159–64, 168–72; Anderson and Sassman, "Mississippian Complexity and Contact Coalescence," 177–78; Blitz, "New Perspectives," 13–14. By the time the English started exploring the Southeast with the intent to settle, the Spanish had inhabited the area for close to a century. By 1670, the Spanish were concentrated in St. Augustine, while up to forty towns of Christian Indians spread through the Guale on the Georgia coast, Timucua in central Florida, and Apalache around present-day Tallahassee. William Hilton, who led a group looking for the proper area for a British settlement in 1663, noted that the Indians he encountered showed evidence of contact with the Spanish, usually through items they carried. In addition, a widespread and sophisticated intertribal trade existed before European contact. See Bushnell, "Ruling the 'Republic of Indians'"; Crane, *Southern Frontier*, 5–12; Drechsel, "Mobilian Jargon," 274–86; Waselkov, "Seventeenth-Century Trade"; Rothrock, "Carolina Traders," 5. Some have argued that even until 1670, some inland groups, such as the Cherokee, remained largely insulated from direct European trade; see Dunway, "Incorporation," 459. Yet others have shown that even groups who did not have face-to-face contact with European traders felt the repercussions of the trade in their production and social systems, as they traded deerskins for European commodities with groups that did have direct contact with European explorers and settlers; see Lapham, *Hunting for Hides*; Waselkov, "Historic Creek Indian Responses."

19. William Hilton, "A True Relation of a Voyage," in Cheves, *Shaftesbury Papers*, 21.

20. Mathew, "Mr. Mathew's Relation," in Cheves, *Shaftesbury Papers*, 169.

21. Armitage, "Three Concepts."

22. Thomas, *Entangled Objects*, 11.

23. David Harris Sacks describes a similar form of trading that developed between Bristol cloth merchants and traders along the Iberian Peninsula in the fifteenth century in which goods were paid off immediately and an extensive system of credit was bypassed; *Widening Gate*, 54–55.

24. Appadurai, *Social Life of Things*, 13–16; Parry and Bloch, *Money and the Morality of Exchange*, 8–9; J. Davis, *Exchange*, 41–42; Gell, "Inter-tribal Commodity Barter," 144.

25. Agnew, *Worlds Apart*, 1–3.

26. F. O'Sullivan to Lord Ashley, September 10, 1670, in Cheves, *Shaftesbury Papers*, 189. See also Ashe, "Carolina, or a Description of the Present State of that Country (1682)," in Salley, *Narratives of Early Carolina*, 150; Barker, "'Much Blood and Treasure,'" 204.

27. Stumpf, "Merchants of Colonial Charlestown," 13–18.

28. Mancall, Rosenbloom, and Weiss, "Indians and the Economy of Eighteenth-Century Carolina," 312.

29. Stephen Bull to Lord Ashley, September 12, 1670, in Cheves, *Shaftesbury Papers*, 104.

30. Memoranda, Wm. Owen, September 15, 1670, in Cheves, *Shaftesbury Papers*, 224.

31. Rivers, *Sketch*, 90; Instructions for Joseph Morton Esq, May 10, 1682, *BPRO-SC*, 1:141–42; September 27, 1671, Records of the Grand Council and Proprietors' Council, John S. Green Transcripts of Journals, 1671–1721, SCDAH, 8. On the settlement Indians, see Browne, "'Carying Awaye Their Corne," 108.

32. Gallay, *Indian Slave Trade*, 51–52.

33. Salley, *Journal of the Grand Council, August 25, 1671–June 24, 1680*, 59.

34. September 27, 1671, Records of the Grand Council and Proprietors' Council, Green Transcripts, SCDAH, 8.

35. Stephen Bull to Lord Ashley, September 12, 1670, in Cheves, *Shaftesbury Papers*, 104. On the Westos, see Browne, "'Carying Awaye Their Corne," 104–14.

36. Agnew, *Worlds Apart*, 68; Shovlin, "War and Peace," 311–16.

37. Leng, "Commercial Conflict," 933, 954; Finkelstein, *Harmony and the Balance*, 22–25, 89–97; Pincus, "Rethinking Mercantilism," 18–19.

38. Shaftesbury, Craven, and Colleton to [?], October 22, 1677, *BPRO-SC*, 1:60.

39. Proprietors to the Governor, Grand Council, and Parliament, September 30, 1683, *BPRO-SC*, 1:258.

40. Gauci, *Politics of Trade*, 112–15; Pincus, *1688*, 376–77, 385; L. Johnson, "Business of War," 460; Stump, "Economic Consequence of 1688," 28–35; March 15, 1632/3, in Stock, *Proceedings*, 58. That trade could be regulated to benefit the public good, see Finkelstein, *Harmony and the Balance*, 66–67; Keirn, "Monopoly," 427–66. For debates about the East India Company, see Vaughn, "Politics of Empire," 131–35, 162–64; Stern and Wennerlind, *Mercantilism Reimagined*, 178–95; Pettigrew, *Freedom's Debt*, 28–34, 40–43, 83–113.

41. Steele, *Politics of Colonial Policy*, 67; South Carolina, General Assembly, "Report of the Committee," 16. See also, for Virginia's unsuccessful efforts to create

a monopoly, Franklin, "Virginia and the Cherokee Indian Trade," 4. See also, for Virginia's antimonopoly argument against South Carolina, Oatis, *Colonial Complex*, 76.

42. Roper, *Conceiving Carolina*, 51–68; Browne, "Dr. Henry Woodward's Role," 82–86.

43. Address to Seth Sothel, 1690, in Rivers, *Sketch*, appendix, 424. Note that this pamphlet was written in 1690 when the proprietors temporarily reasserted monopoly rights when they declared martial law; Sirmans, *Colonial South Carolina*, 47–48.

44. Roper, *Conceiving Carolina*, 63; Browne, "Dr. Henry Woodward's Role," 82–86.

45. Earl of Shaftesbury and P. Colleton to Andrew Percivall and Maur. Mathews, March 9, 1680/1, *BPRO-SC*, 1:112; Proprietors to Gov. Joseph Blake and Council, December 20, 1697, *BPRO-SC*, 3:234; Instructions for Nicholas Trott, March 8, 1697/8, *BPRO-SC*, 4:13; Mr. Amy to James Moore, August 28, 1698, *BPRO-SC*, 4:71; Sirmans, "Politics in Colonial South Carolina," 33–55; Gallay, *Indian Slave Trade*, 57–69, 215–16; Hewitt, "State in the Planters' Service," 53–54.

46. Greene, *Quest for Power*, 310–29.

47. For the process of establishing trade regulations, see Minutes, February 3, 4, 10, and 12, 1702/3, *JCHA 1703*, 32, 35, 38, 41; Minutes, September 20, 1710, *JCIT*, 3; Oatis, *Colonial Complex*, 46, 53–54; Crane, *Southern Frontier*, 142–44. For the historiography about free versus regulated trade, see Ramsey, *Yamasee War*, 81.

48. An Act Appointing a Special Court for the Speedy Deciding of Controversies between Merchant and Merchant, or Mariner and Mariner, or Merchants and Mariners, about Freight, Damage, and Other Maritime Cases, 1661, in *Acts of Assembly, Passed in the Island of Barbadoes*, 12–13. On the increasing use of judicial outlets to resolve trading disputes in the early modern period, see Muldrew, *Economy of Obligations*, 199–271.

49. For the proprietors' use of the Grand Council to resolve trading disputes, see Minutes, February 24, 1672/73, March 4, 1672/73, and February 2, 1673, in Salley, *Journal of the Grand Council of South Carolina*, 1:54, 55, 66–67; Proprietors to Joseph West and others, May 17, 1680, *BPRO-SC*, 1:97–102; see also Instructions for Joseph Morton Esq, May 10, 1682, *BPRO-SC*, 1:142.

50. Minutes, July 27, 1711, *JCIT*, 11.

51. Minutes, August 3, 1711, *JCIT*, 14.

52. Minutes, July 9, 1712, *JCIT*, 31.

53. In this way, the southeastern borderland was similar to the concept laid out in Hämäläinen and Truett, "On Borderlands."

54. Pincus, "Rethinking Mercantilism," 18–21.

55. Lieberman, "Property, Commerce, and the Common Law," 144–45; "A Bill of Complaint in Chancery, 1700"; Pocock, *Virtue, Commerce, and History*, 56. The proprietors defended Native American ownership of land as well as of personal property; see Proprietors to the Governor, Grand Council, and Parliament, September 30, 1683, *BPRO-SC*, 1:258.

56. Minutes, September 21, 1710, *JCIT*, 4; Minutes, March 9, 1711, *JCIT*, 6; Minutes, July 28, 1711, *JCIT*, 11; Minutes, August 2, 1711, *JCIT*, 13; Minutes, March 21, 1712, *JCIT*, 20; Minutes, April 17, 1712, *JCIT*, 23; Minutes, April 18, 1712, *JCIT*, 23; Ramsey, *Yamasee War*, 88. On differing categorizations of slaves, see Perdue, *Slavery and the Evolution of Cherokee Society*, 4–18.

57. Minutes, March 9, 1711, *JCIT*, 6; Minutes, August 3, 1711, *JCIT*, 14; Minutes, June 10, 1712, *JCIT*, 27.

58. Minutes, October 28, 1710, *JCIT*, 5. See also Minutes, April 17–18, 1712, *JCIT*, 23.

59. Minutes, March 2, 1716, *JCIT*, 262.

60. Canoe values varied based on size and condition. A canoe in Hugh Campbell's estate was valued at ten shillings; Inventories of Estates, 1744, microfilm ST0446, SCDAH. But canoes could be valued for up to twenty times that amount. The Commissioners for the Indian Trade offered to pay Colonel John Barnwell ten pounds for a canoe; December 5, 1716, *JCIT*, 136.

61. A. Moore, *Nairne's Muskhogean Journals*, 56.

62. South Carolina, General Assembly, "Report of the Committee," 8.

63. A. Moore, *Nairne's Muskhogean Journals*, 56.

64. See, for instance, the dispute between Henry Woodward and the Third Baron Cadross; Crane, *Southern Frontier*, 29–30.

65. The South Carolina Indian traders' license agreements specified that they were allowed to trade only with "Indians in amity with this Government"; see Commissioners to Theophilus Hastings, July 24, 1716, *JCIT*, 85; Instructions to Theophilus Hastings, July 19, 1718, *JCIT*, 310. For traders forming partnerships with individuals of other nations, see Cherokee Traders before the Governor and Council, July 6, 1753, *DRIA*, 1:446; Affidavit of David Dowey, May 25, 1751, *DRIA*, 1:57; Governor Henry Ellis to John Rae, Lachlan McGillivray, Francis McCartan Esquires, December 7, 1759, document GLC05228.02, Gilder Lehrman Institute of American History, New York, N.Y.

66. Lud. Grant to Governor Glen, March 4, 1752, *DRIA*, 1:223.

67. Minutes, March 9, 1711, *JCIT*, 6.

68. Affidavit of Lachland McIntosh, November 14, 1752, *DRIA*, 1:343.

69. Minutes, July 17, 1713, *JCIT*, 47.

70. Representation upon Ordinance Passed in South Carolina the 26th June 1736 for Ascertaining and Maintaining the Rights and Privileges of His Majesty's Subjects of the Said Province, CO 5/401, accessed November 25, 2015. http://www.colonialamerica.amdigital.co.uk/Documents/Details/CO_5_401_093.

71. Lieutenant Governor Dinwiddie to Governor Glen, August 5, 1754, *DRIA*, 1:529.

72. Commissioners to John Wright, May 30, 1711, *JCIT*, 8.

73. Minutes, May 4, 1714, *JCIT*, 53–56. See also Riggs, "Reconsidering Chestowee."

74. Agnew, *Worlds Apart*, 40–42; Sacks, *Widening Gate*, 78; Zahedieh, "Overseas Expansion."

75. Breen, *Marketplace*, 137–40; Defoe, *Complete English Tradesman*, 25; Agnew, *Worlds Apart*, 3.

76. Woodbridge, "Peddler," 143–70, esp. 164.

77. Beaumont, *The royal merchant*, 6.

78. Woodbridge, "Peddler,"144; Barlow, *The justice of peace*, 7–9, 726. For South Carolina's punishment of rogues and vagabonds, see Minutes, *JCHA, November 8, 1734–June 7, 1735*, 55, 61, 79, 159. For Barbadian vagrant legislation, see An Act to Prevent the Prejudice That May Happen to This Island by Loose and Vagrant Persons in and about the Same, n.d., in *Acts of Assembly, Passed in the Island of Barbadoes*, 37. Barbados outlawed traveling merchants in 1668. See An Act Prohibiting Wandering Persons from Carrying Goods and Wares in Packs, or Otherwise, from House to House in This Island, in ibid., 64.

79. Spufford, *Great Reclothing*, 10. J. G. A. Pocock argues that the debates regarding virtue and movable/landed property began in earnest in the 1690s, twenty years after the first settlement in South Carolina; *Virtue, Commerce, and History*, 65–66. See also Berger, *Most Necessary Luxuries*, 32.

80. Woodbridge, "Peddler," 52, 63, 145; Spufford, *Great Reclothing*, 21–31.

81. Act against Vagabonds, February 29, 1764 *CRG*, 18:588.

82. Act 269, in Cooper and McCord, *Statutes at Large of South Carolina*, 2:309.

83. May 16, 1751, in Hawes, "Proceedings of the President and Assistants in Council of Georgia," 50.

84. Minutes, *JCHA, June 2, 1724–June 16, 1724*, 4; May 16, 1751, in Hawes, "Proceedings of the President and Assistants in Council of Georgia," 50.

85. *JCHA, June 2, 1724–June 16, 1724*, 4.

86. Proprietors to Governor and Council, March 7, 1680/1, *BPRO-SC*, 1:115.

87. Proprietors to Governor and Council, February 21, 1680/1, *BPRO-SC*, 1:104.

88. Proprietors to Governor and Council, March 7, 1680/1, *BPRO-SC*, 1:116.

89. By 1708 Indian slaves made up 25 percent of South Carolina's slave population; Ramsey, *Yamasee War*, 37.

90. Bailyn, *Origins of American Politics*, 86–87.

91. Scheme for Regulating the Indian Trade, 1751, *DRIA*, 1:89.

92. Talk of the Cherokee Indians to Governor Glen, November 15, 1751, *DRIA*, 1:181–83; *DRIA*, 1:446–49.

93. The Red Coat King to Governor Glen, July 26, 1753, *DRIA*, 1:380; Governor Glen to the Cherokee Head Men, June 13, 1754, *DRIA*, 1:521.

94. Minutes, August 3, 1711, *JCIT*, 16. See also Minutes, March 25, 1713, *JCIT*, 42.

95. Colonel Mackey to Theopilus Hastings, July 24, 1716, *JCIT*, 86. William Ramsey argues that this episode underlines the dangers posed by having two competing discourses in the Southeast, trade talk and treaty talk; *Yamasee War*, 79–97.

96. Agnew, *Worlds Apart*, 44–49; Muldrew, *Economy of Obligation*, 63; Sacks, *Widening Gate*, 77–79; Lloyd, *Alien Merchants*, 2–3.

97. Barlow, *The justice of peace*, 206.

98. Minutes, April 13, 1692, in Salley, *Journal of the Grand Council*, April 11, 1692–September 26, 1692, 5. This measure grew out of the history of South Carolinians trading with pirates; see Sirmans, *Colonial South Carolina*, 7, 39–43, 45, 50, 53, 54.

99. An Act to Prevent Abuses by False Weights and Measures, 1710, in Trott, *Laws of the Province of South-Carolina*, 59, 168. See also An Act for Settling a Fair and Markets, 1723, ibid., 409–11. Similar laws were passed in Barbados: see An Act for Weights and Measures, 1652, in *Acts of Assembly, Passed in the Island of Barbadoes*, 6; An Act for Establishing Market Days, 1661, Repeal in 1668, ibid., 58; An Act concerning Forestallers and Ingrossers of Provisions, 1672, ibid., 83–88; An Act to Prevent the Inconveniencies upon the Inhabitants of This Island by Forestallers, Ingrossers and Regulators, 1676, ibid., 96–98; An Act for the Better Regulating of Outcries in Open Market, 1688, ibid., 128–29.

100. Ditz, "Secret Selves," 219. See also Finkelstein, *Harmony and the Balance*, 15–16, 22–25.

101. "White Indian" is a term used by James Axtell to describe Europeans who chose to join Native American communities. Axtell, *Invasion Within*, 302–27. For a general historiographical essay on cultural brokerage, see Hinderaker, "Translation and Cultural Brokerage," 357–75. For the uneasy position of people who spanned two cultures in colonial America, see Kupperman, *Indians and English*, 212–40; Lepore, *Name of War*, 21–47; Merrell, "'Cast of His Countenance'"; Merrell, *Into the American Woods*, 37–38, 64–65, 94–95, 289–94. For a French description of an English trader, see Galloway, "Choctaws at the Border," 338–39.

102. Barker, "Indian Traders," 142. For relationships between Native American women and British Indian trader men, see Barker, "'Much Blood and Treasure,'" 149–67; Braund, *Deerskins and Duffels*, 36, 78, 83–86; Hatley, *Dividing Paths*, 52–63; Perdue, "'Sprightly Lover,'" 165–78; Piker, *Okfuskee*, 166–76.

103. Agnew, *Worlds Apart*, 68; Woodbridge, "Peddler," 160; Muldrew, *Economy of Obligation*, 148.

104. Dionne and Mentz, "Introduction: Rogues and Early Modern English Culture," 1–2; Barnwell, "Tuscarora Expedition," 43; Deposition of James Francis, June 1, 1751, *DRIA*, 1:24; Governor James Glen Talk, November 14, 1751, *DRIA*, 1:197; Brewer and Baillie, "Journal of George Pawley's 1746 Agency," 18. For the disguises of itinerant workers, see Fumerton, "Making Vagrancy (In)Visible."

105. Pennington, "South Carolina Indian War of 1715," 254.

106. Minutes, July 16, 1715, *JCIT*, 56–57.

107. Oral Report to the Commissioners of Trade, July 26, 1715, *JCIT*, 62.

108. Oral Report to the Commissioners of Trade, July 15, 1715, Great Britain, *JCIT*, 2:54.

109. This trope persisted long after South Carolina became a royal colony; see Boulware, "'Traders, Pedlars, and Idle Fellows,'" 53–72; Minutes, *JCHA, November 8, 1734–June 7, 1735*, 20; Minutes, May 16, 1751, *DRIA*, 1:50–51; January 8–January 12, 1760, in Warren and Lowery, *South Carolina Newspapers*. It used to be standard for historians to accept the colonists' interpretation of the causes of

the Yamasee War; see Axtell, *Indians' New South*, 49; Schrager, "Yamasee Indians," 173. For a synopsis of the Yamasee War historiography, see Ramsey, "'Something Cloudy in Their Looks,'" 44–49. Recently, a handful of historians have worked against this trend of blaming Indian traders for the strife in the Southeast; see Ramsey, *Yamasee War*, 13–53; Hann, "'Trade Do's Not Flourish as Formerly'"; Hall, *Zamumo's Gifts*, 117–44; Kelton, "Shattered and Infected."

110. Minutes, July 17, 1716, *JCIT*, 81.

111. Crane, *Southern Frontier*, 197–98.

112. Samuell Muckleroy and Joseph Thompson to Eleazer Wiggan, July 6, 1716, *JCIT*, 71; Minutes, July 10, 1716, *JCIT*, 73–74; An Act for the Better Regulation of the Indian Trade (n.d.), *JCIT*, 327.

113. Instructions to the Storekeeper, &c., July 6, 1716, *JCIT*, 72; An Account of Prices of Goods negotiated on April 30, 1716, *JCIT*, 89.

114. Crane, *Southern Frontier*, 200; Scheme for Regulating the Indian Trade, 1751, *DRIA*, 1:136.

115. Records of His Majesty's Council in South Carolina, July 17, 1725, SCDAH, 63–64.

116. February 29, 1764, *CRG*, 18:588–98.

117. The original of the Evans journal, which includes entries from 1700 to 1715, is split between the Library of Congress and the South Caroliniana Library. The South Caroliniana Library has handwritten transcriptions of some, but not all, of the journal portions housed at the Library of Congress. James H. Merrell discusses the Evans journal as a personal rather than an official document; *Indians' New World*, 73. Despite the fact that in parts of the journal Evans discusses conducting inquiries among the Tuscarora Indians about a murder, substantial evidence confirms that colonial officials did not commission or collect this journal. Personal receipts, promissory notes, and accounts of exchanges are interspersed throughout its pages, and there is no stamp or signature confirming official processing. In addition to these few clues, Evans's journal differs from diplomatic journals of the time in content and concentration. Indian traders who were commissioned to carry out diplomatic missions for colonial governments recorded with great detail the physical and social characteristics of the peoples they visited. If colonial officials instructed them to meet with particular leaders to negotiate specific problems, the traders transcribed both their own words and the words of the Indians they met with, including impressions of the sincerity of the Indians. The amount of detail expected of diplomatic journals is not surprising; colonial officials wanted to be apprised of all dimensions of potentially hostile communities. Further, officials wanted to be sure that their ambassadors were saying and doing the right things. The Evans journal reveals surprisingly little about the Indian towns he visited. Unlike existing official documents, Evans's journal fails to record how many people lived in their towns, the extent of their weaponry, or their loyalty toward the colonists. Only one entry speaks directly about the Indians he visits, and from it one can garner only the following cultural specificities: first, Tuscarora leaders hunted and traveled long distances to trade for salt, facts we learn because Evans is unable to speak to the two leaders who have gone

hunting and salt trading; second, the Tuscaroras had a town-based form of government, which we learn because the Tuscarora Indians as a whole are not able to give a firm decision because the leaders are elsewhere. To compare the Evans journal to known official journals, see Journal of Tobias Fitch, South Carolina Council Journal, 3:50–59, SCDAH; Brewer and Baillie, "Journal of George Pawley's 1746 Agency"; Salley, Journal of Colonel John Herbert; A. Moore, Naire's Muskhogean Journals.

118. Evans accounts for "money spent in Carolina" in his journal; Evans Journal, SCL, 3. On March 22, 1711, South Carolina gave an Indian license to David Crawly, John Evans, and Richard Jones of Virginia; JCIT, 7. Evans also took out trading licenses in Virginia; see Palmer et al., Calendar of Virginia State Papers, 1:155–56.

119. Evans Journal, SCL, 1, 5.

120. Evans Journal, LOC, 18.

121. Although not all of the place-names that Evans gives match up, the distances do. Enough of the names are common to conclude that Evans was discussing the same places but giving the alternate English and Native American place-names; Evans Journal, LOC, 14.

122. In Evans's journal he describes traveling through much of the land he would later purchase. Evans purchased 1,001 acres in Prince George County on Stony Creek, December 23, 1714. On November 13, 1721, he bought land that spanned Sappone Creek at the Trading Branch. He bought 200 acres on the south side of Nottoway River and the Little Swamp, which is probably the swamp he referred to as "Small Swamp" in his journal; Nugent and Virginia State Library, Cavaliers and Pioneers, 3:166, 231, 303.

123. Barker, "'Much Blood and Treasure,'" 93–94; Pressly, Rim of the Caribbean, 178, 201; Bossy, "Godin & Co." For the prerequisites for holding positions of power in the colonial Southeast, see Gallay, Formation of a Planter Elite, 68. In this way, Indian traders who were operating in the field were similar to the larger Indian trading firms in Charles Town who were both merchants and planters; Sirmans, Colonial South Carolina, 110–11.

124. For a surveying example, see "Journal of the Proceedings of the Commissioners Appointed to Ascertain and Mark the Boundary Lines Agreeably to Treaties between the Indian Nations and the United States," in Hawkins, Collected Works of Benjamin Hawkins, 144, 149–51. Evans did not use surveying instruments, but rather estimated distances based on the time it took to travel; Pett-Conklin, "Cadastral Surveying in Colonial South Carolina," 4, 69–104. For a compelling argument about the creation of a hybrid cartography that combined Native American path maps and European senses of space, see Paulett, Empire of Small Places, 23–30.

125. Minutes, August 3, 1711, JCIT, 16. See also Minutes, March 25, 1713, JCIT, 42; Colonel Mackey to Theopilus Hastings, July 24, 1716, JCIT, 86.

126. James Adair to Wm. Pinckney, May 7, 1751, DRIA, 1:56. See also James Beamer to Governor Glen, May 27, 1754, DRIA, 1:507.

127. Cornelius Dogharty to Governor Glen, July 31, 1751, DRIA, 1:115.

128. Anthony Dean to Cornelius Doharty, May 1, 1751, *DRIA*, 1:73. For settler rhetoric, see Yirush, *Settlers, Liberty, and Empire*, 222–26.

129. Brown, Rae, and Company, to the Honorable Trustees, February 13, 1750, *CRG*, 26:153.

130. John Campbell to Governor Glen, September 18, 1750, *DRIA*, 1: 6.

131. Petition of Lachlan McGillivray, *DRIA*, 1:518.

132. Cashin, "Gentlemen of Augusta," in *Colonial Augusta*, 39.

133. Brewer and Baillie, "Journal of George Pawley's 1746 Agency," 12.

134. July 19, 1718, *JCIT*, 306.

135. Proceedings of the Council concerning Indian Affairs, May 31, 1753, *DRIA*, 1:398–99.

136. Scheme for Regulating the Indian Trade, 1751, *DRIA*, 1:88. See also "An Account of Prices of Goods &c. Settled between Col. James Moore and the Conjuror, the 30th Day of April, 1716," *JCIT*, 89; "A Schedule of the Stated Prices of the Goods, as They Are to Be Disposed of, to the Indians in Barter," August 9, 1716, *JCIT*, 104; Instructions to Captain Bartholomew Gaillard, October 2, 1716, *JCIT*, 116; September 10, 1717, *JCIT*, 205; "A Table of Rates to Barter By," April 23, 1718, *JCIT*, 269; Commissioners to Captain Glover, Creek Prices of Goods, June 3, 1718, *JCIT*, 281; July 19, 1718, *JCIT*, 306; Proceedings of the Council concerning Indian Affairs, May 28, 1753, *DRIA*, 1:388; Oglethorpe and Lower Creek Indians, "Oglethorpe's Treaty," 14–15; *Mississippi Provincial Archives*, 3:303; Records of the Georgia Trustees, October 9, 1734, *CRG*, 2:73; H. Berenger de Beaufain to Georgia Governor, October 10, 1743, *CRG*, 24:126.

137. Shovlin, "War and Peace," 318–19.

138. Instructions for Waties, August 7, 1716, *JCIT*, 95.

139. Instructions to Bartholomew Gaillard, October 2, 1716, *JCIT*, 115–16.

140. October 18, 1716, *JCIT*, 119; November 26, 1716, *JCIT*, 132; March 7, 1718, *JCIT*, 259; July 5, 1718, *JCIT*, 298.

141. March 7, 1718, *JCIT*, 259.

142. December 5, 1717, *JCIT*, 238; January 16, 1718, *JCIT*, 248.

143. Skiagunsta, the Warrior of Keowee, to James Glen, November 26, 1751, *DRIA*, 1:193; Proceedings of the Council concerning Indian Affairs, July 5, 1753, *DRIA*, 1:439.

144. Instructions to Eleazar Wiggan, January 31, 1717, *JCIT*, 156.

145. Muldrew, *Economy of Obligation*, 43.

146. Ibid.

147. Sacks, *Widening Gate*, 313–15; Leng, "Epistemology."

148. March 10, 1736, *CRG*, 21:138–39. For an account of the grim economic reality in early Savannah, see Pressly, *Rim of the Caribbean*, 13–15.

149. Journal of Earl Egmont, March 13, 1739, *CRG*, 5:353.

150. Journal of Earl Egmont, January 8, 1739, *CRG*, 5:236.

151. T. H. Breen argues that sellers and buyers were fully aware of current market values; Breen, *Marketplace*, 120.

152. Here I disagree with Steven Hahn, who I believe overstates the Creeks' understanding of the marketplace; *Invention of the Creek Nation*, 118. For an impressive

reconstruction of the economic conditions that influenced the trade with Southeastern Native Americans prior to the Yamasee War, see Ramsey, *Yamasee War*, 57–78.

153. November 22, 1751, *DRIA*, 1:147.

154. Scheme for Regulating the Indian Trade, *DRIA*, 1:88.

155. Journal of an Indian Trader, *DRIA*, 2:63.

156. H. Berenger de Beaufain to the Georgia Governor, October 10, 1743, *CRG*, 24:126.

157. George Chicken, August 3, 1725, "Colonel Chicken's Journal," in S. Williams, *Early Travels*, 104.

158. Journal of an Indian Trader, *DRIA*, 2:65.

159. Scheme for Regulating the Indian Trade, *DRIA*, 1:87–88.

160. Journal of Thomas Bosomworth, January 1, 1753, *DRIA*, 1:326.

161. Proceedings of the Council concerning Indian Affairs, June 2, 1753, *DRIA*, 1:406–7.

162. Though they were not allowed to negotiate prices personally, traders were not completely excluded from the price determination process. If traders protested that they simply could not afford to sell at a particular price, colonial officials would raise the official price of the item; see Governor Glen's Talk to the Cherokee Indians, November 22, 1751, *DRIA*, 1:147.

163. Proceedings of the Council concerning Indian Affairs, June 2, 1753, *DRIA*, 1:407. For other episodes of Creek Indian irritation over government refusal to lower prices, see Piker, *Okfuskee*, 58.

164. Historians have noted that Indian women who married European traders had more access to goods than other members of Native American communities. Perdue, "'Sprightly Lover,'" 172–73; Piker, *Okfuskee*, 168.

165. Waselkov and Braund, *William Bartram on the Southeastern Indians*, 47.

166. July 16, 1715, in Great Britain, Board of Trade, *Journal of the Commissioners for Trade and Plantations*, 2:56–57.

167. Silverman, *Thundersticks*, 75–76.

168. Affidavit of William Thomson, undated, *DRIA*, 1:51.

169. July 11, 1735, G. Jones and Peucher, "'We Have Come to Georgia with Pure Intentions,'" 117.

170. Breen, *Tobacco Culture*, 94–95.

171. Muldrew, *Economy of Obligation*, 174; Robert Raper, October 17, 1759, Robert Raper Letter Book, 1759–70, South Carolina Historical Society, Charleston, S.C.

172. John Brownfield to the Georgia Trustees, March 10, 1736, *CRG*, 21:138–39; Defoe, *Complete English Tradesman*, 87.

173. Act of the Georgia Legislature, February 2, 1757, *CRG*, 18:172–81.

174. Harman Verelst to George Oglethorpe, August 11, 1738, *CRG*, 30:5.

175. Gallay, *Formation of a Planter Elite*, 58–59.

176. A. Moore, "Thomas Nairne's 1708 Western Expedition," 34–35.

177. Adair, *History of the American Indians*, 416–17.

178. Ramsey, *Yamasee War*, 20–21.

179. Hahn, *Invention of the Creek Nation*, 76; Ramsey, *Yamasee War*, 24–25. An individual could harvest between twenty and one hundred deerskins a year; Waselkov, "Eighteenth-Century Anglo-Indian Trade," 202. Paul Pressly estimates that on the eve of the American Revolution, merchants in South Carolina and Georgia who dealt in deerskins owed the equivalent of 670,000 pounds of deerskins to British creditors, which would require that every Southeastern Indian individual repay an entire season's worth of skins; *Rim of the Caribbean*, 210.

180. March 25, 1713, *JCIT*, 42; Minutes, September 25, 1713, *JCIT*, 50–51; January 25, 1717, *JCIT*, 150; Ramsey, *Yamasee War*, 25.

181. Salley, *Journal of Colonel John Herbert*, 4.

182. June 10, 1712, *JCIT*, 26.

183. Hahn, *Invention of the Creek Nation*, 81–82.

184. Adair, *History of the American Indians*, 416–17.

185. June 10, 1712, *JCIT*, 26.

186. Agreed upon Instructions for the Commissioners Met at the House of Mr. Geo. Hadderell, July 10, 1712, *JCIT*, 36. The commissioners added this rule to the Indian Agent Instruction List on December 18, 1712; *JCIT*, 39.

187. December 18, 1712, *JCIT*, 39.

188. Sirmans, *Colonial South Carolina*, 107–11.

189. Breen, *Tobacco Culture*, 94; see also 133–41, 161–75. See also Breen, *Marketplace*, 137–39; Jowett, "Middleton and Debt in *Timon of Athens*"; Wrightson, *Earthly Necessities*, 191, 293–94; Howell, *Commerce before Capitalism*, 25–30; Waddell, *God, Duty and Community*, 49–50.

190. Lud. Grant to Governor Glen, March 27, 1755, *DRIA*, 2:42.

191. Sherman, *Finance and Fictionality*, 15.

192. William Stephens to the Georgia Trustees, March 16, 1739, *CRG*, 22.1:365–66.

193. Hunt, *Middling Sort*, 24, 80; Sacks, *Widening Gate*, 61, 65–66; Hancock, *Citizens of the World*, 83–84; Bosher, "Huguenot Merchants," 77–102. The Indian trade also was organized around family; Barker, "Indian Traders," 148–49.

194. Muldrew, *Economy of Obligation*, 3; see also 125–47. See also Wrightson, *Earthly Necessities*, 300–303.

195. Sherman, *Finance and Fictionality*, 14–54.

196. Pocock, *Virtue, Commerce, and History*, 98.

197. Thomas Causton to the Trustees, November 26, 1736, *CRG*, 21:273.

198. John Brownfield to the Trustees, March 10, 1736, *CRG*, 21:138–39.

199. Commissioners to Theophilus Hastings, July 24, 1716, *JCIT*, 86; Crane, *Southern Frontier*, 152–53. Tom Hatley states that the Cherokee had difficulty understanding that an item given on credit was not a gift, a position I am uncomfortable with precisely because it mimics the accusations of colonial officials against those they considered economically incompetent; *Dividing Paths*, 48.

200. Piker, *Okfuskee*, 161.

201. Commissioners to Theophilus Hastings, July 24, 1716, *JCIT*, 86.

202. November 1, 1716, *JCIT*, 120–21.

203. July 10, 1725, Records of His Majesty's Council in South Carolina, 3:59.

204. Salley, *Journal of Colonel John Herbert*, 18–19.

205. Ibid., 18.

206. Talk between James Glen and Cherokee of Hiwasee, Stecoe, Tuccoigia, Toxoway, November 14, 1752, *DRIA*, 1:191–92.

207. For an early example of debt extension, see Journal of John Evans, 1702–1715, SCL, 4.

208. Adair, *History of the American Indians*, 416–17. Earlier in his work (p. 319), Adair discussed an incident in which the Georgia governor forgave all Indian debts.

209. January 9, 1759, William Richardson, "Diary, 1758–1759," transcribed by William B. Jack, p. 26, http://www.parsonjohn.org/images/Richardson.pdf, accessed July 29, 2014.

210. Boulware, *Deconstructing the Cherokee Nation*, 41.

211. Beck, "Persuasive Politics and Domination," 20; G. Wilson, Marcoux, and Koldehoff, "Square Pegs in Round Holes," 44, 46.

212. Ramsey, *Yamasee War*, 25.

213. For evidence of individuals trading on their own behalf, see Instructions to Agent John Wright, May 30, 1711, *JCIT*, 9; Instructions to Agent John Wright, August 3, 1711, *JCIT*, 14; April 17, 1712, *JCIT*, 23; June 20, 1712, *JCIT*, 27; October 25, 1712, *JCIT*, 38; March 26, 1713, *JCIT*, 43; July 27, 1716, *JCIT*, 92; November 26, 1716, *JCIT*, 132; January 25, 1717, *JCIT*, 150; July 5, 1718, *JCIT*, 298.

214. January 25, 1717, *JCIT*, 151–52.

215. Cherokee of Hiwasee, Stecoe, Tuccoigia, Toxoway Talk to James Glen, November 15, 1751, *DRIA*, 1:181. See also Talk of the Cherokee Indians to Governor Glen, November 14, 1751, *DRIA*, 1:175; Upper and Lower Creek Talk, May 31, 1753, *DRIA*, 1:388–408; Talk of Caneecatee of Chote and Others, April 22, 1751, *DRIA*, 1:253–54; Tasate and Chickee to Governor Glen, October 6, 1752, *DRIA*, 1:356; Warriors of Highwassee and Tommothy to Governor Glen, *DRIA*, 1:505; Wallace, "'Building Forts in Their Hearts,'" 26.

216. Brown, Rae, and Co. to William Pinckney, May 15, 1751, *DRIA*, 1:59; Talk of the Cherokee Towns to Governor Glen, May 6, 1751, *DRIA*, 1:172–73; Talk of the Cherokee Towns to Governor Glen, November 14, 1751, *DRIA*, 1:176; Anthony Dean to Governor Glen, April 13, 1752, *DRIA*, 1:260; Proceedings of the Council concerning Indian Affairs, May 28, 1753, *DRIA*, 1:392.

217. R. White, *Roots of Dependency*, 52–53, 74–75, 80; Hall, *Zamumo's Gifts*, 87; Beck, *Chiefdoms, Collapse, and Coalescence*, 157, 236–37, 243.

218. July 9, 1712, *JCIT*, 32, 36.

219. Instructions to Theophilus Hastings, July 19, 1718, *JCIT*, 311; *DRIA*, 1:72, 175, 232, 305, 414, 451; Brewer and Baillie, "Journal of George Pawley's 1746 Agency," 15; Piker, *Four Deaths of Acorn Whistler*, 89; Sweet, *Negotiating for Georgia*, 40–60.

220. September 12, 1717, Council Journal, Green Copy, SCDAH, 122.

221. May 9, 1717, *JCIT*, 178; Piker, *Four Deaths of Acorn Whistler*, 86–87.

222. "All the ceremonies," "Historical Relation of Facts Delivered by Ludovick Grant," 57; December 29, 1758, Richardson, "Diary, 1758–1759," 21.

223. Piker, *Four Deaths of Acorn Whistler*, 100–103, 136–41; Beck, *Chiefdoms, Collapse, and Coalescence*, 240–41.

224. [Talks] of the King[s], Chiefs and Warriors of the Chickasaw Nation [to] the Governor [of] Georgia, undated, TCC, Document TCC223, 2, accessed June 2, 2015.

225. "Historical Relation of Facts Delivered by Ludovick Grant," 65–68. Note that I find Ouconecaw's account more reliable than Alexander Cuming's; "Journal of Sir Alexander Cuming (1730)," in S. Williams, *Early Travels*, 115–46. Cuming had a vested interest in overstating the import of his mission, as he was attempting to secure a place for himself within the empire, was in debt, and also viewed his mission as part of a grand apocalyptic narrative; Sir Alexander Cuming, London Saturday De.r. 18/19, 1764, Commonplace Book, 1739–65, Folder 2, 3–7; The Humble Memorials of Sir Alexander Cuming, Baronet, Commonplace Book, 1755, Folder 3, Sir Alexander Cuming Papers, Newberry Library, Vault Ayer MS 204. For the importance of age to Southeastern Indian leaders, see LeMaster, *Brothers Born of One Mother*, 74–77; Wallace, "'Building Forts in Their Hearts,'" 175–77; Shoemaker, *Strange Likeness*, 119.

226. Hatley, *Dividing Paths*, 160; Tortora, *Carolina in Crisis*, 17–20. For other instances of the inability of the British to choose and control Southeastern Indian leaders, see Wallace, "Building Forts in Their Hearts," 171; Brewer and Baillie, "Journal of George Pawley's 1746 Agency," 13.

227. Tlahlo (Chehaws), Oakalpetchie (Oakmulges), Youlialie (Oucatchees), Toposokoie (Palochucholes) Talk to Georgia Governor James Oglethorpe, SCDAH, 785; *DRIA*, 1:126, 506.

228. Talk of Governor Glen to the Cherokees concerning Their Treaty, November 26, 1751, *DRIA*, 1:191. For the ongoing concern about weights and measures, see Knox, "Christian Priber's Cherokee 'Kingdom of Paradise,'" 324–25; Scheme for Regulating the Indian Trade, 1751, *DRIA*, 1:88; Talk of Governor Glen to the Cherokee Indians, November 20, 1751, *DRIA*, 1:185–86; Lud. Grant to Governor Glen, May 3, 1752, *DRIA*, 1:262; Lud. Grant to Governor Glen, March 27, 1755, *DRIA*, 2:41–42; Benjamin Martyn to the President and Assistants of Georgia, July 10, 1751, *CRG*, 31:235.

229. *DRIA*, 1:254. See also *DRIA*, 1:262–63.

230. An Act to Prevent Abuses by False Weights and Measures, 1710, in Trott, *Laws of the Province of South-Carolina*, 59, 168. See also An Act for Settling a Fair and Markets, 1723, in Trott, *Laws of the Province of South-Carolina*, 409–11; March 7, 1755, Georgia Legislature Minutes, *CRG*, 18:83.

231. January 23, 1717, *JCIT*, 149.

232. Letter to Agent, May 14, 1713, *JCIT*, 45; September 10, 1717, *JCIT*, 205; *DRIA*, 1:113.

233. October 4, 1717, *JCIT*, 216.

234. June 27, 1716, *JCIT*, 77; July 14, 1716, *JCIT*, 78; July 17, 1716, *JCIT*, 81; August 10, 1717, *JCIT*, 202; June 18, 1717, *JCIT*, 192; August 10, 1717, *JCIT*, 202; March 11, 1717, *JCIT*, 170; June 7, 1717, *JCIT*, 186.

235. May 8, 1718, *JCIT*, 272.

236. July 10, 1716, *JCIT*, 73.

237. Instructions to Theophilus Hastings, January 30, 1717, *JCIT*, 157.

238. January 29, 1717, *JCIT*, 154–55.

239. January 30, 1717, *JCIT*, 157.

240. November 23, 1717, *JCIT*, 231.

241. November 5, 1717, *JCIT*, 223.

242. July 17, 1716, *JCIT*, 81; July 23, 1716, *JCIT*, 83; July 24, 1716, *JCIT*, 84; June 27, 1716, *JCIT*, 77.

243. December 9, 1717, *JCIT*, 239.

244. July 24, 1716, *JCIT*, 84. See also Letter to Mr. Charlesworth Glover, February 27, 1717, *JCIT*, 167.

245. September 20, 1717, *JCIT*, 211.

246. June 4, 1718, *JCIT*, 282. Note that the one Native American who was hired as a packhorseman was paid about a third as much (3 pounds versus 10–12 pounds) as white men holding the same job; June 11, 1718, *JCIT*, 286.

247. Paulett, *Empire of Small Places*, 49–51, 123, 127–29, 136–41.

248. Defoe, *Complete English Tradesman*, 196.

249. August 30, 1725, Records of His Majesty's Council in South Carolina, 3:120–21.

250. Commissioners to Theophilus Hastings, July 24, 1716, *JCIT*, 86.

251. Ships did not leave port with only deerskins, and thus one needed to be able to negotiate with ship captains or South Carolina merchants who owned ships for transport space; see Charles Town Port Clearings, 1717–1721, SCDAH, 195000. On networks between deerskin exporters and British merchants, see Barker, "'Much Blood and Treasure,'" 78–83.

252. For Indian trader debts to larger merchants, see THJR; John Bee and William Loughton vs. Alexander Parris, Judgment Roll, 1720, S136002, Box 016A, Item 0136A, SCDAH; Robert Gouedy vs. Samuel Benn and Aaron Price, Judgment Roll, 1763, S136002, Box 057B, Item 0009A; South Carolina, General Assembly, "Report of the Committee"; Miscellaneous Records, vol. 76: 8–9, SCDAH. For late seventeenth- and early eighteenth-century relationships between Indian traders and Charlestown merchants, see Bossy, "Godin & Co."

253. Paulett, *Empire of Small Places*, 78–114; Braund, *Deerskins and Duffels*, 42–49; Cashin, "Gentlemen of Augusta," 29–58; Robert Pringle to Andrew Pringle, February 2, 1744, in Pringle, *Letterbook of Robert Pringle*, 1:808.

254. Braund, *Deerskins and Duffels*, 45.

255. Paulett, *Empire of Small Places*, 124–25; Pressly, *Rim of the Caribbean*, 18.

256. Letter from the President and Assistants, February 28, 1751, *CRG*, 26:168–69; H. Berenger de Beaufain to the Georgia Governor, October 10, 1743, *CRG*, 24:126; Journal of Thomas Bosomworth, *DRIA*, 1:329; Barker, "'Much Blood and Treasure,'" 97–100; Cashin, "Gentlemen of Augusta," 35–36.

257. See note 40 in this chapter.

258. Brown, Rae, and Company to the Honorable Trustees, February 13, 1750, *CRG*, 26:153–55.

259. Paulett, *Empire of Small Places*, 148–49; "Memorial of Robert Bunning and Others," November 22, 1751, *DRIA*, 1:148–51.

260. William discusses Levy Taylor, who appears in the Macartan and Campbell account book; Macartan and Campbell, Augusta, Ga., MS (R), August 1762–June 1766, SCL, 296, 340. The Mr. Scot that William mentions may be the Thomas Scott listed in the account book, 302, 307, 319, 329.

261. Anonymous Journal of a Visit to Indian Country, 1767, MS 10, GHS.

262. Ibid.

263. Ibid.

264. Ibid.

265. Journal of an Indian Trader, April 22, 1755, *DRIA*, 2:62.

266. October 18, 1716, *JCIT*, 119. See also November 26, 1716, *JCIT*, 132.

Chapter Three

1. Commissioners to Jos. Thomas, July 14, 1716, *JCIT*, 79; Commissioners to Theophilus Hastings, July 24, 1716, *JCIT*, 84.

2. Jansson, "Measured Reciprocity," 348.

3. Instructions to Meredith Hughes, February 20, 1717, *JCIT*, 163. See also Bonnefoy, "Journal of Antoine Bonnefoy," in S. Williams, *Early Travels*, 157.

4. Copy of a letter from Andrew Rutledge Esq. to Major General Oglethorpe, April 15, 1747, CO 5/655 part 2, accessed November 25, 2015, http://www.colonialamerica.amdigital.co.uk/Documents/Details/CO_5_655_PART2_05.

5. Piker, *Four Deaths of Acorn Whistler*, 46–49; Mercantini, *Who Should Rule at Home?*, 68–86.

6. Ben-Amos, *Culture of Giving*, 156–80, 215–27.

7. Ibid., 170.

8. Greene, *Quest for Power*, 318–21.

9. On Glen's belief that Native American affairs were central to empire, see Piker, *Four Deaths of Acorn Whistler*, 30–34, 46–48. On Georgia governor Henry Ellis's use of gift giving and his sense that securing Native American alliances was central to his mission, see Cashin, *Governor Henry Ellis*, 73–94.

10. Piker, *Four Deaths of Acorn Whistler*, 33, 40, 46–48.

11. S. Smith, *Sermon Preached . . . 1731*, 11, 15–19; Burton, *Sermon Preach'd . . . 1732*, 20; Ridley, *Sermon Preach'd . . . 1746*, 15.

12. August 13, 1777, KRC, Document KRC080.

13. April 28, 1752, *DRIA*, 1:211.

14. LeJau, "Letter of Francis LeJau," 261.

15. Thomas Jones Account, October 23, 1741, *CRG*, 23:123–24; for clothes as gifts, see also January 31, 1759, in Richardson, "Diary," 47.

16. Reck, *Von Reck's Voyage*, 46.

17. Longe, "Small Postscript," 30.

18. LaCombe, *Political Gastronomy*, 1, 77–79, 139.

19. Muller, *Mississippian Political Economy*, 83–87; L. Johnson, "Material Translations," 43–44.

20. Woodward, "Faithfull Relation," in Salley, *Narratives of Early Carolina*, 132.

21. Captain Raymond Demere to Governor Littleton, June 23, 1756, *DRIA*, 2:126. See also Boyd, "Diego Pena's Expedition," 22.

22. Sanford, "The Port Royal Discovery," in Cheves, *Shaftesbury Papers*, 66, 74.

23. Ibid., 224.

24. September 5, 1716, *JCIT*, 107.

25. Salley, *Journal of Colonel John Herbert*, 27.

26. Anonymous, April 12, 1736, in M. Lane, *General Oglethorpe's Georgia*, 1:260. For a similar eyewitness account, see Gordon, "An Account of the First Settling of the Colony of Georgia," KRC, Document KRC080, 27.

27. May 2, 1733, "Travel Diary of the Two Pastors Messrs. Boltzius and Gronau," in G. Jones, *Detailed Reports on the Salzburger Emigrants*, 1:81.

28. LeMahieu, "Gift Exchange," 129–42.

29. "The Humble Memorial of Edward Loughton and Richard Tranter," *BPRO-SC*, 4:196. For records of subsequent gifts for Native Americans, see Mancall, Rosenbloom, and Weiss, "Indians and the Economy of Eighteenth-Century Carolina," 306. For Georgia Trustee accounts for yearly funds attributed to Indian presents, see *CRG*, 3:85, 86, 93, 116, 117, 241, 255, 329, 341. For earlier South Carolina Indian presents, see *JCHA 1703*, 32, 47–48, 61, 106.

30. Jansson, "Measured Reciprocity," 355; Heal, *Hospitality*, 188–91, 204, 208; LaCombe, *Political Gastronomy*, 109–14, 136–40.

31. Thomas Causton to the Georgia Trustees, June 20, 1735, in M. Lane, *General Oglethorpe's Georgia*, 1:196. See also Georgia Governor and Council Record, November 13, 1754, *CRG*, 7:35.

32. William Stephens's Journal, February 13, 1739, *CRG*, 4:278–80.

33. Georgia Governor and Council Record, April 21, 1757, *CRG*, 7:546.

34. November 23, 1751, *DRIA*, 1:161–62. Southeastern Native American consumer tastes are discussed in chapter 4.

35. August 30, 1725, Record of the Majesty's Council in South Carolina, 3:125, SCDAH; William Stephens's Journal, May 4, 1740, *CRG*, 4:567; Presents Given to the Cherokee Indians, November 23, 1751, *DRIA*, 1:161–62; Receipts from the Headmen and Warriors of the Chickasaw Nation to Jerome Courtonne for Presents, March 30, 1756, *DRIA*, 2:114; "Deposition of Messrs. Burleigh (Quaker) and Simpson (Charles Town Merchant), December 8, 1736," South Carolina General Assembly, "Report of the Committee appointed to examine into the proceedings of the people of Georgia,"116; Mancall, Rosenbloom, and Weiss, "Indians and the Economy of Eighteenth-Century Carolina," 307.

36. L. Johnson, "Material Translations," 119–20.

37. Bienville to Pontchartrain, November 27, 1711, Mississippi Department of Archives and History, *Mississippi Provincial Archives*, 3:159.

38. That "present" and "reward for services" were synonymous in their interactions with the Cherokees during the Seven Years' War was suggested by Dowd, "'Insidious Friends.'"

39. Records of the Trustees, April 16, 1735, *CRG*, 2:95; Gordon, "An Account of the First Settling," 90.

40. Herbert, *Female Alliances*, 52–77; LaCombe, *Political Gastronomy*, 76–77.

41. July 24, 1716, *JCIT*, 84.

42. December 2, 1717, *JCIT*, 236.

43. January 30, 1717, *JCIT*, 155.

44. Munn, *Fame of Gawa*; Weiner, *Inalienable Possessions*; Mauss, *The Gift*.

45. Chickasaw Head Men and Warriors to Governor Glen, June 26, 1754, *DRIA*, 1:513.

46. Georgia, Trustees of, "Brief Account," 12.

47. Upper and Lower Creek Talk with Governor James Glen, May 31, 1753, *DRIA*, 1:398–99.

48. Information of George Johnson, October 2, 1754, *DRIA*, 2:11.

49. September 3, 1768, in Warren and Jones, *Georgia Governor and Council Journals*, 3:25.

50. James Wright Talk to the Creek Indians, undated, *CRG*, 38.1:249.

51. Journal of Tobias Fitch, July 10, 1725, Records of the Majesty's Council in South Carolina, SCDAH, 3:55.

52. Brewer and Baillie, "Journal of George Pawley's 1746 Agency," 15. See also Barker, "'Much Blood and Treasure,'" 142–43; November 14, 1717, *JCIT*, 228; Talk of Old Hop, the Governor of Chota, to the Governor of Virginia, July 23, 1756, in *Account of Major Lewis's Mission to the [Cherokee], Including Messages from Old Hop and Otassity to the Governor of Virginia*, CO 5/17 part 3, accessed November 19, 2015, http://www.colonialamerica.amdigital.co.uk/Documents/Details/CO_5_17 Part3_015. Silverman, *Thundersticks*, 77, 82–85.

53. Baden, *Tomotley*, appendix 2; Silverman, *Thundersticks*, 87.

54. Chaplin, *Subject Matter*, 206–7.

55. Silverman, *Thundersticks*, 16.

56. Governor Glen's Talk to the Cherokee, November 13, 1751, *DRIA*, 1:158; Journal of Tobias Fitch, July 10, 1725, Records of the Majesty's Council in South Carolina, SCDAH, 3:55.

57. *BPRO-SC*, 2:66. Although it is beyond the scope of this book, it seems likely that other European nations did this as well. For a sixteenth-century example of the Spanish deploying gifts of weapons to persuade Southeastern Indians to help them in their imperial battle, see Raymond de Fourquevaux (Ambassador of the French Court in Spain) to Charles IX, February 18, 1566, David B. Quinn Papers, Box 75, fol. 1, LOC.

58. January 26, 1717, *JCIT*, 153.

59. Salley, *Journal of Colonel John Herbert*, 25.

60. De Beauchamp, "Journal of De Beauchamps' Journey to the Choctaws," in Mereness, *Travels*, 279–80.

61. January 13, 1756, *DRIA*, 2:98.

62. Nathan Brownson, Talk Given to the Creek, 1781, TCC, Document TCC267.

63. Ibid.

64. John Martin, Talk Delivered at Savannah to the Tallesee King and the Headmen and Warriors of the Upper and Lower Creek Nations, October 29, 1782, TCC, Document TCC272.

65. Journal of the President and Assistants, August 17, 1749, *CRG*, 6:274

66. Captain Raymd. Demere to Governor Littleton, November 18, 1756, *DRIA*, 2:249. See also Dowd, "'Insidious Friends,'" 135–38.

67. Don Gregorio de Salinas Varona, Governor of Pensacola, September 9, 1717, in Boyd, "Documents Describing the Second and Third Expeditions of Lieutenant Diego Pena," 129.

68. Herman Verelst to Patrick Graham, August 24, 1749, *CRG*, 31:158.

69. Patrick Mackay to Thomas Causton, March 27, 1735, *CRG*, 20:290.

70. April 1, 1752, *DRIA*, 1:226.

71. John Highrider to James Glen, October 24, 1750, *DRIA*, 1:38–40.

72. Benjamin Martyn to WP and Assistants, March 11, 1751, *CRG*, 31:226–27.

73. Talk of Governor Glen to the Cherokees concerning Their Treaty, November 26, 1751, *DRIA*, 1:195.

74. De Beauchamp, "Journal of De Beauchamps' Journey to the Choctaws," 272.

75. Georgia Governor and Council Report, January 12, 1763, *CRG*, 9:17.

76. Talk of Governor Glen to the Cherokees concerning Their Treaty, November 26, 1751, *DRIA*, 1:195.

77. Talk of the Cherokee of Hiwassee, Stecoe, Tuccoigia and Toxoway, November 14, 1751, *DRIA*, 1:181.

78. Talk from Jud's Friend to Governor Glen, March 31, 1752, *DRIA*, 1:244.

79. Cherokee of Hiwasee, Stecoe, Tuccoigia, Toxoway Talk to Governor James Glen, November 28, 1751, *DRIA*, 1:197–98.

80. Journal of Tobias Fitch, July 10, 1725, Records of the Majesty's Council in South Carolina, SCDAH, 3:55.

81. See essays throughout Ethridge and Shuck-Hall, *Mapping the Mississippian Shatter Zone*; Beck, *Chiefdoms, Collapse, and Coalescence*, 99–222. David Silverman refers to this process as "the gun frontier"; *Thundersticks*.

82. James Oglethorpe to the Georgia Trustees, December 29, 1739, CO 5/654 part 2, accessed November 24, 2015, http://www.colonialamerica.amdigital.co.uk /Documents/Details/CO_5_654_Part2_005.

83. Chickasaw Head Men and Warriors to Governor Glen, June 26, 1754, *DRIA*, 1:513. See also [Talks] of the King[s], Chiefs and Warriors of the Chickasaw Nation [to] the Governor [of] Georgia, undated, TCC, Document TCC223, 2–3, accessed June 2, 2015; Talk of the Upper Creeks to Governor Glen, undated, *DRIA*, 1:225–26; Talgier and Wyawnoy, Chief War Captains of the Cheehaws, April 22, 1743, CO 5/655 part 2, accessed November 25, 2015, http://www.colonialamerica.amdigital .co.uk/Documents/Details/CO_5_655_PART2_007.

84. Killa Cunsta to Governor Glen, July 6, 1764, *DRIA*, 1:515. For the Chickasaw invoking shared enemies to argue for munitions, see Chickasaw Indian Talk, July 13, 1736, CO5/654 part 1, accessed November 25, 2015, http://www.colo nialamerica.amdigital.co.uk/Documents/Details/CO_5_654_Part1_029.

85. Cherokee Talk to the Board of Trade, September 9, 1730, CO5/4 part 2, accessed November 24, 2015, http://www.colonialamerica.amdigital.co.uk/Documents /Details/CO_5_4_Part2_014.

86. Cherokee to Governor Glen, April 1, 1752, *DRIA*, 1:227.

87. Coulter, *Journal of William Stephens*, 1:111, 116.

88. Talk of the Upper Creeks to Governor Glen, undated, *DRIA*, 1:225–26.

89. Lud. Grant to Governor Glen, May 3, 1752, *DRIA*, 1:262.

90. October 16, 1736, *CRG*, 21:214.

91. Swanson, *Social Organization*, 171.

92. Andrew Grant, Hugh Sterling, Patrick Tailfer and Patrick Houstoun to the Georgia Trustees, March 15, 1735, *CRG*, 20:266.

93. July 12, 1735, in G. Jones, *Detailed Reports on the Salzburger Emigrants*, 2:109.

94. July 26, 1735, in ibid., 2:113.

95. Orders by Captain Rayd. Demere, August 25, 1756, *DRIA*, 2:172.

96. Matthew Toole to Governor Glen, October 28, 1752, *DRIA*, 1:358–59.

97. July 26, 1735, in G. Jones, *Detailed Reports on the Salzburger Emigrants*, 2:113.

98. Cherokee Talk to the Board of Trade, September 9, 1730, CO 5/4 part 2.

99. Letters of Timothy Barnard, May 2, 1786, GDAH, 51–54. On white wings acting as symbols of peace during the peace negotiations between different Southeastern Indian groups, see A Discourse with the Indians in South Carolina, January 24–26, 1727, CO 5/387, 246, 247, accessed November 25, 2015, http://www.colonialamerica.amdigital.co.uk/Documents/Details/CO_5_387_084.

100. Waselkov and Braund, *William Bartram on the Southeastern Indians*, 49.

101. Cherokee Grant of Land to South Carolina, November 23, 1734, Records of the Secretary of the Province of SC, 1732–34, Book BB, 303–4, SCDAH.

102. Brewer and Baillie, "Journal of George Pawley's 1746 Agency," 15.

103. Journal of the Georgia President and Assistants, August 17, 1749, *CRG*, 6:271.

104. Henry Ellis to the Creek Nation, May 26, 1760, TCC, Document TCC263. See also Cussetaw and Buzzard Roost Indian Talk to Edward Telfair, May 27, 1786, in Letters of Timothy Barnard, 52–54, GDAH; Tallessee King to Governor of Georgia, April 11, 1787, in Letters of Timothy Barnard, 73, GDAH.

105. Martin, Talk Delivered at Savannah to the Tallesee King . . . , TCC, Document TCC272.

106. Talk of the White Lieutenant of the Oakfurkeys, August 15, 1792, in Creek Letters, part 1, 254, GDAH.

107. *CRG*, vol. 38, part 1 unpublished, on microfilm at GDAH, 256.

108. "Mr. Ingham's Journal," in Reese, *Our First Visit in America*, 175.

109. Ramsey, *Yamasee War*, 79–97.

110. "New Voyage to Georgia," 62.

111. "Mr. Ingham's Journal," 175. Given that the Southeastern Indians did not domesticate animals for milk, this episode is curious. It may be that Ingham is misidentifying the drink as dairy milk, when it could be a different liquid, such as hickory milk. It could also be that Scenauky acquired dairy milk from a colonist and is presenting it as an emblem of assimilation. Cattle became representative of colonization, and cows were often singled out by Native Americans for death during warfare because they served as such a strong emblem of colonization.

112. Appadurai, *Social Life of Things*, 23.

113. Cherokee Talk to the Board of Trade, September 9, 1730, CO 5/4 part 2.

114. Journal of the Proceedings of the Commissioners Appointed to Treat with the Southern Indians, 1785-86, TCC, DocumentTCC794.

115. Ibid.

116. Ibid.

117. Ibid.

118. Colonel Chicken to the Council, August 30, 1725, Records of His Majesty's Council in South Carolina, 3:125, SCDAH; Instructions to Bartholomew Gilliard, Factor at Santee, October 2, 1716, *JCIT*, 116.

119. Ulrich, *Age of Homespun*, 41–74.

120. Instructions Given to the Agent, July 9, 1712, *JCIT*, 33.

121. September 5, 1716, *JCIT*, 107. See also *JCIT*, 199, 206, 209, 310.

122. Instructions for the Agent, July 9, 1712, *JCIT*, 33.

123. September 26, 1716, *JCIT*, 112–13.

124. Ben-Amos, *Culture of Giving*, 208–14.

125. Governor Glen to King Malatchi, October 2, 1754, *DRIA*, 2:9.

126. For an examination of the networks that carried curiosities to Britain, see Murphy, "Portals of Nature"; Waselkov and Braund, *William Bartram on the Southeastern Indians*, 144–45.

127. Ashe, "Carolina, or a Description of the Present State of that Country," in Salley, *Narratives of Early Carolina*, 156. See also Governor Glen's Talk to the Cherokees, November 13, 1751, *DRIA*, 1:158.

Chapter Four

1. After the Yamasee War, most of the guns that entered Southeastern Indian territory did so as gifts. Therefore, the discussion of their consumption is primarily confined to chapter 3.

2. Hentschell, "Treasonous Textiles." For the class and gender implications of clothing, see Mowry, "Dressing Up and Dressing Down." See also A. Jones and Stallybrass, *Renaissance Clothing*, 1–14, 66; Loren, *Archaeology of Clothing*, 7–10, 27–28.

3. Mancall, Rosenbloom, and Weiss, "Indians and the Economy of Eighteenth-Century Carolina," 312.

4. Blanch, *The art of tanning*, 85; *Case of the leather-sellers*.

5. Clarkson, "Organization of the English Leather Industry," 245–56.

6. Staples, "'Useful, Ornamental or Necessary,'" 65.

7. For the complicated histories that surrounded goods that were unavoidably exotic, see Peck, *Consuming Splendor*.

8. Bickham, *Savages within the Empire*, 21–64.

9. Stallybrass, "Marx's Coat," 186.

10. Kuchta, "Making of the Self-Made Man"; Graeber, *Toward an Anthropological Theory of Value*, 95–96.

11. A. Jones and Stallybrass, *Renaissance Clothing*, 7.

12. Haulman, *Politics of Fashion*, 13–14, 17–18, 25–31, 46, 48, 81–216; Waldstreicher, "Why Thomas Jefferson"; Breen, *Marketplace*.

13. Chaplin, *Subject Matter*, 201–42.

14. Waselkov, "Eighteenth-Century Anglo-Indian Trade," 202.

15. Ashe, "Carolina, or a Description of the Present State of That Country," in Salley, *Narratives of Early Carolina*, 156; Hill, *Weaving New Worlds*, 9. Ambiguities in the basket trade make it difficult to know how many settlers utilized Southeastern Indian baskets. Extant written records may give the deceptive impression that the trade in baskets was nonexistent. It must be kept in mind, however, that baskets were not taxed as deerskins were, and thus may be invisible for that very reason. If baskets comprised a large portion of the Indian trade, however, the commissioners would have taken greater notice of them. Notably, officials did not dictate the price of baskets, as they did with deerskins.

16. Waselkov and Braund, *William Bartram on the Southeastern Indians*, 96, 144.

17. November 23, 1716, *JCIT*, 129. See also November 1, 1716, *JCIT*, 120; Opinion of the House of Commons in Relation to the Late Demands of Col. Theophilus Hastings, *JCIT*, 126.

18. January 23, 1717, *JCIT*, 149.

19. John Williams owned three Indian baskets, which were valued at a total of fifteen shillings; John Williams Estate, March 21, 1737, Microfilm ST 0467, 87, Inventories of Estates, vol. 68, SCDAH. Hannah Guerard left three Indian baskets as part of her estate; Hannah Guerard Estate, Microfilm ST 0467, Inventories of Estates, vol. 68, SCDAH.

20. Miscellaneous Records, vol. 62A: 437, SCDAH. For Holms's involvement in the trade monopoly, see September 6, 1716, *JCIT*, 108; November 1, 1716, *JCIT*, 121; September 12, 1717, *JCIT*, 207.

21. Darquier Estate, Microfilm ST 0489, Inventories of Estates, vol. 94A, 1771–74, SCDAH.

22. LeBass Estate, May 20, 1738, Microfilm ST 0467, 256, Inventories of Estates, vol. 68, SCDAH; McKenzie and Roche Estate, Microfilm ST 0470, Inventories of Estates, vol. 71 (original vol. KK), 1739–43, 49.

23. Bint Estate, October 30, 1745, Microfilm ST 0446, SCDAH.

24. Orlin, "Fictions of the Early Modern English Probate Inventory."

25. Poplin et al., "Archaeological Investigation of Schieveling Plantation," SCIAA; Calhoun et al., "Home Upriver," SCIAA.

26. List of deerskin exporters taken from W. Moore, "Largest Exporters of Deerskins." Thirteen exporter inventories were examined, none containing Indian-made products.

27. Groover, "Of Mindset and Material Culture"; Poplin et al., "Archaeological Investigation of Schieveling Plantation"; Bastian, "Fort Independence," SCIAA.

28. For a similar commitment in other parts of America by those who moved to rural areas to maintain their metropolitan identity, see Bushman, *Refinement of America*, 219–37.

29. Zierden, Calhoun, and Hacker-Norton, *Archdale Hall*. English borderlands may differ in this regard, for archaeological excavations at some other colonial settlements suggest that settlers did meld styles; Loren, *Archaeology of Clothing*, 59–88.

30. F. Moore, "A Voyage to Georgia," in Reese, *Our First Visit in America*, 123.

31. March 21, 1736/7, Microfilm ST 0467, 87, Inventories of Estates, vol. 68, SCDAH.

32. Baumgarten, *What Clothes Reveal*, 68; Haulman, *Politics of Fashion*, 161–62.

33. Merrell, *Indians' New World*, 33.

34. Braund, *Deerskins and Duffels*, 121.

35. Ray and Freeman, *"Give Us Good Measure"*; Ray, "Indians as Consumers in the Eighteenth Century," 320–43; Carlos and Lewis, *Commerce by a Frozen Sea*.

36. This chapter draws most heavily on four such orders: (1) a list of the initial goods that South Carolina settler Henry Woodward purchased in 1674, while he was trading with neighboring groups such as the Kiawah, and in 1675, after he established a trade with the Westo Indians; HWA; (2) an itemized account of three sizable purchases the experienced trader Theophilus Hastings made for the Cherokee trade in July 1713 and May and June 1714, which is included in the 1719 lawsuit that the South Carolina merchants Samuel Wragg and Jacob Satur brought against Hastings for defaulting on his debts; THJR; (3) records and advertisements that the Directors of the Cherokee Trade placed in the *South Carolina Gazette* soliciting particular goods needed to restock the public trading factory at Fort Prince George near the Lower Cherokee town of Keowee during its operation from 1762 to 1764; Journal of the Directors of the Cherokee Trade, 1762–1765, *DRIA*, 2:509–600; and (4) the account book of purchases made at George Galphin's Silver Bluff, Georgia, trading post from 1767 to 1772; GSB. For Creek Indians mentioning that they traded at the Silver Bluff Store, see "A Talk Delivered at Silver Bluff the Third Day of November 1779 to George Galphin Esq. Commissioner of Indian Affairs in Southern Departments by the Tallassee King," in George Galphin Letters (manuscript): Silver Bluff [Ga.], to Benjamin Lincoln, General and Commander in Chief of the Troops in the Southern Department, 1778–80, Newberry Library, Vault box Ayer MS 313, Folder 1.

37. Loren, *Archaeology of Clothing*, 5, 23–29.

38. Commissioners to Theophilus Hastings, February 27, 1717, *JCIT*, 168; Commissioners for the Indian Trade Instructions to Traders, April 23, 1718, *JCIT*, 269.

39. A State of the Province of Georgia, Attested upon Oath in the Court of Savannah, November 10, 1740, *CRG*, 2:72.

40. Brown, "Early Indian Trade," 123.

41. Sir William Keith, "A Short Discourse on the Present State of the Colonies in America with Respect to the Interest of Great Britain," 1728, CO 5/4 part 2:6, accessed November 24, 2015, http://www.colonialamerica.amdigital.co.uk/Doc uments/Details/CO_5_4_Part2_006.

42. DuPlessis, "Cloth and the Emergence of the Atlantic Economy," 75.

43. "A Description of the Golden Islands, with an Account of the Undertaking Now on Foot for Making a Settlement There," in Reese, *Most Delightful Country*, 43.

44. William Bull to the Lords Commissioners for Trade, July 20, 1738, *CRG*, 22.1:212–14.

45. Montgomery, *Textiles in America*, 177–79.

46. Slave Act, 1735, in Cooper and McCord, *Statutes at Large of South Carolina*, 7:396.

47. Baumgarten, *What Clothes Reveal*, 78–84.

48. Axtell, "First Consumer Revolution," 138; Braund, *Deerskins and Duffels*; DuPlessis, "Cloth and the Emergence of the Atlantic Economy."

49. May 22, 1674, HWA.

50. Reck, *Von Reck's Voyage*, 40; January 20, 1737, in G. Jones, *Detailed Reports on the Salzburger Emigrants*, 1:4, 8.

51. Journal of John Buckles, May 18, 1753, *DRIA*, 1:385.

52. THJR, 140–42.

53. *DRIA*, 2:568, 577; Public Cherokee Trade, Account Book, Goods Sold and Delivered out of the Fort Prince George Factory, August 31, 1762–September 29, 1763; original at the New-York Historical Society; copy at SCDAH. This account book records purchases that nearby settlers and soldiers and officers stationed at Fort Prince George purchased out of the public Cherokee trading fort. Although this document can be used to ascertain the variety of goods available to the Cherokee for purchase, it does not illuminate their actual purchasing behavior.

54. June 1, 1763, *DRIA*, 2:527; November 17, 1763, *DRIA*, 2:535; April 20, 1764, *DRIA*, 2:539.

55. Hawes, *Letter book of Thomas Raspberry*, 111–12.

56. Linen is mentioned in the advertisements of June 1, 1763, *DRIA*, 2:527; November 17, 1763, *DRIA*, 2:535; April 20, 1764, *DRIA*, 2:539. Wool is mentioned in the advertisements of October 7, 1762, *DRIA*, 2:516, and November 17, 1763, *DRIA*, 2:535.

57. November 19, 1762, *DRIA*, 2:519.

58. December 10, 1716, *JCIT*, 137.

59. December 31, 1716, *JCIT*, 142.

60. Ibid., 144.

61. Report of William Waties to the Commissioners, February 12, 1717, *JCIT*, 160.

62. April 29, 1717, *JCIT*, 176–77.

63. Baden, *Tomotley*, appendix 2. For other Southeastern Indian modifications of European goods, see Piker, *Okfuskee*, 147; Elliott and Folse Elliott, *Mount Pleasant*, 41, 51, 54; M. Smith et al., "Archaeological Investigations at Tomassee"; M. Harmon, "Eighteenth Century Lower Cherokee Adaptation," 132.

64. Letter to John Colleton, December 8, 1759, Robert Raper Letter Book (34/511), South Carolina Historical Society, Charleston, S.C., 22–23. See also January 16, 1716, *JCIT*, 147–48.

65. For description and sample of plains, see Queen, *Textiles for Colonial Clothing*, 16. See also Staples, "'Useful, Ornamental or Necessary.'" Half thicks were grouped with plains on some of the official price lists, indicating that they were of similar quality; A Table of Rates to Barter By, April 23, 1718, *JCIT*, 269; Agreement for the Prices of Goods with the Creek Indians, June 3, 1718, *JCIT*, 281; Montgomery, *Textiles in America*, 256, 272–73.

66. THJR, 140–42.

67. Oglethorpe and Lower Creek Indians, "Oglethorpe's Treaty with the Lower Creek Indians"; C. Jones, *Historical Sketch of Tomochichi*.

68. "Indian Half Breeds" are listed as Abraham and James Ladson. Timothy Barnard, Hannah, and Edward Hayns exhibited buying patterns consistent with purchases made for the Indian trade, particularly large quantities of goods such as cloth, beads, bells, and trading shirts; GSB, 27, 30, 34, 35, 38, 39, 44, 50, 56, 60, 67, 69, 70.

69. Daybook kept by John Blackwood and Alexander Nisbet, GD237/1/151, National Archives of Scotland. For a description of osnaburg, see Montgomery, *Textiles in America*, 313. Captain Raymond Demere of Fort Prince George requested osnaburgs for making bullet bags; *DRIA*, 2:173.

70. Cash book of Robert Nisbet, GD237/1/150, National Archives of Scotland.

71. THJR, 140–42.

72. November 17, 1763, *DRIA*, 2:535.

73. Montgomery, *Textiles in America*, 238. For a sample, see Queen, *Textiles for Colonial Clothing*, 14.

74. Queen, *Textiles for Colonial Clothing*, 14.

75. Baumgarten, *What Clothes Reveal*, 43; Montgomery, *Textiles in America*, 354.

76. THJR; Table of Goods and Prices for the Indian Trade, *DRIA*, 2:567.

77. For gifts of plains, see Mancall, Rosenbloom, and Weiss, "Indians and the Economy of Eighteenth-Century Carolina," 307. For purchases of plains for the Indian trade monopoly, see November 8, 1716, *JCIT*, 124 (300 yards); Commissioners to Theophilus Hastings, February 27, 1717, *JCIT*, 168 (unspecified amount); September 5, 1717, *JCIT*, 204 (unspecified amount); Commissioners to Charlesworth Glover, June 24, 1718, *JCIT*, 295 (unspecified amount); January 30, 1717, *JCIT*, 155; February 27, 1717, *JCIT*, 167 (191¾ yards of half thicks to Savano Town); Commissioners to Charlesworth Glover, April 29, 1717, *JCIT*, 176–177 (52½ yards to Savano Town); August 10, 1717, *JCIT*, 202–3 (six blankets, a mixture of duffels and half thicks, to Wineau [Winyaw]).

78. Waselkov and Braund, *William Bartram on the Southeastern Indians*, 121.

79. Adair, *History of the American Indians*, 70.

80. Hawes, *Letter book of Thomas Raspberry*, 49.

81. Ibid., 92.

82. Robert Pringle to Andrew Pringle, May 19, 1753, *Letterbook of Robert Pringle*, 2:552.

83. G. Jones, *Detailed Reports on the Salzburger Emigrants*, 1:208. See also Axtell, "First Consumer Revolution," 138; Adair, *History of the American Indians*, 8.

84. May 4, 1752, *DRIA*, 1:238; Potter, "Matchcoat"; Braund, *Deerskins and Duffels*, 122–23.

85. Elliott, "Yuchi in the Lower Savannah River Valley," 77–80.

86. Reck, *Von Reck's Voyage*, 128–29. Throughout the eighteenth century, Southeastern Indians continued to use skins to construct matchcoats; Adair, *History of the American Indians*, 69.

87. Elliott, "Yuchi in the Lower Savannah River Valley," 87.

88. LeMaster, *Brothers Born of One Mother*, 121–22.

89. Braund, *Deerskins and Duffels*, 130–31; M. Morris, *Bringing of Wonder*, 75.

90. *DRIA*, 2:527, 535, 539.

91. Ostenaco had another goal as well—to supplant the position of Attakullakulla (Little Carpenter); Tortora, *Carolina in Crisis*, 178.

92. D. King, *Memoirs of Lt. Henry Timberlake*, 59.

93. Ibid., 133fn.172.

94. Ibid., 75. For his rendition of Cherokee fashion, see also 24–25.

95. Francis Parsons and Joshua Reynolds painted their portraits while their subjects sat for them; Foreman, *Indians Abroad*, 70–71; Pratt, "Reynolds' 'King of the Cherokees,'" 149; D. King, *Memoirs of Lt. Henry Timberlake*, 134–35fn.176. There is some scholarly debate about whether the matchcoats (which some scholars call mantles or cloaks) the Cherokee visitors were depicted wearing should be characterized as English or Native clothing. Pratt refers to their "Europeanized dress," but she appears to categorize it as such because the clothing was manufactured in London; *American Indians in British Art*, 52. Gail DeBuse Potter, director of the Museum of the Fur Trade, on the other hand, believes that the construction of the covering in the Parsons portrait resembles other accounts we have of matchcoats, and thus categorizes it as a matchcoat; "The Matchcoat." The consistency of the components of the coverings in the portraits, particularly the lace hedging and cord, and the Cherokee purchasing habits, as well as Timberlake's account, lead me to believe that Timberlake instructed the London manufacturer to produce an item that resembled a matchcoat.

96. For the identities and names of the Cherokee visitors, see Vaughan, *Transatlantic Encounters*, 167–68.

97. Hudson, *Southeastern Indians*, 144–45, 166–67, 386–87; Rodning, "Late Prehistoric and Protohistoric Shell Gorgets," 36.

98. October 10, 1716, *JCIT*, 117; April 16, 1717, *JCIT*, 174; April 27, 1717, *JCIT*, 176.

99. THJR, 140–42.

100. Mathins is not a known Indian trader, and the amount of blue cloth he purchased, 3¾ yards, was not terribly substantial. During this same transaction, however, he did buy 4½ dozen hair buttons, which indicates this purchase may have been Indian trade–related; GSB, 7.

101. July 17, 1716, *JCIT*, 81.

102. June 27, 1716, *JCIT*, 77.

103. July 23, 1716, *JCIT*, 83.

104. July 24, 1716, *JCIT*, 84.

105. November 22, 1716, *JCIT*, 125–27.

106. December 31, 1716, *JCIT*, 143; January 28, 1717, *JCIT*, 154; November 27, 1717, *JCIT*, 232; *JCIT*; February 20, 1717, *JCIT*, 162; Commissioners to Meredith Hughes, February 20, 1717, *JCIT*, 163.

107. "Daily Register of the Two Pastors, Mr. Boltzius and Mr. Gronau," May 2, 1735, in G. Jones, *Detailed Reports on the Salzburger Emigrants*, 2:83.

108. There has been no extensive study of Native American acceptance of, or rejection of, European currency. It is possible that colonists dissuaded the Native

Americans from adopting European currency by accepting only skins and furs in exchange for goods; Directors to Edward Wilkinson, March 2, 1763, *DRIA*, 2:583.

109. Baden, *Tomotley*, appendix 2.

110. Thomas, *Entangled Objects*, 100; A. Jones and Stallybrass, *Renaissance Clothing*, 17, 273–75.

111. Letters of Mr. Matthews and Mr. Carteret, in Cheves, *Shaftesbury Papers*, 165–69. For the incorporation of foreign objects, see Renfrew, "Varna and the Emergence of Wealth in Prehistoric Europe," 52; Calloway, *New Worlds for All*, 45; Lohse, "Trade Goods," 397.

112. May 22, 1764, HWA; Woodward, "Faithfull Relation," in Salley, *Narratives of Early Carolina*, 132. On the Westos' history of militarization, see Browne, "'Carying Away Their Corne."

113. THJR, 140–42.

114. At the Cherokee site of Tomassee, for instance, archaeologists recovered brass buttons that had been drilled and laced with iron wire, indicating that they were used as jewelry; M. Smith et al., "Archaeological Investigations at Tomassee."

115. November 17, 1763, *DRIA*, 2:535; September 20, 1765, *DRIA*, 2:553.

116. GSB, 38, 43, 50, 51, 70.

117. Marcoux, "Glass Trade Beads,"157–84; personal correspondence with Jon Marcoux, June 13, 2013.

118. Hawes, *Letter book of Thomas Raspberry*, 49.

119. September 20, 1717, *JCIT*, 211–12.

120. Directors to Edward Wilkinson, November 4, 1762, *DRIA*, 2:574.

121. Directors to Edward Wilkinson, November 20, 1762, *DRIA*, 2:580.

122. Reck, *Von Reck's Voyage*, 40.

123. Baden, *Tomotley*, appendix 2; Elliott and Folse Elliott, *Mount Pleasant*, 49–50.

124. Table of Goods and Prices for the Indian Trade, *JCIT*, 89; Tables of Goods and Prices for the Cherokee Trade, *DRIA*, 2:567.

125. Personal correspondence with Jon Marcoux, June 13, 2013.

126. Directors to Edward Wilkinson, November 20, 1762, *DRIA*, 2:580.

127. Tortora, *Carolina in Crisis*, 172–74.

128. Directors to Edward Wilkinson, November 4, 1762, *DRIA*, 2:574.

129. Directors to Edward Wilkinson, March 2, 1763, *DRIA*, 2:583.

130. Ultimately, Fort Prince George lost the public close to £4,000; December 19, 1765, *DRIA*, 2:555.

131. July 20, 1765, *DRIA*, 2:551.

132. The directors complained about the fact that the Cherokees were not cleaning and dressing the skins properly; Directors to Edward Wilkinson, June 21, 1763, *DRIA*, 2:587. William Ramsey argues that the Southeastern Indians changed the way they dressed skins to increase their exchange value in the early seventeenth century as well; *Yamasee War*, 72.

133. Directors to Edward Wilkinson, December 3, 1763, *DRIA*, 2:588; Directors to Edward Wilkinson, April 25, 1764, *DRIA*, 2:590

134. For other examples of Southeastern Indians refashioning European manufactures, see Samuel Hollinshed to Moses Thomson, Esq., December 28, 1751, *DRIA*, 1:217; G. Jones, *Detailed Reports on the Salzburger Emigrants*, 2:113; Narrative of Father Marquette (1673), in S. Williams, *Early Travels*, 43–45; D. Elliott and Folse Elliott, *Mount Pleasant*, 41, 51, 54; Baden, *Tomotley*, appendix 2; M. Harmon, "Eighteenth Century Lower Cherokee Adaptation"; M. Smith et al., "Archaeological Investigations at Tomassee."

135. John Gendron to Governor Glen, September 24, 1751, *DRIA*, 1:121.

136. Cherokee Talk to the Board of Trade, September 9, 1730, CO 5/4 part 2, accessed November 24, 2015, http://www.colonialamerica.amdigital.co.uk /Documents/Details/CO_5_4_Part2_014.

137. Clayton, Knight, and Moore, *De Soto Chronicles*, 68; Lederer, *Discoveries of John Lederer*, 24; De Beauchamp, "Journal of De Beauchamps' Journey to the Choctaws," in Mereness, *Travels*, 270; Reck, *Von Reck's Voyage*, 44; "Journal of Alexander Cuming, 1730," in S. Williams, *Early Travels*, 126.

Conclusion

1. Hawes, *Letter Book of Thomas Raspberry*, 23.

2. Ibid., 58.

3. Ibid., 61.

4. Ibid., 49.

5. Ibid., 18, 48–51.

6. Ibid., 55, 62.

7. Ibid., 88–89.

8. For complaints about the Bristol strouds being too small, see ibid., 32.

9. Ibid., 55, 62.

10. John Habersham of Georgia claimed that Creek leather was prized over Cherokee leather in London; Habersham to Joseph Tuckwell at Wallingford, May 18, 1765, James Habersham Papers, GHS. The story from the point the ship docks is conjecture, based on standard practices in the leather industry in early modern England as elucidated in Clarkson, "Organization of the English Leather Industry," 245–56; R. Bateman, "Strouds, Deer, War and Breeches."

11. In August, Raspberry assured John he would supply him, while in September he wrote to Thomson canceling the orders; Raspberry to John Ulrich, August 23, 1760, in Hawes, *Letter Book of Thomas Raspberry*, 118; Raspberry to Thomson, September 1, 1716, in Hawes, *Letter Book of Thomas Raspberry*, 119.

12. Raspberry to William Thomson, June 2, 1760, in Hawes, *Letter Book of Thomas Raspberry*, 111–12.

13. Tobler's Friend is an invented name, but it follows the logic of some Native American names that were created to mimic one's relationship with an Indian trader.

14. For British confusion about the Creeks' allegiance to the British in 1760, see Thomas Raspberry to William Thomson, June 2, 1760, in Hawes, *Letter Book of Thomas Raspberry*, 111–12; Piker, *Okfuskee*, 52–63.

15. At Lower Cherokee sites, the archaeologist Michael Harmon found a number of bullets with teeth marks; "Eighteenth Century Lower Cherokee Adaptation," 86–87.

16. Southeastern Native Americans continued to use bows and arrows in addition to European firearms. See Stephen Johnson to Governor George Walton, April 20, 1789, Creek Letters, GDAH, part 1, 196–97.

17. Hunting camps by midcentury were usually composed of a single nuclear family or a couple of families who were members of the same clan; Braund, *Deerskins and Duffels*, 67; Piker, *Okfuskee*, 78–79.

18. For Southeastern Indian deerskin production, see Braund, *Deerskins and Duffels*, 68.

19. Settled Indian traders complained that Robert Goudy intercepted Indians with deerskins while they were at their hunting camps and offered to trade with them illegally; Journal of an Indian Trader, April 22, 1755, *DRIA*, 2:62.

20. The historian Joshua Piker argues that after midcentury, Creek Indians sold more of their raw skins to unlicensed traders; *Okfuskee*, 150–52.

21. For the interrelationship between Southeastern Indian male and female roles and desires in the trade, see LeMaster, *Brothers Born of One Mother*, 118–48.

22. Galphin's Silver Bluff account book includes sales of raw and dressed deerskin from individuals who are not registered as licensed traders; GSB, 14, 15, 29. For estimates about the amount of rum that was purchased by Southeastern Indians see Pressly, *Rim of the Caribbean*, 206–8.

23. One might only look at the evolving arguments made by the eminent historian James Merrell to see this trend clearly. In 2006 Merrell revisited an essay he wrote in 1989 about intercultural exchange in the Carolina piedmont. In 1989 he had described the indigenous actors as operating in a system of economic thought that was similar to that of the European colonists. In the intervening seventeen years the scholarly consensus had determined that Native Americans did not exchange goods outside of the context of kinship or diplomacy. Merrell expressed regret about his earlier decision to refer to the Southeastern Indians as business-minded consumers; Merrell, "'Our Bonds of Peace," 269–70. In the past few years the tendency to depict Native American and British American cultures as starkly different has given way to studies that identify significant similarities between the groups, a movement this book embraces; see Richter, *Before the Revolution*; Shoemaker, *Strange Likeness*; LaCombe, *Political Gastronomy*.

24. I am consciously invoking Richard White's "middle ground," which emerged from his study of the French and Native American relationships formed in the Great Lakes region, and Dan Usner's "frontier economy," which he used to describe the informal trade economy created among French settlers, slaves, and Native Americans in the Lower Mississippi Valley. Both of these works demonstrate the ability of seemingly dissimilar groups operating a long distance from strong imperial oversight to create interdependent relationships; R. White, *Middle Ground*; Usner, *Frontier Exchange Economy*.

25. Piker, *Okfuskee*, 75–88, 95–96, 148–61.

26. Beck, *Chiefdoms, Collapse, and Coalescence*, 236–37.

27. Ramsey, *Yamasee War*, 61–74.

28. As quoted in Saunt, *New Order of Things*, 34.

29. On the defining characteristics and goals of ethnohistory, see Axtell, "Ethno-history." On the historiography of ethnohistory, see Harkin, "Ethnohistory's Ethnohistory." In excavating knowledge about pre- and postcontact indigenous cultures, ethnohistorians revealed that Native Americans adopted ideas and manufactures from Europeans in a piecemeal fashion and, even then, altered those ideas and manufactures to fit into their preexisting cultural and social systems. Rather than viewing Native Americans as victims, ethnohistorians highlighted the agency and ingenuity of Native American actors. For the culmination of these arguments, see Richter, *Facing East*. For a critical appraisal of *Roots of Dependency* from the ethnohistorical perspective, see Van Hoak, "Untangling the Roots of Dependency." Note that historians do still explicitly engage with dependency theory: Carson, *Searching for the Bright Path*; Ramsey, *Yamasee War*, 14; Silverman, *Thundersticks*. For the most recent casual reference to Southeastern Indians being dependent on European goods by the middle of the eighteenth century, see, Tortora, *Carolina in Crisis*, 16.

30. R. White, *Roots of Dependency*, 52–53, 74–75, 80; Hall, *Zamumo's Gifts*, 87; Beck, *Chiefdoms, Collapse, and Coalescence*, 157, 236–37, 243 264.

31. Mathew, "Mr. Mathew's Relation," in Cheves, *Shaftesbury Papers*, 169; Hilton, "A True Relation of a Voyage," ibid., 21.

32. A. King, "Leadership Strategies," 73–90; Beck, "Persuasive Politics," 24–28, 35; G. Wilson, Marcoux, and Koldehoff, "Square Pegs in Round Holes," 43–44, 50–51, 64–65; Payne, "Foundations of Leadership," 104–6; Schroeder, "Walls as Symbols," 134–35; Myers, "Leadership at the Edge," 159, 172; Gougeon, "Different but the Same," 178–81, 189–90.

33. R. White, *Roots of Dependency*, xvii, xix.

34. Guha, *Dominance without Hegemony*.

Bibliography

Manuscript Sources

Athens, Georgia
  Hargrett Rare Book and Manuscript Library, University of Georgia Libraries
    Keith Read Collection. Available online at Galileo Digital Library of
      Georgia, Southeastern Native American Documents, 1730–1842.
    Telamon Cuyler Collection. Available online at Galileo Digital Library of
      Georgia, Southeastern Native American Documents, 1730–1842.
Atlanta, Georgia
  Georgia Department of Archives and History
    Creek Indian letters, talks, and treaties, 1705–1839, in four parts. Compiled,
      copied, and bound with authority of John B. Wilson, Secretary of State,
      under direction of Mrs. J. E. Hays, State Historian; WPA
      Project P.P. 665-34-3-224.
    Records of Colonial Georgia, unpublished volumes 33–39, edited by
      Allen D. Candler, on microfilm.
    Unpublished letters of Timothy Barnard, 1784–1820. Compiled by Louise
      Frederick Hays.
Charleston, South Carolina
  South Carolina Historical Society
    John Guerard Letter Book, 1752–54. 34/0321 OvrSz.
    Robert Raper Letter Book, 1759–70. 34/511.
Chicago, Illinois
  Newberry Library
    George Galphin Letters, 1778–80, Vault Ayer MS 313.
    John Howard Payne Papers, 1791–1852, Vault Ayer MS 689.
    Sir Alexander Cuming Papers, 1734–67, Vault Ayer MS 204.
Columbia, South Carolina
  South Carolina Department of Archives and History
    Charles Town Port Clearings, 1717–21.
    Henry Woodward, Accounts as Indian Agent of the First Earl of Shaftesbury,
      1674–78.
    Public Cherokee Trade. Account Book. Goods Sold and Delivered out of
      the Fort Prince George Factory, 1762–63 (duplicate of original at
      New-York Historical Society).
    Records of the Grand Council and Proprietors' Council. John S. Green
      Transcripts of Journals, 1671–1721.
    Records of His Majesty's Council in South Carolina Journals, 1725–34.

Records of the South Carolina Court of Common Pleas Judgment Rolls, 1703–63.

Secretary of State. Recorded Instruments. Inventories of Estates, WPA Transcripts, 1736–74. Miscellaneous Records, Proprietary Series, 1671–1725. Miscellaneous Records, Interregnum Series, 1721–33. Miscellaneous Records, Main Series, 1732–63.

Secretary of State. Surveyor General's Office. Colonial Plat Books, 1731–75.

South Carolina Institute of Archaeology and Anthropology

Bastian, Beverly. "Fort Independence: An Eighteenth Century Frontier Homesite and Militia Post in South Carolina." In Russell Papers. Atlanta: Interagency Archaeological Service Division, National Park Service, 1982.

Calhoun, Jeanne A., et al. "Home Upriver: Rural Life on Daniel's Island, Berkeley County, South Carolina." South Carolina Department of Highways and Public Transportation, 1987.

Poplin, Eric, et al. "Archaeological Investigation of Schieveling Plantation." Brockington and Associates Inc., 2004.

Smith, Marvin T., et al. "Archaeological Investigations at Tomassee (38OC186): A Lower Cherokee Town." Research Manuscript Series No. 206, 1988.

South Caroliniana Library, University of South Carolina

James Glen Papers, 1738–77.

John Evans Journal, 1702–15.

Macartan & Campbell Account Book, Augusta Store, August 1762–June 1766.

Durham, North Carolina

Duke University, Special Collections Library

Thomas Coster, To the Kings Most Excellent Majesty, 1734.

Edinburgh, Scotland

National Archives of Scotland

Cash book of Robert Nisbet, merchant in Charles Town, South Carolina, 1720–23. GD237/1/150.

Daybook kept by John Blackwood and Alexander Nisbet, first in Charles Town, South Carolina, to September 29 1729, and thereafter in London and Edinburgh, 1727–30. GD237/1/151.

Letter book, containing copies of letters written by John Murray of Murraythwaite, whilst resident in Charleston, South Carolina. GD219/290.

Kew, Britain

British Public Record Office

Colonial Office 5, accessed digitally through Adam Matthew, Colonial America, www.colonialamerica.amdigital.co.uk.

New York, New York

Gilder Lehrman Institute of American History

Governor Henry Ellis to John Rae, Lachlan McGillivray, Francis McCartan Esquires, December 7, 1759. GLC05228.02.

Providence, Rhode Island
  John Carter Brown Library
    Thomas Nairne. "A Description of Carolina" [1710?]. Manuscript of
      published edition, Codex Eng. 10.
Savannah, Georgia
  Georgia Historical Society
    Anonymous Journal of a visit to Indian Country, 1767. MS 10.
    George Galphin account books, 1767–72. MS 269.
    James Habersham Papers, 1747–75. MS 337.
Washington, D.C.
  Library of Congress
    David B. Quinn Papers, 1109–1994.
    Sir Hans Sloane Collection, 1660–1763.
    Journal of John Evans, Indian Trader, 1709–15.

Newspapers

Georgia Gazette, Savannah, Georgia, 1763
South Carolina Gazette, Charles Town, South Carolina, 1732

Published Primary Sources

Acts of Assembly, Passed in the Island of Barbadoes, from 1648, to 1718. London: John
  Baskett, 1732.
Adair, James. *The History of the American Indians.* Edited by Kathryn E. Holland-
  Braund. Tuscaloosa: University of Alabama Press, 2005.
Barlow, Theodore. *The justice of peace: a treatise containing the power and duty of
  that magistrate, . . . Together with a table . . . By Theodore Barlow, . . . To which is
  added an appendix.* London: In the Savoy: Printed by Henry Lintot (assignee
  of Edward Sayer Esq;) for John and Paul Knapton and John Nourse, 1745.
Barnwell, Colonel John. "The Tuscarora Expedition: Letters of Colonel John
  Barnwell." *South Carolina Historical Magazine* 9 (January 1908): 28–54.
Bateman, Edmund. *A Sermon Preach'd before the Trustees for Establishing the
  Colony of Georgia in America and the Associates of the Late Rev. Dr. Bray; at Their
  Anniversary-Meeting, March 19, 1740-1, at the Parish Church of St. Bride, Alias
  St. Bridget, in Fleetstreet, London.* London: Trustees and Associates, 1741.
Beaumont, Francis. *The royal merchant: or, beggars bush. A comedy. As it is acted at the
  Theatre-Royal in Smock-Alley. . . . Written by Beaumont and Fletcher.* Dublin, 1736.
Best, William. *A Sermon Preach'd before the Trustees for Establishing the Colony of
  Georgia in America and the Associates of the Late Rev. Dr. Bray; at Their
  Anniversary Meeting, March 18, 1741-2, at the Parish Church of St. Bride, in
  Fleetstreet. In Which Some Notice Is Taken of a Late Abusive Pamphlet, a True and
  Historical Narrative of the Said Colony.* London: Trustees and Associates, 1742.
"A Bill of Complaint in Chancery, 1700." *South Carolina Historical Magazine* 21
  (October 1920): 139–43.

Blanch, John. *The art of tanning and currying leather: with an account of all the different processes made use of in Europe and Asia for dying leather red and yellow. To which are added, Mr. Philippo's method of dying.* London: Dublin Society and J. Nourse, 1774.

Boyd, Mark, ed. "Diego Pena's Expedition to Apalachee and Apalachicola in 1716." *Florida Historical Quarterly* 28 (1949): 1–27.

———, ed. "Documents Describing the Second and Third Expeditions of Lieutenant Diego Pena to Apalachee and Apalachicolo in 1717 and 1718." *Florida Historical Quarterly* 31, no. 1 (July 1952): 109–39.

Brewer, T. F., and J. Baillie, eds. "The Journal of George Pawley's 1746 Agency to the Cherokee." *Journal of Cherokee Studies* 16 (1991): 3–22.

Bruce, Lewis. *A Sermon Preach'd before the Trustees for Establishing the Colony of Georgia in America and the Associates of the Late Rev. Dr. Bray; at Their Anniversary Meeting, March 15, 1743, at the Parish Church of St. Margaret, Westminister [sic].* London: Trustees and Associates, 1743.

Burton, John. *A Sermon Preach'd before the Trustees for Establishing the Colony of Georgia in America, and before the Associates of the Late Rev. Dr. Thomas Bray, for Converting the Negroes in the British Plantations, and for Other Good Purposes. At Their Anniversary-Meeting, in the Parish Church of St. Mary-Le-Bow. On Thursday March 15, 1732.* London: Trustees and Associates, 1732.

Candler, Allen Daniel, et al. *The Colonial Records of the State of Georgia.* 32 vols. Atlanta, Ga.: Franklin Printing and Publishing Co., 1904.

Case of the leather-sellers and leather-dressers of the cities of London and Westminster, and parts adjacent, humbly offered to the consideration of the honourable the knights, citizens, and burgesses in Parliament assembled. N.p., [1711].

Cheves, Langdon, ed. *The Shaftesbury Papers and Other Records Relating to Carolina and the First Settlement on the Ashley River prior to the Year 1676.* Columbia, S.C.: South Carolina Historical Society, 2000 [1897].

Clayton, Lawrence A., Vernon J. Knight, and Edward C. Moore. *The De Soto Chronicles: The Expedition of Hernando de Soto to North America in 1539–1543.* 2 vols. Tuscaloosa: University of Alabama Press, 1993.

Cooper, Thomas, and Daniel J. McCord, eds. *The Statutes at Large of South Carolina.* 10 vols. Columbia, S.C.: A. S. Johnson, 1836–41.

Coulter, E. Merton, ed. *The Journal of William Stephens, 1741–1743.* 2 vols. Athens: University of Georgia Press, 1958.

Cox, Thomas. *Magna Britannia et Hibernia, antiqua & nova. Or, a new survey of Great Britain, Collected and composed by an impartial hand. . . .* Vol. 5. London: E and R Nutt, 1730.

Davies, K. G., ed. *Calendar of State Papers, Colonial America and West Indies.* Vol. 43. London: Her Majesty's Stationery Office, 1963. Available online at http://www.british-history.ac.uk/cal-state-papers/colonial/america-west-indies/vol43.

De Brahm, William. "Plan of the Environs in the Neck of Tanasee and Telequo Rivers about Fort Loudoun, 1773." In *The Southeast in Early Maps,* edited by William Patterson Cumming and Louis De Vorsey, plate 66A. Chapel Hill: University of North Carolina Press, 1998.

Defoe, Daniel. *The Complete English Tradesman*. London: Charles Rivington, 1726.

Gallardo, Jose Miguel, trans. "Testimony of Thomas Vide, Hugh Jordan and Charles Miller to the Governor of Florida." *South Carolina Historical Magazine* 37 (July 1936): 94–99.

Georgia, Trustees of. "A Brief Account of the Establishment of the Colony of Georgia under Gen. James Oglethorpe, February 1, 1733." *American Colonial Tracts Monthly* 1 (1897) [1733]: 3–16.

Great Britain. Board of Trade. *Journal of the Commissioners for Trade and Plantations*. 14 vols. London: H. M. Stationery Office, 1920–38.

Hawes, Lilla Mills, ed. *The Letter Book of Thomas Raspberry, 1758–1761*. Savannah, Ga.: Georgia Historical Society, 1959.

———, ed. "Proceedings of the President and Assistants in Council of Georgia, 1749–1751, Part II." *Georgia Historical Quarterly* 36 (March 1952): 46–70.

Hawkins, Benjamin. *The Collected Works of Benjamin Hawkins, 1796–1810*. Edited by Thomas Foster. Tuscaloosa: University of Alabama Press, 2003.

"Historical Relation of Facts Delivered by Ludovick Grant, Indian Trader, to His Excellency, the Governor of South Carolina." *South Carolina Historical and Genealogical Magazine* 10 (January 1909): 54–68.

Jones, Calvin, and Charles Hicks. "Manners and Customs of the Cherokees." *Niles Register* 16 (October 13, 1818): 100–101.

Jones, George Fenwick, ed. *Detailed Reports on the Salzburger Emigrants Who Settled in America*. 18 vols. Athens: University of Georgia Press, 1968–1995.

Jones, George Fenwick, and Paul Martin Peucher. "'We Have Come to Georgia with Pure Intentions': Moravian Bishop August Gottlieb Spangenberg's Letters from Savannah, 1735." *Georgia Historical Quarterly* 82 (Spring 1998): 84–120.

King, Duane H., ed. *The Memoirs of Lt. Henry Timberlake*. Cherokee, NC: Museum of the Cherokee Indian Press, 2007.

Lane, Mills, ed. *General Oglethorpe's Georgia: Colonial Letters, 1733–1743*. 2 vols. Savannah, Ga.: Beehive Press, 1975.

Lawson, John, and Hugh Talmage Lefler. *A New Voyage to Carolina*. Chapel Hill: University of North Carolina Press, 1967 [1709].

Lederer, John. *The Discoveries of John Lederer, with Unpublished Letters by and about Lederer to Governor John Winthrop, Jr., and an Essay on the Indians of Lederer's Discoveries*. Charlottesville: University of Virginia Press, 1958.

Le Jau, Francis. "Letter of Francis LeJau." In "The South Carolina Indian War of 1715, as Seen by the Clergymen," edited by Edgar Legarè Pennington. *South Carolina Historical Magazine* 32, no. 4 (October 1931): 251–69.

Locke, John. *Second Treatise of Government*. Edited by C. B. Macpherson. Indianapolis, Ind.: Hackett Publishing, 1980.

Longe, Alexander. "Alexander Longe's 'A Small Postscript to the Ways and Manners of the Indians Called Cherokees, and Contents of the Whole So That You May Find Everything by the Pages.'" Edited by David Corkran. *Southern Indian Studies* 21 (October 1969): 3–49.

Mante, Thomas. *The history of the late war in North-America, and the islands of the West-Indies, including the campaigns of MDCCLXIII and MDCCLXIV against His Majesty's Indian enemies.* London: Printed for W. Strahan; and T. Cadell, 1772.

McDowell, William L., Jr., ed. *Documents Relating to Indian Affairs, May 21, 1750–August 7, 1754* [vol. 1]. Columbia, S.C.: South Carolina Department of Archives and History, 1992 [1958].

———, ed. *Documents Relating to Indian Affairs, 1754–1765* [vol. 2]. Columbia, S.C.: South Carolina Department of Archives and History, 1992 [1970].

———, ed. *Journals of the Commissioners of the Indian Trade: September 20, 1710–August 29, 1718.* Columbia, S.C.: South Carolina Department of Archives and History, 1992 [1955].

McMurtrie, Douglas C, ed. "The Correspondence of Peter Timothy, Printer of Charlestown, with Benjamin Franklin." *South Carolina Historical Magazine* 35 (October 1934): 123–29.

Mereness, Newton D., ed. *Travels in the American Colonies.* New York: Macmillan, 1916.

Mississippi Provincial Archives, French Dominion. Edited by Mississippi Department of Archives and History, Dunbar Rowland, A. G. Sanders, and Patricia Kay Galloway. 4 vols. Jackson, Miss.: Press of the Mississippi Department of Archives and History, 1927–84.

Moore, Alexander, ed. *Nairne's Muskhogean Journals: The 1708 Expedition to the Mississippi River.* Jackson: University Press of Mississippi, 1988.

Morgan, Joseph. *The Nature of Riches, Shewe'd from the Natural Reasons of the Use and Effects Thereof: Together with Some Improvements Made Upon the Considerations of the Nature and Effects of Riches.* Philadelphia: B. Franklin, 1732.

Newe, Thomas. "Letters of Thomas Newe from South Carolina, 1682." *American Historical Review* 12 (January 1907): 322–27.

"A New Voyage to Georgia. By a Young Gentleman. Giving an Account of his Travels to South Carolina, and Part of North Carolina. To which is added, A Curious Account of the Indians, by an Honorable Person. And a Poem to James Oglethorpe, Esq., on His Arrival from Georgia (1737)." *Collections of the Georgia Historical Society* 2 (1842): 37–68.

"Notes and Documents: Some Ancient Georgia Lore." *Georgia Historical Quarterly* 15 (June 1931): 191–98.

Nugent, Nell Marion, and Virginia State Library. *Cavaliers and Pioneers: Abstracts of Virginia Land Patents and Grants.* 3 vols. Richmond, Va.: Press of the Dietz Print Co., 1934.

Oglethorpe, James Edward, and Lower Creek Indians. "Oglethorpe's Treaty with the Lower Creek Indians." *Georgia Historical Quarterly* 4 (March 1920): 3–16.

Palmer, William Pitt, et al. *Calendar of Virginia State Papers and Other Manuscripts Preserved in the Capitol at Richmond.* 11 vols. Richmond, Va.: R. F. Walker, 1875.

Pennington, Edgar Legaré, ed. "The South Carolina Indian War of 1715, as Seen by the Clergymen." *South Carolina Historical and Genealogical Magazine* 32 (October 1931): 251–69.

Priestley, Herbert Ingram, ed. *The Luna Papers: Documents Relating to the Expedition of Don Tristan de Luna y Arellano for the Conquest of La Florida in 1559–1561*. Vol. 1. Deland: Florida State Historical Society, 1928.

Pringle, Robert. *The Letterbook of Robert Pringle*. 2 vols. Edited by Walter B. Edgar. Columbia: University of South Carolina Press, 1972.

Reck, Philipp Georg Friedrich von. *Von Reck's Voyage: Drawings and Journal of Philip Georg Friedrich von Reck*. Edited by Kristian Hvidt. Savannah, Ga.: Beehive Press, 1990.

Reese, Trevor R. *The Clamorous Malcontents: Criticisms and Defenses of the Colony of Georgia, 1741–1743*. Savannah, Ga.: Beehive Press, 1973.

———, ed. *Our First Visit in America: Early Reports from the Colony of Georgia, 1732–1740*. Savannah, Ga.: Beehive Press, 1974.

———, ed. *The Most Delightful Country of the Universe: Promotional Literature of the Colony of Georgia, 1717–1734*. Savannah, Ga.: Beehive Press, 1972.

Richardson, William. "Diary, 1758–1759." Transcribed by William B. Jack, http://www.parsonjohn.org/images/Richardson.pdf.

Ridley, Glocester. *A Sermon Preach'd before the Trustees for Establishing the Colony of Georgia in America and the Associates of the Late Rev. Dr. Bray; at Their Anniversary Meeting, March 20, 1746, at the Parish Church of St. Margaret, Westminister [sic]*. London: Trustees and Associates, 1746.

Sainsbury, Noel, ed. *Records in the British Public Records Office Relating to South Carolina, 1663–1782*. 36 vols. London, 1860–1919.

Salley, Alexander S., Jr., ed. *Journal of Colonel John Herbert, Commissioner of Indian Affairs for the Province of South Carolina: October 17, 1727 to March 19, 1727/8*. Columbia, S.C.: Historical Commission of South Carolina by the State Company, 1936.

———, ed. *Journal of the Grand Council of South Carolina, April 11, 1692–September 26, 1692*. Columbia, S.C.: Historical Commission of South Carolina, 1907.

———, ed. *Journal of the Grand Council of South Carolina, August 25, 1671–June 24, 1680*. Columbia, S.C.: Historical Commission of South Carolina, 1907.

———, ed. *Journals of the Commons House of Assembly of South Carolina for 1703*. Columbia, S.C.: Printed by the State Company, 1934.

———, ed. *Journals of the Commons House of Assembly of South Carolina for the Sessions Beginning January 30, 1696, and Ending March 17, 1696*. Columbia, S.C.: Printed by the State Company, 1908.

———, ed. *Journals of the Commons House of Assembly of South Carolina for the Two Sessions of 1697*. Columbia, S.C.: Printed by the State Company, 1913.

———, ed. *Journals of the Commons House of Assembly of South Carolina, March 6, 1705/6–April 9, 1706*. Columbia, S.C.: Printed by the State Company, 1937.

———, ed. *Journals of the Commons House of Assembly of South Carolina, June 2, 1724–June 16, 1724*. Columbia, S.C.: Printed by the State Company, 1944.

——, ed. *Journals of the Commons House of Assembly of South Carolina, November 1, 1725–April 30, 1726*. Columbia, S.C.: Printed by the State Company, 1945.

——, ed. *Journals of the Commons House of Assembly of South Carolina, November 8, 1734–June 7, 1735*. Columbia, S.C.: Printed by the State Company, 1947.

——, ed. *Narratives of Early Carolina, 1650–1708*. New York: Charles Scribner's Sons, 1911.

Smith, Samuel. *A Sermon Preach'd before the Trustees for Establishing the Colony of Georgia in America, and before the Associates of the Late Rev. Dr. Thomas Bray, for Converting the Negroes in the British Plantations, and for Other Good Purposes. At Their First Yearly-Meeting, in the Parish Church of St. Augustin*. London: Trustees and Associates, 1731.

South Carolina. General Assembly. "Report of the Committee appointed to examine into the proceedings of the people of Georgia, with respect to the province of South-Carolina, and the disputes subsisting between the two colonies." Charles-Town, S.C.: Lewis Timothy, 1736.

Stewart, John. "Letters from John Stewart to William Dunlop, 1690." *South Carolina Historical and Genealogical Magazine* 32 (January 1931): 1–33.

Stock, Leo Francis, ed. *Proceedings and Debates of the British Parliaments Respecting North America*. Washington, D.C.: Carnegie Institution of Washington, 1924.

Tailfer, Patrick, et al. "A True and Historical Narrative of the Colony of Georgia." *American Colonial Tracts Monthly* 1 (1897): 42–44.

Trenchard, John, and Thomas Gordon. *Cato's Letters: Or, Essays on Liberty, Civil and Religious, and Other Important Subjects*. 2 vols. Edited by Ronald Hamowy. Indianapolis: Liberty Fund, 1995.

Trott, Nicholas. *The Laws of the Province of South-Carolina, in Two Parts*. Charles-Town, S.C.: Printed by Lewis Timothy, 1736.

Warren, Mary Bondurant, and Jack Moreland Jones, eds. *Georgia Governor and Council Journals*. 7 vols. Danielsville, Ga.: Heritage Papers, 1991–2010.

Warren, Mary Bondurant, and Robert S. Lowery, eds. *South Carolina Newspapers: The South-Carolina Gazette, 1760*. Danielsville, Ga.: Heritage Papers, 1988.

Waselkov, Gregory A., and Kathryn E. Holland Braund. *William Bartram on the Southeastern Indians*. Lincoln: University of Nebraska Press, 1995.

Watts, George. *A Sermon Preach'd before the Trustees for Establishing the Colony of Georgia in America; at Their Anniversary-Meeting, in the Parish Church of St. Bridget, Alias St. Bride, in Fleetstreet, London. On Thursday March 18, 1735*. London: Trustees, 1735.

Williams, Hannah. "Letter to James Petiver." *South Carolina Historical Magazine* 21 (January 1920): 5.

Williams, Samuel Cole, ed. *Early Travels in Tennessee Country, 1540–1800*. Johnson City, Tenn.: Watauga Press, 1928.

Wilson, Thomas. *The knowledge and practice of Christianity made easy to the meanest capacities: or, an essay towards an instruction for the indians. Together with directions and prayers*. London, 1741.

Dissertations and Theses

Barker, Eirlys Mair. "'Much Blood and Treasure'": South Carolina's Indian Traders, 1670–1755." PhD diss., College of William and Mary, 1993.

Bossy, Denise Ileana. "The 'Noble Savage' in Chains: Indian Slavery in Colonial South Carolina, 1670–1733." PhD diss., Yale University, 2007.

Brazeal, Ernestine Erskine. "Labor Problems in Colonial Georgia." Master's thesis, University of Chicago, 1937.

Butler, Jay Jordan. "Agrarianism and Capitalism in Early Georgia, 1732–1743." Master's thesis, University of Wyoming, 1949.

Drechsel, Emanuel Johannes. "Mobilian Jargon: Linguistic, Sociocultural, and Historical Aspects of an American Lingua Franca." PhD diss., University of Wisconsin, 1979.

Groover, Mark D. "Of Mindset and Material Culture: An Archaeological View of Continuity and Change in the South Carolina Backcountry." Master's thesis, University of South Carolina, 1991.

Hallmark, Terrell Lee. "John Locke and 'The Fundamental Constitutions of Carolina.'" PhD diss., Claremont Graduate University, 1998.

Harmon, Michael. "Eighteenth Century Lower Cherokee Adaptation and Use of European Material Culture." Master's thesis, University of South Carolina, 1986.

Johnson, Laura. "Material Translations: Cloth in Early American Encounters, 1520–1750." PhD diss., University of Delaware, 2010.

Lane, Laura E. "Gender, Labor, and Virtue in Eighteenth Century Georgia." PhD diss., University of Miami, 2012

Murphy, Kate. "Portals of Nature: Networks of Natural History in Eighteenth-Century British Plantation Societies." PhD diss., Johns Hopkins University, 2007.

Pett-Conklin, Linda Marie. "Cadastral Surveying in Colonial South Carolina: A Historical Geography." PhD diss., Louisiana State University, 1986.

Schrager, Bradley Scott. "Yamasee Indians and the Challenge of Spanish and English Colonialism in the North American Southeast, 1660–1715." PhD diss., Northwestern University, 2001.

Stumpf, Stuart Owen. "The Merchants of Colonial Charlestown, 1680–1756." PhD diss., Michigan State University, 1971.

Vaughn, James. "The Politics of Empire: Metropolitan Socio-political Development and the Imperial Transformation of the British East India Company, 1675–1775." PhD diss., University of Chicago, 2009.

Wallace, Jessica Lynn, "'Building Forts in Their Hearts': Anglo-Cherokee Relations on the Mid-Eighteenth-Century Southern Frontier." PhD diss., Ohio State University, 2014.

Secondary Sources

Agnew, Jean-Christophe. *Worlds Apart: The Market and the Theater in Anglo-American Thought, 1550–1750*. Cambridge: Cambridge University Press, 1986.

Akin, David, and Joel Robbins. "An Introduction to Melanesian Currencies: Agency, Identity, and Social Reproduction." In *Money and Modernity: State and Local Currencies in Melanesia*, edited by David Akin and Joel Robbins, 1–40. Pittsburgh: University of Pittsburgh Press, 1999.

Albers, Patricia. "Labor and Exchange in American Indian History." In *A Companion to American Indian History*, edited by Philip J. Deloria and Neal Salisbury, 269–86. Malden, Mass.: Blackwell, 2002.

Anderson, David G., and Kenneth E. Sassman. "Mississippian Complexity and Contact Coalescence." In Anderson and Sassman, *Recent Developments in Southeastern Archaeology* (Washington, D.C.: Society for American Archaeology, 2012), 152–90.

Anderson, David G., and Kenneth E. Sassman. *Recent Developments in Southeastern Archaeology*. Washington, D.C.: Society for American Archaeology, 2012.

Appadurai, Arjun, ed. *The Social Life of Things: Commodities in Cultural Perspective*. Cambridge: Cambridge University Press, 1986.

Appleby, Joyce O. *Economic Thought and Ideology in Seventeenth Century England*. Princeton, N.J.: Princeton University Press, 1978.

Armitage, David. "John Locke, Carolina, and the *Two Treatises of Government*." *Political Theory* 32 (October 2004): 602–27.

———. "Three Concepts of Atlantic History." In *The British Atlantic World, 1500–1800*, edited by David Armitage and Michael J. Braddick, 11–27. New York: Palgrave Macmillan, 2002.

Arneil, Barbara. *John Locke and America: The Defence of English Colonialism*. Oxford: Clarendon Press; Oxford University Press, 1996.

Ashcraft, Richard. "Lockean Ideas, Poverty, and the Development of Liberal Political Theory." In *Early Modern Conceptions of Property*, edited by John Brewer and Susan Staves, 43–61. London: Routledge, 1995.

Axtell, James. "Ethnohistory: A Historian's Viewpoint." *Ethnohistory* 26 (Winter 1979): 1–13.

———. "The First Consumer Revolution." In *Beyond 1492: Encounters in Colonial America*, 125–51. Oxford: Oxford University Press, 1992.

———. *The Indians' New South: Cultural Change in the Colonial Southeast*. Baton Rouge: Louisiana State University Press, 1997.

———. *The Invasion Within: The Contest of Cultures in Colonial North America*. Oxford: Oxford University Press, 1985.

Baden, William. *Tomotley: An Eighteenth Century Cherokee Village*. Knoxville: Tennessee Valley Authority, 1983.

Bailyn, Bernard. *The Origins of American Politics*. New York: Vintage Books, 1965.

Barber, Karin. *The Generation of Plays: Yoruba Popular Life in Theater*. Indianapolis: Indiana University Press, 2000.

Barker, Eirlys Mair. "Indian Traders, Charles Town, and London's Vital Links to the Interior of North America, 1717–1755." In *Money, Trade, and Power: The Evolution of Colonial South Carolina's Plantation Society*, edited by Jack P.

Greene, Rosemary Brana-Shute, and Randy J. Sparks, 141–65. Columbia: University of South Carolina Press, 2001.

Bateman, Rebecca B. "Strouds, Deer, War and Breeches—Some Suggestions toward an Economic Analysis of the 18th Century South Carolina Deerskin Trade." Unpublished paper delivered to the Seminar in Atlantic History, Culture, and Society, Johns Hopkins University, 1984 (used with permission from the author).

Baumgarten, Linda. *What Clothes Reveal: The Language of Clothing in Colonial and Federal America*. Williamsburg, Va.: Colonial Williamsburg Foundation in association with Yale University Press, 2002.

Beck, Robin. *Chiefdoms, Collapse, and Coalescence in the Early American South*. New York: Cambridge University Press, 2013.

———. "Persuasive Politics and Domination at Cahokia and Moundville." In *Leadership and Polity in Mississippian Society*, edited by Brian M. Butler and Paul D. Welch, 19–42. Carbondale: Southern Illinois University, Center for Archaeological Investigations, 2006.

Becker, Marshall. "Match Coats and the Military: Mass-Produced Clothing for Native Americans as Parallel Markets in the Seventeenth Century." *Textile History and the Military*, supplement 41.1 (2010): 153–81.

Bell, Amelia Rector. "Separate People: Speaking of Creek Men and Women." *American Anthropologist* 92 (June 1990): 332–45.

Ben-Amos, Ilana Krausman. *The Culture of Giving: Informal Support and Gift-Exchange in Early Modern England*. Cambridge: Cambridge University Press, 2008.

Berger, Ronald. *The Most Necessary Luxuries: The Mercers' Company of Coventry, 1550–1680*. University Park: Pennsylvania State University Press, 1993.

Berry, Christopher J. *Social Theory of the Scottish Enlightenment*. Edinburgh: Edinburgh University Press, 1997.

Bickham, Troy O. *Savages within the Empire: Representations of American Indians in Eighteenth-Century Britain*. Oxford: Oxford University Press, 2005.

Blitz, John H. "New Perspectives in Mississippian Archaeology." *Journal of Archaeological Research* 18 (March 2010): 1–39.

Bosher, J. F. "Huguenot Merchants and the Protestant International in the Seventeenth Century." *William and Mary Quarterly*, 3rd ser., 52 (January 1995): 77–102.

Bossy, Denise I. "Godin & Co.: Charlestown Merchants and the Indian Trade, 1674–1715." *South Carolina Historical Magazine* 114 (April 2014): 96–131.

Boulware, Tyler. "'A Dangerous Sett of Horse-Thieves and Vagrants': Outlaws of the Southern Frontier during the American Revolution." *Eras Journal* 6 (November 2004), http://arts.monash.edu.au/publications/eras/edition-6/boulwarearticle.php.

———. *Deconstructing the Cherokee Nation: Town, Region, and Nation among Eighteenth-Century Cherokees*. Gainesville: University Press of Florida, 2011.

———. "'Traders, Pedlars, and Idle Fellows': Community Boundaries and Collective Identity in the Southeastern Deerskin Trade." In *Global Economies,*

Cultural Currencies of the Eighteenth Century, ed. Michael Rotenberg-Schwartz, 53–72. New York: AMS Press, 2012.

Braund, Kathryn E. Holland. *Deerskins and Duffels: Creek and Indian Trade with Anglo-America, 1685–1815.* Lincoln: University of Nebraska Press, 1993.

Breen, T. H. *The Marketplace of Revolution: How Consumer Politics Shaped American Independence.* New York: Oxford University Press, 2004.

——. *Tobacco Culture: The Mentality of the Great Tidewater Planters on the Eve of Revolution.* Princeton, N.J.: Princeton University Press, 1985.

Brown, Philip M. "Early Indian Trade in the Development of South Carolina: Politics, Economics, and Social Mobility during the Proprietary Period, 1670–1719." *South Carolina Historical Magazine* 76 (July 1975): 118–28.

Browne, Eric E. "'Carying Awaye Their Corne and Children': The Effects of Westo Slave Raids on the Indians of the Lower South." In *Mapping the Mississippian Shatter Zone: The Colonial Indian Slave Trade and Regional Instability in the American South*, edited by Robbie Ethridge and Sheri M. Shuck-Hall, 104–14. Lincoln: University of Nebraska Press, 2009.

——. "Dr. Henry Woodward's Role in Early Carolina Indian Relations." In *Creating and Contesting Carolina: Proprietary Era Histories*, edited by Michelle LeMaster and Bradford J. Wood, 73–93. Columbia: University of South Carolina Press, 2013.

Bushman, Richard. *The Refinement of America: Persons, Houses, Cities.* New York: Vintage Books, 1993.

Bushnell, Amy Turner. "Ruling the 'Republic of Indians' in Seventeenth-Century Florida." In *American Encounters: Natives and Newcomers from European Contact to Indian Removal, 1500–1850*, edited by Peter C. Mancall and James H. Merrell, 311–23. New York: Routledge, 2000.

Butler, Brian M., and Paul D. Welch, eds. *Leadership and Polity in Mississippian Society.* Carbondale: Southern Illinois University, Center for Archaeological Investigations, 2006.

Calloway, Colin. *New Worlds for All: Indians, Europeans, and the Remaking of Early America.* Baltimore: Johns Hopkins University Press, 1997.

Carlos, Ann M., and Frank D. Lewis. *Commerce by a Frozen Sea: Native Americans and the European Fur Trade.* Philadelphia: University of Pennsylvania Press, 2010.

Carson, James Taylor. *Searching for the Bright Path: The Mississippi Choctaws from Prehistory to Removal.* Lincoln: University of Nebraska Press, 1999.

Cashin, Edward, ed. *Colonial Augusta: "Key of the Indian Countrey."* Macon, Ga.: Mercer University Press, 1986.

——. *Governor Henry Ellis and the Transformation of British North America.* Athens: University of Georgia Press, 1994.

Chaplin, Joyce E. *An Anxious Pursuit: Agricultural Innovation and Modernity in the Lower South, 1730–1815.* Chapel Hill: University of North Carolina Press, 1996.

——. *Subject Matter: Technology, the Body, and Science on the Anglo-American Frontier, 1500–1676.* Cambridge, Mass.: Harvard University Press, 2001.

Clarkson, L. A. "The Organization of the English Leather Industry in the Late Sixteenth and Seventeenth Centuries." *Economic History Review*, n.s., 3 (December 1960): 245–56.

Cobb, Charles R. "Mississippian Chiefdoms: How Complex?" *Annual Review of Anthropology* 32 (October 2003): 63–84.

Coclanis, Peter A. "The Hydra Head of Merchant Capital: Markets and Merchants in Early South Carolina." In *The Meaning of South Carolina History: Essays in Honor of George C. Rogers, Jr.*, edited by David R. Chesnutt and Clyde N. Wilson, 1–18. Columbia: University of South Carolina Press, 1991.

Cozma, Cadrina. "John Martin Boltzius and the Early Christian Opposition to Slavery in Georgia." *Georgia Historical Quarterly* 88 (Winter 2004): 457–76.

Crane, Verner W. *The Southern Frontier: 1670–1732*. Durham, N.C.: Duke University Press, 1928.

Davis, John. *Exchange*. Minneapolis: University of Minnesota Press, 1992.

Davis, Ralph. "English Foreign Trade, 1660–1700." *Economic History Review* 7 (December 1954): 150–66.

Dionne, Craig, and Steve Mentz. "Introduction: Rogues and Early Modern English Culture." In *Rogues and Early Modern English Culture*, edited by Craig Dionne and Steve Mentz, 1–29. Ann Arbor: University of Michigan Press, 2004.

Ditz, Toby L. "Secret Selves, Credible Personas: The Problematics of Trust and Public Display in the Writing of Eighteenth-Century Philadelphia Merchants." In *Possible Pasts: Becoming Colonial in Early America*, edited by Robert Blair St. George, 219–42. Ithaca, N.Y.: Cornell University Press, 2000.

Dowd, Gregory Evans. "'Insidious Friends': Gift Giving and the Cherokee-British Alliance in the Seven Years' War." In *Contact Points: American Frontiers from the Mohawk Valley to the Mississippi, 1750–1830*, edited by Andrew R. L. Cayton and Fredrika J. Teute, 114–50. Chapel Hill: University of North Carolina Press, 1998.

Dunway, Wilma. "Incorporation as an Interactive Process: Cherokee Resistance to Expansion of the Capitalist World System: 1560–1763." *Sociological Inquiry* 66 (Fall 1996): 455–70.

DuPlessis, Robert S. "Cloth and the Emergence of the Atlantic Economy." In *The Atlantic Economy during the Seventeenth and Eighteenth Centuries: Organization, Operation, Practice, and Personnel*, edited by Peter A. Coclanis, 72–94. Columbia: University of South Carolina Press, 2005.

Edelson, Max. *Plantation Enterprise in Colonial South Carolina*. Cambridge, Mass.: Harvard University Press, 2006.

Elliott, Daniel T. "Yuchi in the Lower Savannah River Valley: Historical Context and Archaeological Confirmation." In *Yuchi Indian Histories before the Removal Period*, edited by Jason Jackson Baird, 73–100. Lincoln: University of Nebraska Press, 2012.

Elliott, Daniel T., and Rita Folse Elliott. *Mount Pleasant: An Eighteenth-Century Yuchi Indian Town, British Trader Outpost, and Military Garrison in Georgia*. Watkinsville, Ga.: Lamar Institute, 1990.

Ethridge, Robbie. "European Invasion and the Transformation of the Indians of Tennessee, 1540–1715. In *Before the Volunteer State: New Thoughts on Early Tennessee, 1540–1800*, edited by Kristopher Ray, 3–34. Knoxville: University of Tennessee Press, 2014.

———. *From Chicaza to Chickasaw: The European Invasion and the Transformation of the Mississippian World, 1540–1715*. Chapel Hill: University of North Carolina Press, 2010.

Ethridge, Robbie, and Charles Hudson, eds. *The Transformation of the Southeastern Indians, 1540–1760*. Jackson: University Press of Mississippi, 2002.

Ethridge, Robbie, and Sheri M. Shuck-Hall, eds. *Mapping the Mississippian Shatter Zone: The Colonial Indian Slave Trade and Regional Instability in the American South*. Lincoln: University of Nebraska Press, 2009.

Finkelstein, Andrea. *Harmony and the Balance: An Intellectual History of Seventeenth-Century English Economic Thought*. Ann Arbor: University of Michigan Press, 2000.

Forehand, Tammy R., Mark D. Groover, David C. Crass, and Robert Moon. "Bridging the Gap between Archaeologists and the Public: Excavations at Silver Bluff Plantation, the George Galphin Site." *Early Georgia* 32 (Spring 2004): 51–73.

Foreman, Carolyn Thomas. *Indians Abroad, 1493–1938*. Norman: University of Oklahoma Press, 1943.

Foster, Michael K. "Another Look at the Function of Wampum in Iroquois-White Councils." In *The History and Culture of Iroquois Diplomacy*, edited by Francis Jennings, 99–114. Syracuse, N.Y.: Syracuse University Press, 1985.

Franklin, W. Neal. "Virginia and the Cherokee Indian Trade, 1673–1752." *East Tennessee Historical Society Publications* 4 (1932): 3–21.

Frey, Sylvia. "Liberty, Equality, and Slavery: The Paradox of the American Revolution." In *The American Revolution: Its Character and Limits*, edited by Jack P. Greene, 230–52. New York: New York University Press, 1987.

Fumerton, Patricia. "Making Vagrancy (In)visible: The Economics of Disguise in Early Modern Rogue Pamphlets." In *Rogues and Early Modern English Culture*, edited by Craig Dionne and Steve Mentz, 193–210. Ann Arbor: University of Michigan Press, 2004.

Galenson, David W. "The Rise and Fall of Indentured Servitude in the Americas: An Economic Analysis." *Journal of Economic History* 44 (March 1984): 1–26.

Gallay, Alan. *The Formation of a Planter Elite: Jonathan Bryan and the Southern Colonial Frontier*. Athens: University of Georgia Press, 1989.

———. *The Indian Slave Trade: The Rise of the English Empire in the American South, 1670–1717*. New Haven, Conn.: Yale University Press, 200.

Galloway, Patricia. "Choctaws at the Border of the Shatter Zone: Spheres of Exchange and Spheres of Social Value." In *Mapping the Mississippian Shatter Zone: The Colonial Indian Slave Trade and Regional Instability in the American South*, edited by Robbie Ethridge and Sheri M. Shuck-Hall, 333–64. Lincoln: University of Nebraska Press, 2009.

———. "Where Have All the Menstrual Huts Gone? The Invisibility of Menstrual Seclusion in the Late Prehistoric Southeast." In *Reader in Gender Archaeology*, edited by Kelley Hays-Gilpin and David S. Whitley, 197–211. New York: Routledge, 1998.

Gauci, Perry. *The Politics of Trade: The Overseas Merchant in State and Society, 1660–1720*. Oxford: Oxford University Press, 2001.

Gaudio, Michael. *Engraving the Savage: The New World and Techniques of Civilization*. Minneapolis: University of Minnesota Press, 2008.

Gell, Alfred. "Inter-tribal Commodity Barter and Reproductive Gift Exchange in Old Melanesia." In *Barter, Exchange, and Value: An Anthropological Approach*, edited by Caroline Humphrey and Stephen Hugh-Jones, 142–68. Cambridge: Cambridge University Press, 1992.

———. "Newcomers to the World of Goods: Consumption among the Muria Gonds." In *The Social Life of Things: Commodities in Cultural Perspective*, edited by Arjun Appadurai, 110–38. Cambridge: Cambridge University Press, 1986.

———. "Strathernograms, or, The Semiotics of Mixed Metaphors." In *The Art of Anthropology: Essays and Diagrams*, edited by Eric Hirsch, 29–75. New Brunswick, N.J.: Athlone Press, 1999.

Glaisyer, Natasha. *The Culture of Commerce in England, 1600–1720*. Woodbridge, UK: Royal Historical Society, Boydell Press, 2006.

———. "Networking: Trade and Exchange in the Eighteenth-Century British Empire." *Historical Journal* 47 (June 2004): 451–76.

Gougeon, Ramie A. "Different but the Same: Social Integration of Households in the Mississippian Chiefdoms." In *Leadership and Polity in Mississippian Society*, edited by Brian M. Butler and Paul D. Welch, 178–94. Carbondale: Southern Illinois University, Center for Archaeological Investigations, 2006.

Graeber, David. *Toward an Anthropological Theory of Value: The False Coin of Our Own Dreams*. New York: Palgrave, 2001.

Grantham, Bill. *Creation Myths and Legends of the Creek Indians*. Gainesville: University Press of Florida, 2002.

Greene, Jack P. *Imperatives, Behaviors, and Identities: Essays in Early American Cultural History*. Charlottesville: University of Virginia Press, 1992.

———. *The Quest for Power: The Lower Houses of Assembly in the Southern Royal Colonies, 1689–1776*. New York: W. W. Norton, 1972 [1963].

Guha, Ranajit. *Dominance without Hegemony: History and Power in Colonial India*. Cambridge, Mass.: Harvard University Press, 1998.

Hahn, Steven C. "The Cussita Migration Legend: History, Ideology, and the Politics of Mythmaking." In *Light on the Path: The Anthropology and History of the Southeastern Indians*, edited by Thomas J. Pluckhahn and Robbie Franklyn Ethridge, 57–93. Tuscaloosa: University of Alabama Press, 2006.

———. " 'The Indians That Live about Pon Pon': John and Mary Musgrove and the Making of a Creek Indian Community in South Carolina, 1717–1732." In *Creating and Contesting Carolina: Proprietary Era Histories*, edited by Michelle LeMaster and Bradford J. Wood, 343–66. Columbia: University of South Carolina Press, 2013.

———. *The Invention of the Creek Nation, 1670–1763*. Lincoln: University of Nebraska Press, 2004.

———. *The Life and Times of Mary Musgrove*. Gainesville: University Press of Florida, 2012.

———. "The Mother of Necessity: Carolina, the Creek Indians, and the Making of a New Order in the American Southeast, 1670–1763. In *The Transformation of the Southeastern Indians, 1540–1760*, edited by Robbie Ethridge and Charles Hudson, 79–114. Jackson: University Press of Mississippi, 2002.

Hall, Joseph M., Jr. *Zamumo's Gifts: Indian-European Exchange in the Colonial Southeast*. Philadelphia: University of Pennsylvania Press, 2009.

Hämäläinen, Pekka, and Samuel Truett. "On Borderlands." *Journal of American History* 98 (September 2011): 338–61.

Hancock, David. *Citizens of the World: London Merchants and the Integration of the British Atlantic Community, 1735–1785*. Cambridge: Cambridge University Press, 1995.

Hann, Richard L. "The 'Trade Do's Not Flourish as Formerly': The Ecological Origins of the Yamassee War of 1715." *Ethnohistory* 28 (Autumn 1981): 341–58.

Harkin, Michael E. "Ethnohistory's Ethnohistory." *Social Science History* 34 (Summer 2010): 113–28.

Harmon, Alexandra, Colleen O'Neill, and Paul C. Rosier. "Interwoven Economic Histories: American Indians in a Capitalist America." *Journal of American History* 98 (December 2011): 688–722.

Harrison, Ross. *Hobbes, Locke, and Confusion's Masterpiece: An Examination of Seventeenth-Century Political Philosophy*. Cambridge: Cambridge University Press, 2003.

Hatley, M. Thomas. "Cherokee Women Farmers Hold Their Ground." In *Powhatan's Mantle: Indians in the Colonial Southeast*, edited by Gregory A. Waselkov, Peter H. Wood, and Thomas Hatley, 305–35. Lincoln: University of Nebraska Press, 2006 [1989].

———. *The Dividing Paths: Cherokees and South Carolinians through the Era of Revolution*. New York: Oxford University Press, 1993.

———. "The Three Lives of Keowee: Loss and Recovery in the Eighteenth-Century Cherokee Villages." In *American Encounters: Natives and Newcomers from European Contact to Indian Removal, 1500–1850*, edited by Peter C. Mancall and James H. Merrell, 240–60. New York: Routledge, 2000.

Haulman, Kate. *The Politics of Fashion in Eighteenth Century America*. Chapel Hill: University of North Carolina Press, 2011.

Heal, Felicity. *Hospitality in Early Modern England*. Oxford: Oxford University Press, 1990.

Hentschell, Roze. *The Culture of Cloth in Early Modern England: Textual Constructions of a National Identity*. Hampshire, UK: Ashgate, 2008.

———. "Treasonous Textiles: Foreign Cloth and the Construction of Englishness." *Journal of Medieval and Early Modern Studies* 32 (Fall 2002): 543–70.

Herbert, Amanda E. *Female Alliances: Gender, Identity, and Friendship in Early Modern Britain*. New Haven, Conn.: Yale University Press, 2014.

Hewitt, Gary L. "The State in the Planters' Service: Politics and the Emergence of a Plantation Economy in South Carolina." In *Money, Trade, and Power: The Evolution of Colonial South Carolina's Plantation Society*, edited by Jack P. Greene, 49–73. Columbia: University of South Carolina Press, 2001.

Hill, Sarah H. *Weaving New Worlds: Southeastern Cherokee Women and Their Basketry*. Chapel Hill: University of North Carolina Press, 1997.

Hinderaker, Eric. "Translation and Cultural Brokerage." In *A Companion to American Indian History*, edited by Philip Joseph Deloria and Neal Salisbury, 357–75. Malden, Mass.: Blackwell, 2002.

Hood, Adrienne D. *The Weaver's Craft: Cloth, Commerce, and Industry in Early Pennsylvania*. Philadelphia: University of Pennsylvania Press, 2003.

Howell, Martha C. *Commerce before Capitalism in Europe, 1300–1600*. New York: Cambridge University Press, 2010.

Hudson, Charles. *The Southeastern Indians*. Knoxville: University of Tennessee Press, 1976.

Humphrey, Caroline, and Stephen Hugh-Jones. "Introduction: Barter, Exchange, and Value." In *Barter, Exchange, and Value: An Anthropological Approach*, edited by Caroline Humphrey and Stephen Hugh-Jones, 1–20. Cambridge: Cambridge University Press, 1992.

Hundert, E. J. "The Making of Homo Faber: John Locke between Ideology and History." *Journal of the History of Ideas* 33 (January–March 1972): 3–22.

Hunt, Margaret R. *The Middling Sort: Commerce, Gender, and the Family in England, 1680–1780*. Berkeley: University of California Press, 1996.

Ishii, Izumi. *Bad Fruits of the Civilized Tree: Alcohol and Sovereignty of the Cherokee Nation*. Lincoln: University of Nebraska Press, 2008.

Jackson, Jason Baird. *Yuchi Ceremonial Life: Performance, Meaning, and Tradition in a Contemporary American Indian Community*. Lincoln: University of Nebraska Press, 2003.

——, ed. *Yuchi Indian Histories before the Removal Period*. Lincoln: University of Nebraska Press, 2012.

Jansson, Maija. "Measured Reciprocity: English Ambassadorial Gift Exchange in the 17th and 18th Centuries." *Journal of Early Modern History* 9 (2005): 348–70.

Jenkins, Ned J. "Tracing the Origins of the Early Creeks." In *Mapping the Mississippian Shatter Zone: The Colonial Indian Slave Trade and Regional Instability in the American South*, edited by Robbie Ethridge and Sheri M. Shuck-Hall, 188–249. Lincoln: University of Nebraska Press, 2009.

Johnson, Jay. "Stone Tools, Politics, and the Eighteenth-Century Chickasaw in Northeast Mississippi." *American Antiquity* 62 (April 1997): 215–30.

Johnson, Ludwell H., III. "The Business of War: Trading with the Enemy in English and Early American Law." *Proceedings of the American Philosophical Society* 118 (October 1974): 459–70.

Jones, Ann Rosalind, and Peter Stallybrass. *Renaissance Clothing and the Materials of Memory*. Cambridge: Cambridge University Press, 2000.

Jones, C. C. *Historical Sketch of Tomochichi*. Savannah, Ga.: Oglethorpe Press, 1998.

Jonsson, Fredrik Albritton. "'Natural History and Improvement: The Case of Tobacco.'" In *Mercantilism Reimagined: Political Economy in Early Modern Britain and Its Empire*, edited by Philip J. Stern and Carl Wennerlind, 177–233. Oxford: Oxford University Press, 2014.

Jordan, Sarah. "From Grotesque Bodies to Useful Hands: Idleness, Industry and the Laboring Class." *Eighteenth-Century Life* 25 (Fall 2001): 62–79.

Jowett, John. "Middleton and Debt in *Timon of Athens*." In *Money and the Age of Shakespeare: Essays in New Economic Criticism*, edited by Linda Woodbridge, 219–39. New York: Palgrave Macmillan, 2003.

Kagan, Richard, and Philip Morgan, eds. *Atlantic Diasporas: Jews, Conversos, and Crypto-Jews in the Age of Mercantilism, 1500–1800*. Baltimore: Johns Hopkins University Press, 2009.

Keirn, Tim. "Monopoly, Economic Thought, and the Royal African Company." In *Early Modern Conceptions of Property*, edited by John Brewer and Susan Staves, 27–66. New York: Routledge, 1996.

Kelton, Paul. "Shattered and Infected: Epidemics, Depopulation, and the Collapse of the Native Slave Trade, 1696–1715." In *Mapping the Mississippian Shatter Zone: The Colonial Indian Slave Trade and Regional Instability in the American South*, edited by Robbie Ethridge and Sheri M. Shuck-Hall, 312–32. Lincoln: University of Nebraska Press, 2009.

King, Adam. "Creek Chiefdoms at the Temporal Edge of the Mississippian World." *Southeastern Archaeology* 21 (Winter 2002): 221–26.

———. "Leadership Strategies and the Nature of Mississippian Chiefdoms in Northern Georgia." In *Leadership and Polity in Mississippian Society*, edited by Brian M. Butler and Paul D. Welch, 73–90. Carbondale: Southern Illinois University, Center for Archaeological Investigations, 2006.

Knight, Vernon, Jr. "The Formation of the Creeks." In *The Forgotten Centuries: Indians and Europeans in the American South, 1513–1704*, edited by Charles Hudson and Carmen Chaves Tesser, 373–92. Athens: University of Georgia Press, 1994.

Knox, Mellon, Jr. "Christian Priber's Cherokee 'Kingdom of Paradise.'" *Georgia Historical Quarterly* 57 (Fall 1973): 319–31.

Koot, Christian J. "Balancing Center and Periphery." *William and Mary Quarterly*, 3rd ser., 69 (January 2012): 41–46.

Kuchta, David. "The Making of the Self-Made Man: Class, Clothing, and English Masculinity, 1688–1832." In *The Sex of Things: Gender and Consumption in Historical Perspective*, edited by Victoria de Grazia and Ellen Furlough, 54–78. Berkeley: University of California Press, 1996.

Kupperman, Karen. *Indians and English: Facing Off in Early America*. Ithaca, N.Y.: Cornell University Press, 2000.

LaCombe, Michael A. "'A Continuall and Dayly Table for Gentlemen of Fashion': Humanism, Food, and Authority at Jamestown, 1607–1609." *American Historical Review* 115 (June 2010): 669–87.

———. *Political Gastronomy: Food and Authority in the English Atlantic World*. Philadelphia: University of Pennsylvania Press, 2012.

Lapham, Heather A. *Hunting for Hides: Deerskins, Status, and Cultural Change in the Protohistoric Appalachians.* Tuscaloosa: University of Alabama Press, 2005.

LeMahieu, Michael L. "Gift Exchange and Social Hierarchy in Thomas Deloney's Jack of Newbury." In *Money and the Age of Shakespeare: Essays in New Economic Criticism*, edited by Linda Woodbridge, 129–42. New York: Palgrave Macmillan, 2003.

LeMaster, Michelle. *Brothers Born of One Mother: British-Native American Relations in the Colonial Southeast.* Charlottesville: University of Virginia Press, 2012.

LeMaster, Michelle, and Bradford J. Wood, eds. *Creating and Contesting Carolina: Proprietary Era Histories.* Columbia: University of South Carolina Press, 2013.

Leng, Thomas. "Commercial Conflict and Regulation in the Discourse of Trade in Seventeenth-Century England." *Historical Journal* 48 (December 2005): 933–54.

———. "Epistemology: Expertise and Knowledge in the World of Commerce." In *Mercantilism Reimagined: Political Economy in Early Modern Britain and Its Empire*, edited by Philip J. Stern and Carl Wennerlind, 97–116. Oxford: Oxford University Press, 2014.

Lepore, Jill. *The Name of War: King Philip's War and the Origin of American Identity.* New York: Vintage Books, 1998.

Lieberman, David. "Property, Commerce, and the Common Law: Attitudes to Legal Change in the Eighteenth Century." In *Early Modern Conceptions of Property*, edited by John Brewer and Susan Staves, 144–58. London: Routledge, 1995.

Lloyd, T. H. *Alien Merchants in England in the High Middle Ages.* Sussex, UK: Harvester Press, 1982.

Lohse, E. S. "Trade Goods." In *Handbook of North American Indians*, edited by Wilcomb E. Washburn, 396–403. Washington, D.C.: Smithsonian Institution, 1988.

Loren, Diana DiPaolo. *The Archaeology of Clothing and Bodily Adornment in Colonial America.* Gainesville: University of Florida Press, 2010.

Magnusson, Lars. *Mercantilism: The Shaping of an Economic Language.* London: Routledge, 1994.

Mancall, Peter C. *Deadly Medicine: Indians and Alcohol in Early America.* Ithaca, N.Y.: Cornell University Press, 1997.

Mancall, Peter C., Joshua L. Rosenbloom, and Thomas Weiss. "Indians and the Economy of Eighteenth-Century Carolina." In *The Atlantic Economy during the Seventeenth and Eighteenth Centuries: Organization, Operation, Practice, and Personnel*, edited by Peter A. Coclanis, 297–322. Columbia: University of South Carolina Press, 2005.

Marcoux, Jon Bernard. "Glass Trade Beads from the English Colonial Period in the Southeast, ca. A.D. 1607–1783." *Southeastern Archaeology* 31 (Winter 2012): 157–84.

———. *Pox, Empire, Shackles, and Hides: The Townsend Site, 1670–1715.* Tuscaloosa: University of Alabama Press, 2010.

Markley, Robert. "'Land Enough in the World': Locke's Golden Age and the Infinite Extension of 'Use.'" *South Atlantic Quarterly* 98 (Fall 1999): 817–37.

Matson, Cathy. "Imperial Political Economy: An Ideological Debate and Shifting Practices." *William and Mary Quarterly*, 3rd ser., 69 (January 2012): 35–40.

Mauss, Marcel. *The Gift: The Form and Reason for Exchange in Archaic Societies.* New York: W. W. Norton, 2000 [1954].

McIlvenna, Noeleen. *The Short Life of Free Georgia: Class and Slavery in the Colonial South.* Chapel Hill: University of North Carolina Press, 2015.

Menard, Russell. "From Servants to Slaves: The Transformation of the Chesapeake Labor System." *Southern Studies* 16 (Winter 1977): 355–90.

Mercantini, Jonathan. *Who Should Rule at Home? The Evolution of South Carolina Political Culture, 1748–1776.* Columbia: University of South Carolina Press, 2007.

Merrell, James H. "'The Cast of His Countenance': Reading Andrew Montour." In *Through a Glass Darkly: Reflections on Personal Identity in Early America*, edited by Ronald Hoffman, Mechal Sobel, and Fredrika J. Teute, 13–39. Chapel Hill: University of North Carolina Press, 1997.

———. *The Indians' New World: Catawbas and Their Neighbors from European Contact through the Era of Removal.* New York: W. W. Norton, 1989.

———. "The Indians' New World: The Catawba Experience." *William and Mary Quarterly*, 3rd ser., 41 (October 1984): 537–65.

———. *Into the American Woods: Negotiators on the Pennsylvania Frontier.* New York: W. W. Norton, 1999.

———. "'Our Bonds of Peace': Patterns of Intercultural Exchange in the Carolina Piedmont, 1650–1750." In *Powhatan's Mantle: Indians in the Colonial Southeast*, rev. and expanded ed., edited by Gregory Waselkov, Peter H. Wood, and Tom Hatley, 267–304. Lincoln: University of Nebraska Press, 2006 [1989].

Michie, Audrey. "Charleston Textile Imports, 1738–1742." *Journal of Early Southern Decorative Arts* 7 (May 1981): 20–39.

Minchinton, Walter. "The Merchants in England in the Eighteenth Century." *Explorations in Entrepreneurial History* 10 (1957): 22–31.

Mokyr, Joel. *The Enlightened Economy: An Economic History of Britain, 1700–1850.* New Haven, Conn.: Yale University Press, 2009.

Montgomery, Florence M. *Textiles in America, 1650–1870: A Dictionary Based on Original Documents: Prints and Paintings, Commercial Records, American Merchants' Papers, Shopkeepers' Advertisements, and Pattern Books with Original Swatches of Cloth.* New York: W. W. Norton, 1984.

Moore, Alexander. "Thomas Nairne's 1708 Western Expedition: An Episode in the Ango-French Competition for Empire." *Proceedings of the Meeting of the French Colonial Historical Society* 10 (1984): 47–58.

Moore, W. O., Jr. "The Largest Exporters of Deerskins from Charles Town, 1735–1775." *South Carolina Historical Magazine* 74 (July 1973): 144–50.

Moorehead, Warren King, ed. *Explorations of the Etowah Site in Georgia.* Gainesville: University Press of Florida, 2000 [1932].

Morris, Michael P. *The Bringing of Wonder: Trade and the Indians of the Southeast, 1700–1783*. Westport, Conn.: Greenwood Press, 1999.

Morris, Richard B. *Government and Labor in Early America*. New York: Harper and Row, 1946.

Mowry, Melissa. "Dressing Up and Dressing Down: Prostitution, Pornography, and the Seventeenth-Century English Textile Industry." *Journal of Women's History* 11 (Autumn 1999): 78–103.

Muldrew, Craig. *The Economy of Obligation: The Culture of Credit and Social Relations in Early Modern England*. New York: Macmillan, 1998.

Muller, John. *Mississippian Political Economy*. New York: Plenum Press, 1997.

Munn, Nancy. *The Fame of Gawa: A Symbolic Study of Value Transformation in a Massim (Papua New Guinea) Society*. Project Heights, Ill.: Waveland Press, 1986.

Myers, Maureen S. "Leadership at the Edge." In *Leadership and Polity in Mississippian Society*, edited by Brian M. Butler and Paul D. Welch, 156–77. Carbondale: Southern Illinois University, Center for Archaeological Investigations, 2006.

Nabokov, Peter. *A Forest of Time: American Indian Ways of History*. Cambridge: Cambridge University Press, 2002.

Neeson, J. M. *Commoners: Common Right, Enclosure, and Social Change in England, 1700–1820*. Cambridge: Cambridge University Press, 1993.

Newell, Margaret Ellen. "Putting the 'Political' Back in Political Economy (This Is Not Your Parents' Mercantilism)." *William and Mary Quarterly*, 3rd ser., 69 (January 2012): 57–62.

Oatis, Steven J. *A Colonial Complex: South Carolina's Frontiers in the Era of the Yamasee War, 1680–1730*. Lincoln: University of Nebraska Press, 2004.

O'Brien, Greg. *Choctaws in a Revolutionary Age, 1750–1830*. Lincoln: University of Nebraska Press, 2002.

Oliphant, John. *Peace and War on the Anglo-Cherokee Frontier, 1756–63*. Baton Rouge: Louisiana State University Press, 2001.

Orlin, Lena Cowen. "Fictions of the Early Modern English Probate Inventory." In *The Culture of Capital: Property, Cities, and Knowledge in Early Modern England*, edited by Henry S. Turner, 51–84. New York: Routledge, 2002.

Parry, J., and M. Bloch, eds. *Money and the Morality of Exchange*. Cambridge: Cambridge University Press, 1989.

Paulett, Robert. *An Empire of Small Places: Mapping the Southeastern Anglo-American Trade, 1732–1795*. Athens: University of Georgia Press, 2012.

Payne, Claudine. "The Foundations of Leadership in Mississippian Chiefdoms." In *Leadership and Polity in Mississippian Society*, edited by Brian M. Butler and Paul D. Welch, 91–114. Carbondale: Southern Illinois University, Center for Archaeological Investigations, 2006.

Peck, Linda Levy. *Consuming Splendor: Society and Culture in Seventeenth-Century England*. Cambridge: Cambridge University Press, 2005.

Perdue, Theda. *Cherokee Women: Gender and Culture Change, 1700–1835*. Lincoln: University of Nebraska Press, 1998.

———. *Slavery and the Evolution of Cherokee Society, 1540–1866*. Knoxville: University of Tennessee Press, 1979.

———. "'A Sprightly Lover Is the Most Prevailing Missionary': Intermarriage between Europeans and Indians in the Eighteenth-Century South." In *Light on the Path: The Anthropology and History of the Southeastern Indians*, edited by Thomas J. Pluckhahn and Robbie Franklyn Ethridge, 165–78. Tuscaloosa: University of Alabama Press, 2006.

Perlin, Frank. "The Other 'Species' World: Speciation of Commodities and Moneys, and the Knowledge-Base of Commerce, 1500–1900." In *Merchants, Companies, and Trade: Asia, Europe, and India in the Early Modern Era*, edited by Sushil Chaudhury and Michel Morineau, 145–72. Cambridge: Cambridge University Press, 1999.

Pesantubbee, Michelene E. *Choctaw Women in a Chaotic World*. Albuquerque: University of New Mexico Press, 2005.

Pettigrew, William A. *Freedom's Debt: The Royal African Company and the Politics of the Atlantic Slave Trade, 1672–1752*. Chapel Hill: University of North Carolina Press, 2013.

Piker, Joshua Aaron. *The Four Deaths of Acorn Whistler: Telling Stories in Colonial America*. Cambridge, Mass.: Harvard University Press, 2013.

———. *Okfuskee: A Creek Indian Town in Colonial America*. Cambridge, Mass.: Harvard University Press, 2004.

Pincus, Steven. "Rethinking Mercantilism: Political Economy, the British Empire, and the Atlantic World in the Seventeenth and Eighteenth Centuries." *William and Mary Quarterly*, 3rd ser., 69 (January 2012): 3–34.

———. *1688: The First Modern Revolution*. New Haven, Conn.: Yale University Press, 2009.

Pocock, J. G. A. *Virtue, Commerce, and History*. Cambridge: Cambridge University Press, 1985.

Potter, Gail DeBuse. "The Matchcoat." In *Rethinking the Fur Trade: Cultures of Exchange in an Atlantic World*, edited by Susan Sleeper-Smith, 411–13. Lincoln: University of Nebraska Press, 2009.

Pratt, Stephanie. *American Indians in British Art, 1700–1840*. Norman: University of Oklahoma Press, 2005.

———. "Reynolds' 'King of the Cherokees' and Other Mistaken Identities in the Portraiture of Native American Delegations, 1710–1762." *Oxford Art Journal* 21 (1998): 135–50.

Pressly, Paul M. *On the Rim of the Caribbean: Colonial Georgia and the British Atlantic World*. Athens: University of Georgia Press, 2013.

Price, Jacob M. *Capital and Credit in British Overseas Trade: The View from the Chesapeake, 1700–1776*. Cambridge, Mass.: Harvard University Press, 1980.

Queen, Sally A. *Textiles for Colonial Clothing: A Workbook of Swatches and Information*. Arlington, Va.: Q Graphics Production, 2003.

Ramsey, William L. "A Coat for 'Indian Cuffy': Mapping the Boundary between Freedom and Slavery in Colonial South Carolina." *South Carolina Historical Magazine* 103 (January 2002): 48–66.

———. "'Something Cloudy in Their Looks': The Origins of the Yamasee War Reconsidered." *Journal of American History* 90 (June 2003): 44–75.

———. *The Yamasee War: A Study of Culture, Economy, and Conflict in the Colonial South.* Lincoln: University of Nebraska Press, 2008.

Ray, Arthur. "Indians as Consumers in the Eighteenth Century." In *Rethinking the Fur Trade: Cultures of Exchange in an Atlantic World*, edited by Susan Sleeper-Smith, 320–43. Lincoln: University of Nebraska Press, 2009 [1980].

Ray, Arthur, and Donald Freeman. *"Give Us Good Measure": An Economic Analysis of Relations between the Indians and the Hudson's Bay Company before 1763.* Toronto: University of Toronto Press, 1978.

Renfrew, Collin. "Varna and the Emergence of Wealth in Prehistoric Europe," In *The Social Life of Things: Commodities in Cultural Perspective*, edited by Arjun Appadurai, 141–68. Cambridge: Cambridge University Press, 1986.

Richter, Daniel. *Before the Revolution: America's Ancient Pasts.* Cambridge, Mass.: Belknap Press of Harvard University Press, 2011.

———. *Facing East from Indian Country: A Native History of Early America.* Cambridge, Mass.: Harvard University Press, 2001.

Riggs, Brett. "Reconsidering Chestowee: The 1713 Raid in Regional Perspective." In *Yuchi Indian Histories before the Removal Era.* Edited by Jason Baird Jackson, 43–72. Lincoln: University of Nebraska Press, 2012.

Rivers, William James. *A Sketch of the History of South Carolina, to the Close of the Proprietary Government by the Revolution of 1719.* Charleston, S.C.: McCarter and Co., 1856.

Roberts, Justin, and Iam Beamish. "Venturing Out: The Barbadian Diaspora and the Carolina Colony, 1650–1685." In *Creating and Contesting Carolina: Proprietary Era Histories*, edited by Michelle LeMaster and Bradford J. Wood, 49–72. Columbia: University of South Carolina Press.

Rodning, Christopher B. "Late Prehistoric and Protohistoric Shell Gorgets from Southwestern North Carolina." *Southeastern Archaeology* 31 (Summer 2012): 33–56.

Roper, L. H. *Conceiving Carolina: Proprietors, Planters, and Plots, 1662–1729.* New York: Palgrave Macmillan, 2004.

Rosen, Deborah A. *Courts and Commerce: Gender, Law, and the Market Economy in Colonial New York.* Columbus: Ohio State University Press, 1997.

Rothrock, Mary U. "Carolina Traders among the Overhill Cherokees, 1690–1760." *East Tennessee Historical Society's Publications* 1 (1929).

Sacks, David Harris. *The Widening Gate: Bristol and the Atlantic Economy, 1450–1700.* Berkeley: University of California Press, 1991.

Saunt, Claudio. *A New Order of Things: Property, Power, and the Transformation of the Creek Indians, 1733–1816.* Cambridge: Cambridge University Press, 1999.

Schroeder, Sissel. "Walls as Symbols of Political, Economic, and Military Might." In *Leadership and Polity in Mississippian Society*, edited by Brian M. Butler and Paul D. Welch, 115–41. Carbondale: Southern Illinois University, Center for Archaeological Investigations, 2006.

Sherman, Sandra. *Finance and Fictionality in the Early Eighteenth Century: Accounting for Defoe*. Cambridge: Cambridge University Press, 1996.

Shoemaker, Nancy. *A Strange Likeness: Becoming Red and White in Eighteenth-Century North America*. New York: Oxford University Press, 2004.

Shovlin, John. "War and Peace: Trade, International Competition, and Political Economy." In *Mercantilism Reimagined: Political Economy in Early Modern Britain and Its Empire*, edited by Philip J. Stern and Carl Wennerlind, 305–27. Oxford: Oxford University Press, 2014.

Silverman, David. *Thundersticks: Firearms and the Transformation of Native America*. Cambridge, Mass.: Harvard University Press, 2016.

Sirmans, M. Eugene. *Colonial South Carolina: A Political History, 1663–1763*. Chapel Hill: University of North Carolina Press, 1966.

——. "Politics in Colonial South Carolina: The Failure of Proprietary Reform, 1682–1694." *William and Mary Quarterly*, 3rd ser., 23 (January 1966): 33–55.

Smail, John. "The Culture of Credit in Eighteenth-Century Commerce: The English Textile Industry." *Enterprise and Society* 4 (June 2003): 299–325.

Smith, Abbot Emerson. *Colonists in Bondage: White Servitude and Convict Labor in America, 1607–1776*. Chapel Hill: University of North Carolina Press, 1947.

Snyder, Christina. *Slavery in Indian Country: The Changing Face of Captivity in Early America*. Cambridge, Mass.: Harvard University Press, 2010.

Spalding, Phinizy. "Some Sermons before the Trustees of Colonial Georgia." *Georgia Historical Quarterly* 57 (Fall 1973): 332–46.

Spufford, Margaret. *The Great Reclothing of Rural England: Petty Chapmen and Their Wares in the Seventeenth Century*. London: Hambledon Press, 1984.

Staff. "Scraps of Prehistoric Fabric Provide a View of Ancient Life: Kathryn Jakes." *Ohio State Research News* (2004).

Stahl, Ann Brower. "Colonial Entanglements and the Practices of Taste: An Alternative to Logocentric Approaches." *American Anthropologist* 104 (September 2002): 827–45.

Stallybrass, Peter. "Marx's Coat." In *Border Fetishisms: Material Objects in Unstable Spaces*, edited by Patricia Spyer, 183–207. New York: Routledge, 1998.

——. "The Value of Culture and the Disavowal of Things." In *The Culture of Capital: Property, Cities, and Knowledge in Early Modern England*, edited by Henry S. Turner, 275–92. New York: Routledge, 2002.

Staples, Kathleen. "'Useful, Ornamental or Necessary in This Province': The Textile Inventory of John Dart, 1754." *Journal of Early Southern Decorative Arts* 29 (Winter 2003): 39–82.

Steele, Ian K. *Politics of Colonial Policy: The Board of Trade in Colonial Administration, 1696–1720*. Oxford: Oxford University Press, 1968.

Stern, Philip J., and Carl Wennerlind, eds. *Mercantilism Reimagined: Political Economy in Early Modern Britain and Its Empire*. Oxford: Oxford University Press, 2014.

Strathern, Marilyn. *The Gender of the Gift: Problems with Women and Problems with Society in Melanesia*. Berkeley: University of California Press, 1990.

Stump, W. Derrell. "An Economic Consequence of 1688." *Albion* 6 (Spring 1974): 28–35.

Swanton, John Reed. *Creek Religion and Medicine*. Lincoln: University of Nebraska Press, 2000.

———. *Social Organization and Social Usages of the Indians of the Creek Confederacy*. New York: Johnson Reprint, 1970 [1928].

Sweet, Julie Anne. " 'The Excellency and Advantage of Doing Good': Thoughts on the Anniversary Sermons Preached before the Trustees of Georgia, 1731–1750." *Georgia Historical Quarterly* 90 (Spring 2006): 1–34.

———. *Negotiating for Georgia: British-Creek Relations in the Trustee Era, 1733–1752*. Athens: University of Georgia Press, 2005.

———. *William Stephens: Georgia's Forgotten Founder*. Baton Rouge: Louisiana State University Press, 2010.

Swingen, Abigail. "Labor: Employment, Colonial Servitude, and Slavery in the Seventeenth-Century Atlantic." In *Mercantilism Reimagined: Political Economy in Early Modern Britain and Its Empire*, edited by Philip J. Stern and Carl Wennerlind, 46–73. Oxford: Oxford University Press, 2014.

Tanner, Adrian. *Bringing Home the Animals: Religious Ideology and Mode of Production of the Mistassini Cree Hunters*. New York: St. Martin's Press, 1979.

Taussig, Michael. *The Devil and Commodity Fetishism in South America*. Chapel Hill: University of North Carolina Press, 1983.

Thomas, Nicholas. *Entangled Objects: Exchange, Material Culture, and Colonialism in the Pacific*. Cambridge, Mass.: Harvard University Press, 1991.

Tortora, Daniel J. *Carolina in Crisis: Cherokees, Colonists, and Slaves in the American Southeast, 1756–1763*. Chapel Hill: University of North Carolina Press, 2015.

Turner, Henry S., ed. *The Culture of Capital: Property, Cities, and Knowledge in Early Modern England*. New York: Routledge, 2002.

Ulrich, Laurel. *The Age of Homespun: Objects and Stories in the Creation of an American Myth*. New York: Alfred A. Knopf, 2001.

Usner, Daniel H., Jr. "The Frontier Exchange Economy of the Lower Mississippi Valley in the Eighteenth Century." *William and Mary Quarterly*, 3rd ser., 44 (April 1987): 165–92.

———. *Indians, Settlers, and Slaves in a Frontier Exchange Economy: The Lower Mississippi Valley before 1783*. Chapel Hill: University of North Carolina Press, 1992.

———. *Indian Work: Language and Livelihood in Native American History*. Cambridge, Mass.: Harvard University Press, 2009.

VanDerwarker, Amber M., and Kandace R. Detwiler. "Gendered Practice in Cherokee Foodways: A Spatial Analysis of Plant Remains from the Coweeta Creek Site." *Southeastern Archaeology* 21 (Summer 2002): 21–28.

VanDerwarker, Amber M., Jon Marcoux, and Kandace Hollenbach. "Farming and Foraging at the Crossroads: The Consequences of Cherokee and European Interaction through the Late Eighteenth Century." *American Antiquity* 78, no. 1 (January 2013): 68–88.

Van Hoak, Stephen P. "Untangling the Roots of Dependency: Choctaw Economics, 1700–1860." *American Indian Quarterly* 23 (Summer–Autumn 1999): 113–28.

Van Kirk, Sylvia. "'The Custom of the Country': An Examination of Fur Trade Marriage Practices." In *Rethinking the Fur Trade: Cultures of Exchange in an Atlantic World*, edited by Susan Sleeper-Smith, 481–518. Lincoln: University of Nebraska Press, 2009.

Vaughan, Alden T. *Transatlantic Encounters: American Indians in Britain, 1500–1776*. New York: Cambridge University Press, 2006.

Waddell, Brodie. *God, Duty and Community in English Economic Life, 1660–1720*. Woodbridge: Boydell Press, 2012.

Waldstreicher, David. "Why Thomas Jefferson and African Americans Wore Their Politics on Their Sleeves: Dress and Mobilization between American Revolutions." In *Beyond the Founders: New Approaches to the Political History of the Early American Republic*, edited by Jeffrey Pasley, Andrew Roberton, and David Waldstreicher, 79–106. Chapel Hill: University of North Carolina Press, 2004.

Waselkov, G. A. "The Eighteenth-Century Anglo-Indian Trade in Southeastern North America." In *New Faces of the Fur Trade: Selected Papers of the Seventh North American Fur Trade Conference, Halifax, Nova Scotia, 1995*, edited by Jo-Anne Fiske, Susan Sleeper-Smith, and William Wicken, 193–222. East Lansing: Michigan State University Press, 1995.

———. "Historic Creek Indian Responses to European Trade and the Rise of Political Factions." In *Ethnohistory and Archaeology: Approaches to Postcontact Change in the Americas*, edited by J. D. Rogers and S. M. Wilson, 123–31. New York: Plenum Press, 1993.

———. "Seventeenth-Century Trade in the Colonial Southeast." *Southeast Archaeology* 8 (Winter 1989): 117–33.

Waselkov, G. A., and Ashley A. Dumas. "Cultural Revitalization and Recasting Identities in the Post-Mississippian Southeast." In *Forging Southeastern Identities: Social Archaeology and Ethnohistory of the Mississippian to Early Historic South*, edited by Gregory A. Waselkov and Martin T. Smith (Tuscaloosa: University of Alabama Press, forthcoming).

Waselkov, G. A., and Marvin T. Smith. "Upper Creek Archaeology." In *Indians of the Greater Southeast: Historical Archaeology and Ethnohistory*, edited by Bonnie G. McEwan, 242–64. Gainesville: University Press of Florida, 2000.

Weiner, Annette. *Inalienable Possessions: The Paradox of Keeping While Giving*. Berkeley: University of California Press, 1992.

Weir, Robert. "'Shaftesbury's Darling:' British Settlement in the Carolinas at the Close of the Seventeenth Century." In *Oxford History of the British Empire*, vol. 1, *The Origins of Empire: British Oversees Enterprise to the Close of the Seventeenth Century*, edited by Nicholas Canny, 375–97. Oxford: Oxford University Press, 2001.

Welch, Paul. "Interpreting Anomalous Rural Mississippian Settlements: Leadership from Below." In *Leadership and Polity in Mississippian Society*, edited by Brian M. Butler and Paul D. Welch, 214–35. Carbondale: Southern Illinois University, Center for Archaeological Investigations, 2006.

Wennerlind, Carl. "Credit-Money as the Philosopher's Stone: Alchemy and Coinage Problems in Seventeenth-Century England." *History of Political Economy* 35, Annual Supplement (2003): 234–61.

Wesson, Cameron B. "Creek and Pre-Creek Revisited." In *The Archaeology of Traditions: Agency and History before and after Columbus*, edited by Timothy R. Pauketat, 94–106. Gainesville: University Press of Florida, 2001.

———. *Households and Hegemony: Early Creek Prestige Goods, Symbolic Capital, and Social Power*. Lincoln: University of Nebraska Press, 2008.

———. "Prestige Goods, Symbolic Capital, and Social Power in the Protohistoric Southeast." In *Between Contacts and Colonies: Archaeological Perspectives on the Protohistoric Southeast*, edited by Cameron B. Wesson and Mark A. Rees, 110–25. Tuscaloosa: University of Alabama Press, 2002.

White, Richard. *The Middle Ground: Indians, Empires, and Republics in the Great Lakes Region, 1650–1815*. Cambridge: Cambridge University Press, 1991.

———. *The Roots of Dependency: Subsistence, Environment, and Social Change among the Choctaws, Pawnees, and Navajos*. Lincoln: University of Nebraska Press, 1983.

White, Shane, and Graham White. "Slave Clothing and African-American Culture in the Eighteenth and Nineteenth Centuries." *Past and Present* 148 (August 1995): 149–86.

Williams, Mark. *Oconee Old Town: History and Archaeological Excavations*. Lamar Institute Publications 36. Savannah, Ga.: Lamar Institute, 1996.

Wilson, Gregory D., Jon Marcoux, and Brad Koldehoff. "Square Pegs in Round Holes: Organizational Diversity between Early Moundville and Cahokia." In *Leadership and Polity in Mississippian Society*, edited by Brian M. Butler and Paul D. Welch, 43–72. Carbondale: Southern Illinois University, Center for Archaeological Investigations, 2006.

Wood, Betty. *Slavery in Colonial Georgia, 1730–1775*. Athens: University of Georgia Press, 1984.

Wood, Neal. *John Locke and Agrarian Capitalism*. Berkeley: University of California Press, 1984.

Wood, Peter H., Gregory A. Waselkov, and Thomas M. Hatley, eds. *Powhatan's Mantle: Indians in the Colonial Southeast*. Rev. ed. Lincoln: University of Nebraska Press, 2006.

Woodbridge, Linda. "The Peddler and the Pawn: Why Did Tudor England Consider Peddlers to Be Rogues?" In *Rogues and Early Modern English Culture*, edited by Craig Dionne and Steve Mentz, 143–70. Ann Arbor: University of Michigan Press, 2004.

Worth, John E. "The Lower Creeks: Origins and Early History." In *Indians of the Greater Southeast: Historical Archaeology and Ethnohistory*, edited by Bonnie G. McEwan, 265–98. Gainesville: University Press of Florida, 2000.

Wrightson, Keith. *Earthly Necessities: Economic Lives in Early Modern Britain*. New Haven, Conn.: Yale University Press, 2000.

Yirush, Craig. *Settlers, Liberty, and Empire: The Roots of Early American Political Theory, 1675–1775*. New York: Cambridge University Press, 2011.

———. "'Since We Came Out of This Ground': Indigenous Legal Norms in the Eighteenth-Century Ohio Valley." Paper presented at WMQ-EMSI Workshop: Early American Legal Histories, Huntington Library, San Marino, California, May 29, 2015.

Zahedieh, Nuala, "Overseas Expansion and Trade in the Seventeenth Century." In *Oxford History of the British Empire*, vol. 1, *The Origins of Empire: British Oversees Enterprise to the Close of the Seventeenth Century*, edited by Nicholas Canny, 398–422. Oxford: Oxford University Press, 2001.

Zierden, Martha A., Jeanne A. Calhoun, and Demi Hacker-Norton. *Archdale Hall: Investigations of a Lowcountry Plantation*. Charlestown: Charlestown Museum, 1985.

Index

Coosata King (Cherokee), 81

Corn Mother myth, 13, 24–26, 30, 32, 37, 43, 175–76 (n. 44)

Cosmography, British and British American, 35–36, 37–38, 39, 42, 104–5

Cosmography, Southeastern Indian, 24–32; and bodily adornment, 19, 141, 172 (n. 15). *See also* Corn Mother myth; Creek origin myth; Green Corn Ceremony

Cotton, 130, 131, 142, 165, 166

Coweta (Creek town), 28, 96

Credit and debt: cultures and ideologies of, 74–81, 180 (n. 108); and gifts, 1–2, 38, 40, 93, 105, 110–11; harmful effects of, 60, 73–74, 77–78, 80; and the Indian trade, 13, 56, 58, 60, 62–63, 64, 73–74, 76, 77, 79–81, 88, 90–91, 157, 194 (n. 179); and social networks, 1–2, 78, 157

Creek Indians, 8–9, 15, 17, 34, 42, 60, 86, 99, 104–14 passim; consumer taste of, 133, 136, 144, 149, 155; cultural practices of, 22, 25–27, 32–33, 75, 76, 96, 111, 113, 158; and the deerskin trade, 56, 57, 67, 69, 72, 79, 88, 90, 120, 128, 131, 149–55. *See also* Corn Mother myth; Creek origin myth; Green Corn Ceremony; Southeastern Indians; *and individual and town names*

Creek origin myth, 28–29, 96, 121

Cuming, Alexander, 83–84, 196 (n. 225)

Cunneshote (Cherokee), 140

Cussita (Creek town), 76–77, 99, 113

Daniel, Robert, 1, 2, 4

Darquier, Moses, 126

Debt. *See* Credit and debt

Deerskin production, Southeastern Indian, 18–19, 20, 22, 28, 46, 81, 115, 123, 150, 158, 194 (n. 179); influenced by the Atlantic trade, 20–24, 34, 157–58, 209 (n. 132)

Deerskins: British use of, 122–23, 127, 147, 149–50; gifts of, 97–98, 115, 118; importance of to the Atlantic trade, 6, 12, 14, 15, 17, 21, 48, 50, 51, 88, 122–23, 127, 129, 130, 154, 158, 183 (n. 13); Southeastern Indian use of, 27, 132; value of, 63, 70, 73, 76, 92, 93, 118, 145–46, 147, 152, 158, 168 (n. 1). *See also* Leather industry; Trade

Defoe, Daniel, 87

Demere, Raymond, 97, 106–7, 112

Dependency theory, 4–5, 160, 169 (n. 10), 212 (n. 29)

de Soto, Hernando, 8, 97

Devonshire, Reeve & Lloyd, 149

Dinwiddie, Robert, 57–58

Diplomacy. *See* Gifts and gift-giving: and diplomacy

Disease, 8, 25, 33, 34, 141

Dockwra v. Dickenson, 53

Documents Relating to Indian Affairs, 128

Duffel, 109, 130, 131, 132–33, 136, 140, 142, 143, 147, 149

Dumas, Ashley, 33

Eagles and eagle feathers, 28–29, 96, 112–13, 115

Ebenezer, Ga, 112

Edelson, Max, 42

Edisto Garrison, 82, 85, 125

Edisto Island, 97

Egremont, Lord (Charles Wyndham), 139

Elbert, Samuel, 96

Ellis, Henry, 99, 113, 198 (n. 9)

Elsinore, Samuel, 72

Emistesego (Creek), 114

Euchee Indians. *See* Yuchi Indians

Evans, John, 64–66, 190–91 (n. 117), 191 (n. 122)

Evans, Thomas, 66

Everand, Richard, 96

Everleigh, Samuel, 111, 136

Fitch, Tobias, 79, 104–5, 109

Flannel, 134, 140, 147

Flint (Cherokee), 58

Foissin, Elias, 142

Food, Southeastern Indian: and assimilation, 96–97, 104, 148; distribution of, 8, 13, 24, 30, 31; production of, 21–25, 30–31, 34, 36; significance of, 24–26, 30–35, 96–98, 115; traded to Europeans, 20, 21, 23–24, 34, 49–51, 63. *See also* Gifts and gift exchange: of hospitality; Green Corn Ceremony; Warfare: disruptions caused by

Fort Prince George, 97, 112, 131–34 passim, 138, 140, 141, 144, 145, 146–47

Frederica, Ga., 110

Free trade, 13, 49, 53, 54, 89, 92

French, 57, 103, 107, 111, 122; alliances with Southeastern Indians, 60, 89, 99–100, 106–7; competition with British colonies, 67, 94, 95, 109–10

French and Indian War, 15, 106–7, 123, 127, 150, 151, 161

Frontier. *See* Borderland

Frontier exchange economy, 11, 12, 52, 56–58, 62, 82, 92, 157, 211 (n. 24)

Gaillard, Bartholomew, 68

Gaillard, Theodore, 148

Galphin, George, 67, 88, 133, 141, 144, 152

Garlix, 130, 133–34

Gender, 30; and the division of labor, 22–24, 28, 158. *See also* Men, Southeastern Indian; Women, Southeastern Indian

Georgia, 36; anniversary sermons, 37–39, 180 (n. 128); economy of, 70, 75, 78–79, 129–30, 131, 149, 150–51, 155, 183 (n. 13); founding of, 5–6, 9–10, 14, 17, 37, 38–40, 43, 47, 48, 50, 70; government of, 13, 14–15, 40–41, 75, 89; relationships with Southeastern Indians, 17–18, 23, 43–44, 49, 64, 80, 98, 99, 104, 106,

108, 109, 110, 113–17 passim; slavery debate in, 6, 9–10, 15, 41–42. *See also* Salzburgers; Trade; *and specific town names*

Georgia Governor and Council, 108

Georgia President and Assistants, 60, 88–89, 106

Georgia Trustees, 6, 14–15, 17–18, 36, 38–41, 43, 46, 79, 88–89, 99, 109, 119

Gifts and gift-giving, 1, 15, 100, 124, 129, 142; the anthropological study of, 4, 102; and counter-gifts, 2, 74, 98–99, 114, 117; and diplomacy, 17, 32, 46, 84, 93–94, 96, 98–99, 100, 108, 112–15, 116; and hierarchies, 11, 15, 45–46, 82, 94, 97, 98, 112, 119, 135; of hospitality, 34, 94, 96–99, 100, 104, 112, 145, 156; and mythology, 95–96, 104–5, 113; preservation and use of, 15, 107, 115–121, 122, 153; refusal of, 72, 108, 117; restrictions on, 95, 117–18; Southeastern Indian requests for, 108–112; as a tool of British empire, 82–83, 92, 94, 95, 99–108, 110–11, 120, 155–56; as a tool to counter British empire, 92, 96, 97–98, 111–12, 115–17, 119–21, 156; versus commodities and commodity exchange, 1–4, 50, 93–94, 102–3, 127, 129, 135, 145, 146–48, 154–55. *See also* Alcohol: gifts of; Credit and debt: and gifts; Consumption: of gifts versus commodities; Deerskins: gifts of; Guns and ammunition: as gifts; Headmen: and gifts; Labor: and gifts; Scalps

Glen, James, 23, 42, 46, 57–58, 67, 70, 72, 77, 95, 103, 105, 107, 108, 110–11, 112, 119, 161

Glorious Revolution, 47

Glover, Charlesworth, 132

Godalming, Surrey, England, 17–18, 43–44, 171 (n. 1)

Goose Creek Men, 14, 15, 53–54

Gordon, Peter, 41–42

Gordon, Thomas, 42–43
Goudy, Robert, 151–52, 211 (n. 19)
Graeber, David, 169 (n. 6)
Graham, Patrick, 60
Grant, Ludovick, 57, 77–78, 110–11
Green Corn Ceremony, 9, 13, 24, 25,
    29–35, 43, 94, 119, 177–78 (n. 80),
    178 (n. 85)
Grendon, John, 148
Gronau, Israel Christian, 36
Guha, Ranajit, 162
Guns and ammunition, 112, 168 (n. 1);
    British and British American pride
    in, 29, 52, 104–5, 155–56; as com-
    modities, 1, 2, 3, 46, 52, 56, 58, 66,
    80, 93, 130, 132, 143–44, 147, 151; as
    gifts, 1, 2, 3, 4, 15, 93, 95, 99, 102–11,
    120, 155–56; gunsmithing of, 105,
    151, 211 (n. 15); importance of to
    Southeastern Indian societies, 8, 20,
    22, 34, 46, 52, 108–111, 132, 169 (n. 10);
    restrictions on the trading of, 54, 151

Haberdashery, 5, 22, 137–38, 140–41,
    144, 147, 153
Half thicks, 133, 135, 142, 206 (n. 65)
Handsome Man (Creek), 96
Harris and Habersham, 149
Hastings, Theophilus, 79, 81, 86–87,
    102, 124–25, 142; and purchases for
    the Indian trade, 131, 133, 134, 141
Headmen: authority of, 13–14, 22, 29,
    31, 33–34, 45–46, 55, 79–80, 81, 83,
    84, 114, 119, 155, 156, 158, 159–61;
    challenges to, 11, 13, 45, 71, 76–77,
    92, 159, 160; control over trade, 18,
    44, 45–46, 49, 68–69, 73, 80–85 pas-
    sim, 92, 157, 159, 160–61; and gifts,
    45–46, 82, 83, 93–96, 99, 100, 102,
    108, 112–13, 119; responsibilities of,
    14, 22, 24, 27, 29, 31, 46–47, 49, 76,
    82–86 passim, 93, 114, 157, 159–61
Hemp, 133
Hepworth, Thomas, 60
Herbert, John, 79–80, 98, 105

Highrider, John, 107
Hilton, William, 49, 184 (n. 18)
Holms, Francis, 125, 126
Hootleyboyaw (Creek), 82
Horses, 57, 64, 82, 85, 86, 87, 88, 90, 91,
    92, 119, 131, 137, 142, 152, 153
Horton, William, 94
Hudson's Bay Company, 128
Hunting, Southeastern Indian, 19, 64,
    80, 104, 115, 120, 123, 131–32, 147,
    151, 190–91 (n. 117), 194 (n. 179), 211
    (n. 17); disruptions to by warfare,
    109–11, 152; effect of Atlantic Trade
    on, 21–22, 29, 43, 46, 76, 155, 157–58;
    and masculinity, 23, 24, 26, 28, 103;
    myths and rituals of, 9, 26–27, 29, 43,
    95–96, 151, 155; and property rights,
    32, 43, 81, 102, 119, 145–46, 159, 160.
    See also Guns and ammunition

Improvement, 5, 6, 41–42, 48
Indian agent, South Carolina, 54–55,
    57, 71–72, 77, 82, 90, 107, 118. See
    also individual Indian agent names
Indian boots, 127
Indian Forster (Tuscarora), 56
Indian traders, 49, 76, 82, 133, 136;
    agency of, 11, 12–13, 14, 56–58, 64–67,
    71–73, 79, 80, 92, 129, 157, 193 (n. 162);
    camaraderie amongst, 91–92, 157;
    colonists' distrust of, 52–53, 56–64,
    67, 71, 73, 79, 87–88, 156–57; diplo-
    matic role of, 58, 60–61, 66–67, 89,
    114, 157, 190–91 (n. 117); factional-
    ism amongst, 89–90; knowledge of
    Southeastern Indian consumer taste,
    128, 134–35, 141, 143–44; relation-
    ships with Native Americans, 12, 54,
    58, 61–62, 72–73, 87; social standing
    of, 11, 66–67, 157; and trading firms,
    88,   89–92, 157, 191 (n. 123); and
    travel, 59, 63–66, 71, 85; unlicensed,
    68, 89–90, 126, 151–52, 153. See also
    Trade: regulation of; and individual
    Indian traders

Johnson, Nathaniel, 54
Jones, John, 82, 85, 125
Jones, Thomas, 70
Joree (Cherokee town), 109
Journals of the Commissioners of Indian Trade, 128
Judd's Friend. *See* Ostenaco

Keith, William, 130
Keowee (Cherokee town), 97, 112
Kersey, 17, 18, 46, 130
Kiawah Indians, 143
Killa Cunsta (Cherokee), 109–10
Koasati Indians, 9
Kussoe Indians, 51–52

Labor, 3, 76, 159; anthropological theories of, 173 (n. 16), 179–80 (n. 108); communal, 3, 20, 24, 29, 30–32, 35–36, 43–44, 97, 155; effect of the Atlantic trade on, 20–24, 155, 157; gendered division of, 22–24, 28 158; and gifts, 93, 95, 99–104, 119, 142; ideologies of, 3, 5–6, 9–10, 14–15, 17–44 passim, 47, 155–62; individual, 3, 6, 14–15, 19, 20, 27–28, 30–33, 35–37, 42, 43–44, 155; managerial, 3, 6, 17, 19, 38, 41–42, 93, 155, 181 (n. 155); and property rights, 32–33, 37, 41, 42–43, 81, 102, 119, 145–46, 148, 155, 159, 160
Land, British and British American: ideologies about, 5–6, 35–42 passim, 47–48, 67, 100; and political and social power, 6, 12, 14, 40–41, 48, 59, 60, 66, 157
Land, Southeastern Indian: common and household, 23–24, 30, 31, 32; defense of, 4, 18, 51, 84, 96, 97, 98, 111–12, 118, 156, 162; European encroachment on, 152, 162; ideologies about, 25, 28–29, 42
Leather industry, 122–24, 149–50
LeBass, James, 126
Le Jau, Francis, 96

Le Moyne de Bienville, Jean-Baptiste, 99–100
linen, 130–35 passim, 147, 150, 153. *See also specific linen types*
Livestock, 51
Locke, John, 6, 32, 36–37, 69, 97
London, England, 37, 136, 149–50; Native American visits to, 17–18, 46, 83–84, 113, 138–41
Longe, Alexander, 32, 33, 58–62 passim, 96–97, 177–78 (n. 80)
Lords Proprietors. *See* South Carolina Lords Proprietors
Lower House of Assembly. *See* South Carolina Commons House of Assembly

Macartan and Campbell Company, 90–92, 157
Mackay, Patrick, 99, 107
Malatchi (Creek), 33, 46, 103, 107, 113, 119
Malcontents. *See* Georgia: slavery debate in
Markley, Robert, 37
Martin, John, 106, 107, 113–14
Martyn, Benjamin, 40, 107
Marx, Karl, 34–35
Matchcoat, 98, 117, 134, 136–42 passim, 148, 153, 208 (n. 95)
Mathews, Maurice, 49–50
Mathins, John, 141, 208 (n. 100)
McGillivray, Lachlan, 67, 88
Men, Southeastern Indian: as fathers, 26, 28; and masculinity, 23–28 passim, 103, 113, 115–16. *See also* Gender
Mercantilism, 4–7 passim, 47, 48, 51, 52, 56, 59, 62–63, 120, 156–57. *See also* British and British American: economic ideologies of
Merrell, James, 128, 211 (n. 23)
Metal goods, 20, 125, 127, 129, 132, 140, 143–48 passim, 153
Middle ground, 157, 211 (n. 24)
Mingastushka (Chickasaw), 116

CPSIA information can be obtained
at www.ICGtesting.com
Printed in the USA
LVHW030408170822
726097LV00005B/188

9 781469 631486